ᴀISTORICAL SOCIETY

*General Editor*: Alan Crossley

# OXFORD QUARTER SESSIONS ORDER BOOK 1614–1637

Oxford Historical Society
NEW SERIES, VOL. XXIX

# OXFORD QUARTER SESSIONS ORDER BOOK 1614–1637

*Edited by*
ROBIN BLADES

*With an Introduction by*
ALAN CROSSLEY

THE BOYDELL PRESS

OXFORD HISTORICAL SOCIETY

MMIX

© The Oxford Historical Society 2009

First published 2009

An Oxford Historical Society publication
Published by The Boydell Press
an imprint of Boydell & Brewer Ltd
PO Box 9, Woodbridge, Suffolk IP12 3DF, UK
and of Boydell & Brewer Inc.
668 Mt Hope Avenue, Rochester, NY 14620, USA
website: www.boydellandbrewer.com

ISBN 978-0-904107-22-7

A CIP catalogue record for this book is available
from the British Library

The publisher has no responsibility for the continued existence or accuracy of
URLs for external or third-party internet websites referred to in this book, and
does not guarantee that any content on such websites is, or will remain, accurate or
appropriate.

This publication is printed on acid-free paper

Printed in Great Britain by
CPI Antony Rowe,
Chippenham and Eastbourne

# PREFACE

This volume appears as no. 29 in the Society's New Series, replacing the delayed volume originally proposed for that position.

Dr Robert Peberdy suggested that I took on this project and has been a great source of encouragement. I took far longer than anticipated to complete the work and I am very grateful for his patience. At an important stage in preparing the calendar he checked and retyped the whole. I would like to thank Dr Malcolm Graham for much help in the initial planning of the calendar in 1990, a time when the archives of the city of Oxford were held in the Town Hall and in his care. In particular, he arranged for the photocopying of the document so that the work could be carried out at a distance. Since the archives were moved to Oxfordshire Record Office the County Archivist, Carl Boardman, and his staff have been unfailingly helpful, particularly Rose Hamilton, who gave advice on the manuscript's binding. Alan Crossley advised on difficult readings in the manuscript, edited the indexes, kindly agreed to write an introduction and did a huge amount of work to prepare the calendar for publication. I am extremely grateful for his advice and the numerous improvements he has made to the calendar. Last but not least I would like to thank my father, Bill Blades, and my late mother, Kathy Blades, for all their support and encouragement over the years.

Robin Blades, March 2009

# CONTENTS

# ABBREVIATIONS

| | |
|---|---|
| *Acts of P.C.* | *Acts of the Privy Council of England* (32 vols. 1890–1907) |
| ald. | alderman |
| *Cal. Close* | *Calendar of the Close Rolls preserved in the Public Record Office* |
| *Cal. Pat.* | *Calendar of the Patent Rolls preserved in the Public Record Office* |
| Foster, *Alumni Oxoniensis* | J. Foster, *Alumni Oxoniensis, 1500–1886* (8 vols. 1887–92) |
| G.D. | Gaol Delivery |
| *Hist. Univ. Oxon.* | *History of the University of Oxford.* vol. iii, *The Collegiate University*, ed. J. McConica (1986); vol. iv, *The Seventeeenth Century*, ed. N. Tyacke (1997). |
| *N.E.D.* | *New English Dictionary*, the original title for the *Oxford English Dictionary* |
| *O.C.A. 1583–1626* | *Oxford Council Acts, 1583–1626*, ed. H. E. Salter (O.H.S. lxxxvii) |
| O.H.S. | Oxford Historical Society publications |
| O.R.O. | Oxfordshire Record Office |
| psh. | parish |
| Q.S. | Quarter Sessions |
| recogn. | recognizance |
| TNA | The National Archive, formerly the Public Record Office (P.R.O.) |
| Univ. Arch. | Archives of the University of Oxford, housed in the Bodleian Library, Oxford |
| *V.C.H.* | *Victoria History of the Counties of England* |

# INTRODUCTION

By 1390 Oxford had its own justices of the peace and thereafter remained exempt from interference from county magistrates; as elsewhere, quarter sessions were probably held regularly in Oxford from the 14th century.[1] The order book calendared here,[2] supplemented by a few miscellaneous lists described below, provides the earliest substantial record of sessions activity in Oxford, and indeed in Oxfordshire, since comparable records of county sessions survive only from the 1660s.[3]

## THE MANUSCRIPT

In August 1613 the city council resolved that their town clerk, in accordance with his oath, should in future enrol 'all the pleas of this city in parchment'. The council was about to appoint a new clerk, Ralph Radcliffe, who, though not sworn in until July 1614, had been admitted as a freeman in March, and it was probably he who ordered the purchase soon afterwards of two books 'for the office', one for the enrolment of apprentices, the other for the entering of actions.[4] The second was almost certainly this order book, first used at a sessions beginning on 23 June 1614.[5]

It is not parchment but a leather-bound paper volume, paginated 1–283 in two stages in 17th-century hands (including two page 13s and no page 15 or 277), flanked by a contemporary title page and endpaper. When the volume was rebound in the 19th century the original tooled leather covers were retained and further endpapers added.[6] The front cover bears the scrawled and inaccurate title

[1] *Cal. Close*, 1389–92, 298. For the development of quarter sessions after the statute of 12 Ric. II, c. 10 *see* T. G. Barnes, *Somerset, 1625–1640* (Harvard Univ. Press, 1961), 68 sqq.

[2] O.R.O., Oxf. City Arch. QSC/A2/1 (formerly O.5.9).

[3] M. S. Gretton, *Oxon. Justices* (Oxon. Rec. Soc. xvi, 1934).

[4] *O.C.A. 1583–1626*, 228, 232–3, 406.

[5] The other book may be identified as O.R.O., Oxf. City Arch. L.5.2, a much larger volume but similar in character, which contains apprenticeship enrolments from Oct. 1613, the first entries probably made late in the municipal year ending Sept. 1614.

[6] Although the book was supplied by an Oxford bookseller (Geo. Chambers) its original paper (watermark of two entwined columns surmounted by a crown) is probably French: cf. C. M. Briquet, *Les Filigrannes* (facs. edn. Amsterdam, 1968), i, pp. 269–70; iii, no. 4444. The later binding probably dates from 1844, when G. P. Hester, town clerk 1839–76, who reorganized and rebound the city archives, inspected and signed the book.

'Sessions Orders 1614 to 1631', added at some date in the second half of the 17th century.[1] In fact the volume contains entries, admittedly sparse, made after 1631 and until 1637, the mistaken title perhaps based on the sight of an out-of sequence entry for 1631 in the last opening.

The elaborate title page of the order book rather suggests, as did the council resolution of 1613, that the recording of quarter sessions in this way was a new departure rather than established practice. Earlier documents relating to the work of the city justices are few and fragmentary: there is a volume recording alehouse licences from 1579,[2] and another, composite, volume noting collections for the poor from 1579, passports issued 1597–1605, overseers appointed from 1599 with the justices' approval, and taxes levied for maimed soldiers from 1593 and for poor prisoners from 1598.[3] Thus the administrative business of the justices, rapidly enlarged by statute in this period, is at least partially illustrated, but there is no record of their judicial activities until 1614. This seems odd in a city with numerous long-established, well-recorded courts (mayor's, bailiffs', university chancellor's, diocesan, etc.), a large community of court officials, and an evidently efficient secretariat.[4] Yet the scarcity throughout England of early judicial material from quarter sessions suggests that Oxford may not have been unusual in its belated recording.

Moreover, in common with similar sessions records elsewhere, this order book is far from being a full record of the court's business. It comprises the names of the attending justices, decisions and orders made in both criminal and administrative matters, notes of writs entered, recognizances forfeited, royal pardons granted, and so on; there are incidental references to court procedure, such as indictments and jury verdicts, and occasional longer memoranda that reveal justices' attitudes and behaviour, both in and out of sessions.[5] There are, however, neither depositions nor detailed indictments, and verdicts and sentences are unexplained. In these respects the

[1] The front cover of a volume of alehouse licences (1579–1654) bears a title in the same hand and style, evidently added after 1654: O.R.O., Oxf. City Arch. QSC/A5/1.
[2] Ibid.    [3] Ibid. QSC/A5/2, ff. 1–41, 46v.–49.
[4] For an overview of city and university courts and their records, see V.C.H. Oxon. iv. 168–72, 336–40.
[5] E.g. below, 1622A12, 1623D12, 1624A17.

Oxford order book is closely comparable to that for the East Riding of Yorkshire 1647–51.[1]

The orders for a session are usually all written in the same hand, carefully and clearly entered beneath a formal heading, indicating that they were written up from other material. Marginal comments by the clerk show that this process was usually not long delayed, and sometimes may have begun while the court was still sitting.[2] Inevitably there were omissions, revealed by references to decisions made at previous sessions, which cannot be traced in the order book.[3] In general, however, the order book seems to have been kept up scrupulously for many years, making its apparent deterioration as a record in the late 1620s rather puzzling. The number of recorded orders, between 70 and 100 a year before 1619, rose to 150 in 1621, and was still *c.* 140 in 1624. Thereafter numbers fell to *c.* 80 in 1625–7 and only 25 in 1629. From 1630 until the last entry in 1637 only 15 sessions and fewer than 30 orders were recorded. Moreover, there is no mention at all of gaol delivery sessions after 1625, even though commissions of gaol delivery were issued regularly until the Civil War. The continued insertion of formal headings and lists of attending justices, even when there were only one or two recorded orders, seems to imply that this order book was still the main court record, so the apparent lack of business requires explanation. It is inconceivable that the criminal and administrative work of Oxford J.P.s was diminishing at a time when, elsewhere, it was greatly increasing,[4] and evidently the city gaol required regular clearance. Much of the apparent decline of sessions business from the mid 1620s may be attributed to negligence by clerks of the court, shown by the occasional use of the order book for rough minutes, but it may also reflect a greater tendency for justices to deal out of sessions with misdemeanours and administrative matters. Although petty sessions, in the sense of regular meetings of justices between quarter sessions, are thought to be a slightly later development, associated with the Privy Council's Book of Orders issued in 1631,[5] it may be that unrecorded meetings of Oxford justices between sessions had already become established practice. By the time of the next surviving order book, begun in 1656, business in petty sessions

[1] G. C. F. Forster, *East Riding Justices of the Peace in the Seventeenth Century* (E. Yorks. Local Hist. Soc. 30, 1973).

[2] Below, 1614B1, 1615B5, 1623A14.   [3] Ibid. 1618D1.

[4] Barnes, *Somerset*, esp. chapter VII.   [5] Ibid. 80–1, 85, 172 sqq.

was formally recorded in the same manner and in the same book as that in quarter sessions.[1]

## THE BENCH

Commissions of the peace for Oxford included a mix of townsmen and scholars, in recognition of the separate jurisdictions established in the conflicts of the Middle Ages.[2] By the early 15th century the university acquired exclusive jurisdiction over scholars and privileged persons when, to the chancellor's existing powers to try breaches of the peace, was added the right to try treason, felony and mayhem in a special steward's court; in 1459 it was even agreed that the chancellor should have cognizance of breaches of the peace involving only townsmen, if university officers made the arrest.[3] Such separate but overlapping jurisdictions, provoking recurrent dispute into later times, made the joint magistracy of townsmen and scholars a necessity.

Early 17th-century commissions of the peace for Oxford usually contained *c.* 20 names, but in the 1620s numbers rose to *c.* 30, with a peak of 35 in 1622 because of an unexplained increase in university representation.[4] The lists of commissioners were invariably headed by a few dignitaries, in 1614 by Thomas, Lord Ellesmere, Chancellor of England and of the university, John Bridges, bishop of Oxford, and William, Lord Knollys, Treasurer of the Household and High Steward of the city. In 1622, along with Knollys, by then Viscount Wallingford, the dignitaries were William, earl of Pembroke, Chancellor of the university, and John Howson, bishop of Oxford, but named before them, presumably as a matter of form, were the Lord Keeper, the Lord Treasurer and two other high officers of state. In 1630 the arrangement was much the same, but by then Howson was bishop of Durham and no Chancellor of the university was named, the earl of

---

[1] O.R.O., Oxf. City Arch. QSC/A2/2.

[2] For these constitutional developments, *see V.C.H. Oxon.* iv. 53–9. For 15th- and 16th-century commissions, which included some county dignitaries, *see Cal. Pat.* 1422–9, 568; 1429–36, 623; 1436–41, 588; *Records of the City of Oxf.*, ed. W. H. Turner (1880), 2, 9, 14.

[3] *Medieval Arch. Univ.* i. (O.H.S. lxx), 20, 226–30, 243–7.

[4] Oxf. commissions of the peace are collected as follows: TNA, C 181/2, ff. 71, 133v., 165, 192, 202, 251v., 289 (1608, 1610, 1612, 1613, 1614, 1616, 1617); ibid. C 181/3, ff. 2v., 43v., 84, 156, 225v. (1620, 1622, 1623, 1625, 1627); ibid. C 181/4, f. 57 (1630); ibid. C 181/5, pp. 157, 245 (1637, 1639).

Pembroke having just died.[1] In 1637 the dignitaries comprised only the Lord Keeper, the Lord Treasurer, and John Bancroft, bishop of Oxford; the Lord Treasurer, however, was William Juxon, who, as a head of house and vice-chancellor, had been an active Oxford J.P. since the early 1620s, and Bancroft, too, as a former master of University College, had been on the Bench for a similar period.[2] Except for those two men only Bishop Howson of the dignitaries mentioned attended a recorded session.

After the dignitaries the vice-chancellor and mayor were named as *ex officio* members of all commissions of the peace until the Civil War. The vice-chancellor's nomination was frequently claimed as a right under the university's disputed 1523 charter, which in fact merely confirmed established practice.[3] On all commissions the vice-chancellor was named before the mayor, although the latter was chairman of the Bench and Custos Rotulorum, and at sessions sat beneath the royal arms, with the vice-chancellor on his right and the recorder on his left. Shortly before this order book began the compromise over precedence was rudely disturbed when a visiting assize judge took the chair at sessions, leaving the mayor and vice-chancellor to dispute the seat at his right hand.[4] Vice-chancellors were present at almost all the recorded quarter sessions in this period, and in lists of attenders were invariably named before the mayor.

Most commissions of the peace achieved a rough balance between the representation of city and university. The university representatives, invariably named before the townsmen, comprised in 1614 six doctors of theology, all heads of houses, headed by William Goodwin, dean of Christ Church; all were of the quorum. Of the seven townsmen nominated, all aldermen or assistants, only two were of the quorum. In 1620 the university contingent, headed by Sir Henry Savile of Merton, included William Laud, then president of St John's. In 1622, in addition to Savile, twelve doctors of theology and two doctors of civil law were named but only eight city councillors. The following year, however, the number of doctors fell to eleven, and there were seven townsmen, of whom four were of the quorum. In 1630 the balance was much the same, but by 1637 had shifted towards

[1] *Oxf. D.N.B.* s.v. Herbert, Wm. (3rd earl).
[2] For Juxon and Bancroft *see Oxf. Dictionary of National Biography (D.N.B.).*
[3] *Hist. Univ. Oxon.* iii. 89–90.　　　　　　　　　　[4] Ibid. iv. 120.

the town, with only five doctors and ten councillors, of whom four were of the quorum.

Crucial in all the commissions were men, usually named between the university and city groups, who formed the 'professional' element on the Bench. In 1612 and 1613 these were the city's recorder, Thomas Wentworth, and two lawyers, William Ryves and John Hawley. Wentworth was temporarily removed from the commission, probably at the behest of the university, which regarded him as a 'most malicious and implacable' enemy; he was restored by 1617 and continued until his death in 1627.[1] His deputy and successor, John Whistler, first commissioned in 1623, was named on all commissions as recorder from 1627. William (later Sir William) Ryves was deputy steward of the university but resigned in 1620 to become a prominent judge in Ireland;[2] strangely he continued to be named on every commission of the peace until the Civil War, but in fact attended no sessions after 1619. John Hawley, principal of Gloucester Hall, was a civil lawyer and judge of the chancellor's court, and he remained on the commission until his death in 1626.[3] Another university J.P., Thomas James, commissioned after 1616 among the doctors, had been initially nominated in 1613 in the professional group. Although not a lawyer, he was a major figure in university business at that time, deeply involved in the building of Bodley's library, of which he became the first librarian;[4] his fellow magistrate, John Hawley, was site overseer of the Bodleian building works,[5] and for many years these two men were clearly the most active university J.P.s. Later members of the professional group on the Oxford commissions included Thomas Flexney (from 1620) and Charles Holloway (from 1627), both resident barristers. Flexney, a sergeant-at-law, was son of the bishop's registrar of the same name (d. 1623) and may have succeeded him in that office.[6] He infuriated

[1] Ibid. iv. 108–9; *V.C.H. Oxon.* iv. 148–9, 151–2, 155; *Oxf. D.N.B.*, where his death is incorrectly dated.
[2] *Reg. Univ. Oxf.* ii (1) (O.H.S. x), 242; A. R. Ingpen, *Middle Temple Bench Book* (1912), 180; F. Elrington Ball, *Judges in Ireland* (1926), 336.
[3] Foster, *Alumni Oxoniensis*; *Hist. Univ. Oxon.* iv. 151, 561; M. Underwood, 'The structure ... of the Oxford chancellor's court', *Jn. Soc. Archivists*, vi (1978), 21.
[4] *Oxf. D.N.B.*                                        [5] *Hist. Univ. Oxon.* iv. 151.
[6] *Wood's City of Oxf.* iii (O.H.S. xxxvii), 163; *Members of the Inner Temple, 1547–1660* [ed. W. H. Cooke] (1877), 171, which, perhaps mistakenly, identifies the younger Thos. as registrar. For the father as registrar, *see* J. Howard-Drake, *Oxf. Church Court Depositions, 1616–22*, page v and *passim*. Thos. jun. does not appear as registrar in diocesan court records (e.g. ibid. *1629–34*), although his brother Wm. was clerk of the court in 1623: O.R.O., MS. Oxf. Dioc. d 11, ff. 228, 337.

the city council in 1620 by demanding payment for his attendance at sessions: evidently no other J.P.s claimed the statutory fee (4s. a day), and the fact that Flexney, as a privileged person of the university, secured judgment in the matter against the city bailiffs in the chancellor's court in 1622 only increased the outrage over a claim 'so rare and unknown in this corporation'.[1] The dispute may have been resolved, since Flexney continued as an active J.P. throughout the period. Charles Holloway, also of the Inner Temple and later sergeant-at-law, was in effect another university member of the Bench, unlikely to have been popular with his fellow city J.P.s: he was the university's lawyer in a period of bitter city–university disputes, yet remained on commissions of the peace until the Civil War.[2]

Although the city's gaol (Bocardo) could be, and indeed was, delivered (i.e. its prisoners brought to trial) by justices acting under commissions of the peace,[3] it continued to be the practice in Oxford to obtain separate commissions of gaol delivery.[4] Usually the city bailiffs made (and paid for) such applications: it was in their financial interest to do so, since they were entitled *inter alia* to profits of courts and felons' goods in return for paying the annual fee-farm of the city.[5] Commissions were issued for a limited period, usually a year, and it was stipulated that at least four commissioners should be present, including two of the quorum. Despite a stipulation in the 1523 charter that the university should be represented on gaol commissions it was still seeking inclusion in 1585.[6] By 1605, however, the vice-chancellor was a commissioner,[7] and by 1615 headed the list before the mayor and Thomas Wentworth, the recorder, although only they were of the quorum; the total of twelve names

---

[1] *O.C.A. 1583–1626*, 291–3, 307–8. For the lengthy action *see* chancellor's court act book 1618–22: Oxf. Univ. Arch. Hyp/A/33, ff. 186 and *passim*. This sessions order book was actually produced in court to verify Flexney's attendance record: ibid. Hyp/B/5, deposition of 2 May 1621.

[2] *Reg. Univ. Oxf.* ii (1) (O.H.S. x), 281; *Wood's Life and Times*, ii (O.H.S. xxi), 220, 397, 469; iv. 57, 59, 65.

[3] For a discussion of gaol delivery by magistrates in this period, *see* J. S. Cockburn, *Hist. Eng. Assizes, 1558–1714* (1972), 87–9; idem, *Cal. of Assize Records: Introduction* (HMSO, 1985), 20–5.

[4] Oxf. commissions of gaol delivery are collected as follows: TNA, C 181/2, ff. 78v., 223v., 228, 307, 337v. (1609, Feb. 1615, May 1615, 1618, 1619; ibid. C 181/3, ff. 72, 84v., 115, 225v. (1622, 1623, 1624, 1627); ibid. C 181/4, ff. 62, 129v., 159v. (1630, 1632, 1634); ibid. C 181/5, pp. 57, 309 (1635, 1639).

[5] *O.C.A. 1583–1626*, xxiii, 116–17, 378.          [6] *V.C.H. Oxon.* iv. 170.

[7] *Royal Letters addressed to Oxf.*, ed. O. Ogle (1892), 248–9.

was made up with six city councillors, the lawyers William Ryves and John Hawley mentioned above, and Anthony Blencowe, provost of Oriel, civil lawyer and chancellor of the diocese.[1] Numbers continued to be much smaller than those on commissions of the peace, sometimes 14 in the 1620s and at most 16 in the 1630s. In 1623, after the vice-chancellor, mayor and recorder, the commissioners comprised two doctors of civil law, John Hawley and William Juxon (later vice-chancellor), two more lawyers John Whistler (deputy recorder) and Thomas Flexney, and seven city councillors; the last six councillors were not of the quorum. In the 1630s university representation was further reduced: in 1635 the vice-chancellor, mayor and recorder were followed only by Flexney, then twelve city councillors, all members of the inner council known as the Thirteen with the exception of James Chesterman, an attorney in the city courts.[2]

Attendance lists in the order book, together with incidental references to the work of individual justices out of sessions, show that the increasing burden of the magistracy was carried by relatively few of the many justices named in commissions of the peace or of gaol delivery. On average the Bench comprised fewer than ten justices; at only five recorded sessions were there more than twelve, and the highest recorded attendance was sixteen. Of the city justices three aldermen, Thomas Harris, William Potter and William Wright, made over sixty appearances and two others, John Bird and Oliver Smith were similarly active over a shorter period. Of the university group John Prideaux, either as vice-chancellor or as rector of Exeter, attended nearly fifty sessions, but even greater contributions were made by John Hawley and Thomas James, mentioned above, with fifty or sixty appearances in lists and as many incidental references to out-of-sessions activity. Statutory provisions that 'men learned in the law' should be present at sessions were clearly observed in Oxford, and in 1618 it was deemed worthy of remark that a death sentence had to be delivered in the absence of the recorder and William Ryves (evidently regarded as the senior professionals), albeit that their stand-in was John Hawley, the civil lawyer.[3] Of the 'professional' group, along with successive recorders, Thomas Flexney was the most regular attender.

[1] Foster, *Alumni Oxonienses*; Howard-Drake, *Depositions 1609–1616*, p. v.
[2] *O.C.A. 1583–1626*, 317.          [3] Below, 1618DI.

## THE COURTS

In accordance with the statute of 1388 Oxford sessions of the peace
were held quarterly near Epiphany, Easter, Trinity and Michaelmas; the
summer sessions, for example, began invariably on the first Thursday
after Trinity (the feast of Corpus Christi). Sessions were held in the
Guildhall, beginning on a Thursday[1] and probably most lasted for the
three days enjoined by statute: Saturday was seen as a deadline in various
court orders, and at Easter 1620, for example, sentencing (probably, as
elsewhere, reserved to the end of proceedings) certainly took place on
a Saturday morning.[2] Gaol delivery sessions, also held in the Guildhall, began on various midweek days, frequently on the Monday or
Tuesday before a Thursday quarter sessions, suggesting that they were
not expected to be prolonged. It is clear from the timing of Oxford
gaol deliveries that the argument, adduced for some places, that separate
gaol commissions were acquired in order to clear prisons in the inter-
vals between quarter sessions does not stand up:[3] indeed in 1615 and
1618 adjourned gaol deliveries were fixed to coincide with forthcoming
quarter sessions, and in January 1619 the gaol delivery session took the
place of what would have been the second day of a quarter session.[4]
In 1624 and 1625 Oxford's sessions of the peace and of gaol delivery
were combined. Even before then there was considerable overlap in the
business conducted in the two courts: since many justices were on both
commissions it would not have seemed improper for a gaol delivery
session, as in 1615, to turn directly from a murder trial to a problem over
church attendance.[5]

   The revised peace commission of 1590 introduced a *casus difficultatis*
clause requiring the presence of an assize judge for the trial of serious
felonies[6] and William Lambarde, in his great justices' manual of
the period, argued that magistrates had no power to deliver felony
suspects and asserted that few felonies now came before sessions.[7]
This order book, however, supports a conclusion, based on contemporary quarter sessions material for other places, that many serious
felonies were not referred to assizes, but were tried by justices

---

[1] An exception was the Easter sessions in 1617, opened on Wednesday 30 April, presumably in the vain hope of avoiding May Day festivities: below, 1617B; ibid. 1617B5.
[2] Below, 1620B34. Cf. 1622E19 for reservation of sentencing to the final day.
[3] Cockburn, *Hist. Eng. Assizes*, 87–9.                    [4] Below, 1615E2, 1618D5, 1619B.
[5] Ibid. 1615D6, 8.                    [6] Cockburn, *Hist. Eng. Assizes*, 46.
[7] W. Lambarde, *Eirenarcha* (1619), 548–53.

acting under peace or gaol delivery commissions.[1] In the absence of contemporary assize records for the Oxford circuit it is impossible to assess the apportionment of cases between assizes and sessions. Certainly the Oxford justices co-operated closely with their circuit judges,[2] consulting them twice over bigamy cases, asking them to decide whether the actions of two apprentices towards their master could be defined as felony and referring as a 'case of difficulty' an action involving a deaf and dumb girl against whom they felt unable to proceed.[3] Yet in 1619, when the gaol delivery commissioners challenged the removal of a murder case by *habeas corpus* to assizes (because it involved a privileged person of the university), the circuit judge confirmed their right to try such serious offences committed within Oxford's liberties; the case was then returned to sessions, where a verdict of manslaughter was recorded.[4]

That case suggests continued reluctance on the university's part to use the city's courts. Its claim to exclusive jurisdiction over scholars and privileged persons had not been given up, but in practice rarely extended to felonies. By the later 16th century the chancellor's court dealt with only minor criminal offences, such as breaches of the peace and petty larceny.[5] The university steward's court for felonies was moribund by the early 17th century, although convened in 1634 largely to demonstrate a theoretical privilege.[6] Oxford's quarter sessions in this period tried serious felonies involving privileged persons (notably manslaughter),[7] as well as many lesser crimes such as thefts from colleges. Probably other such felonies went directly to assizes, no doubt still the preferred course in the university's view: certainly in 1624 a privileged cook seems to have chosen to transfer a felony action from quarter sessions to assizes, and in 1627, when a Lincoln College man was convicted of murder in sessions, the case was quickly removed to assizes by *habeas corpus*.[8]

---

[1] Cf. Cockburn, *Cal. Assize Recs: Intro.* 22–5. Cf. Barnes, *Somerset*, 50 sqq. arguing that serious felonies were mostly tried in assizes by this period.

[2] For names of Oxf. Circuit judges, *see* idem, *Hist. Eng. Assizes*, 269–72.

[3] Below, 1616H11, 1618A15, 23, 1618B17, 1618E11, 1626A6.

[4] Ibid. 1619F3. 1619I4.

[5] e.g. Univ. Arch. Hyp/A/8 (chancellor's court Act bk. 1567–78). Cf. ibid. Hyp/A/33 (chanc. ct. reg. 1618–22).

[6] *V.C.H. Oxon.* iv. 170.       [7] Index, s.v. Griffith, Chas.; Moore, Ferryman

[8] Below, 1624E27, 28, 1627A12.

## CRIME AND PUNISHMENT

Procedure in the Oxford sessions in felony cases was evidently
identical to that in assizes, indictments being first approved or
rejected in private by the grand jury, followed by arraignment and
trial in open court and a verdict by the petty jury, frequently called
the 'jury of life and death'.[1] The order book records the passing of as
many as twenty-nine death sentences for crimes of murder, burglary
and grand larceny; all but three of the sentences seem to have been
carried out.[2] In the same period some twenty-five other capital
convictions, for offences ranging from manslaughter and cattle
stealing to the theft of a salt cellar, were commuted by the grant of
benefit of clergy, under which the offender was 'burnt on the hand'
(branded on the thumb);[3] two of this group were pardoned, and
two others, evidently recidivists, were later among the twenty-six
who were hanged.[4] As elsewhere, the conviction rate in capital
trials seems to have been relatively low, with petty juries returning
over forty verdicts of not guilty, i.e. in some forty per cent of the
recorded trials.[5] It is likely, too, that many offenders escaped capital
trial altogether: probably many more felony indictments were
rejected at the grand jury stage than the handful of recorded verdicts
of 'not found' or *ignoramus* might suggest.[6] Grand juries in Oxford,
as elsewhere, also averted many potential capital trials by undervaluing
alleged stolen goods at 12d. or less, so that charges might be reduced;[7]
and in one case, probably not unusual, a man charged with theft of
goods valued by the grand jury at 5s. was found guilty by the petty
jury of theft to the value of 10d., and was therefore punished for
petty larceny.[8]

[1] For a full discussion, *see* J. H. Baker, 'Criminal Courts and Procedure, 1550–1800', in *The Legal Profession and the Common Law* (1986), 259–303.
[2] For those pardoned, *see* index, s.v. Gray, Tim.; Hayes, Jn.; Huntley, Joan.
[3] For benefit of clergy, *see* Cockburn, *Cal. Assize Recs: Intro.* 117–21; Baker, 'Criminal Courts', 292–3.
[4] For those pardoned, *see* index, s.v. Miles, Ric.; Moore, Ferryman. For those hanged, s.v. Kellam, Thos.; Rogers, Thos.
[5] It is not always clear that acquittals were for capital offences. For comparable rates *see* Cockburn, *Cal. Assize Recs: Intro.* 113; Forster, *East Riding Justices*, 45.
[6] For discussion of the grand jury and indictments, *see* Baker, 'Criminal Courts', 263–5; Cockburn, *Cal. Assize Recs: Intro.* 53, 73–87.
[7] e.g. below, 1619D15, 1624B28. For undervaluation elsewhere, *see* Forster, *East Riding Justices*, 44; Cockburn, *Hist. Eng. Assizes*, 97; Barnes, *Somerset*, 51 sqq.
[8] Below, 1624E32, 45.

Much of the judicial work recorded in this order book was
concerned with petty larceny, which has been found to be the most
common criminal offence in other quarter sessions records.[1] In
Oxford the wide range of stolen goods, as might be expected in a
city, was dominated by clothing, household chattels and shop goods,
but there were probably more valuables than normal, reflecting the
relative prosperity of the citizens and perhaps the availability of college
plate. Other common criminal offences were assault and battery,
abusive behaviour, drunkenness, and various other misdemeanours
(a class of offence greatly enlarged by Tudor legislation).[2] Many actions
proceeded from indictment, some from presentations by the grand
jury. In 1617, and perhaps routinely, the Oxford grand jury presented
all those suspected of statutory misdemeanours, and warrants were
then made out.[3] Whereas procedure on indictment was swift, usually
completed in a session, in misdemeanours the offender could bring in
a traverse (pleading an exception), and so initiate a lengthier process
with plea and counter plea, as in a civil action. Informants and sworn
testimony were often used.[4]

Punishment for lesser crimes and misdemeanours was sometimes
dictated by statute, but much was left to the discretion of the Bench.
The better-off were frequently allowed to find sureties for good
behaviour. Fines, sometimes backed by temporary imprisonment until
payment, were typically 6s. 8d. for assault and battery or breaches of
the peace, 5s. for drunkenness. Much heavier fines, 20s. or more, were
levied for assaults on court officials or constables, and one particularly
'barbarous' assault on a woman attracted a fine of £6 13s. 4d.[5] The
offender's ability to pay was taken into account: the clerk recorded
that a 'lewd fellow' fined 10s. for assault would have been fined more
if he were not so poor; another, allowed a reduced fine because of
his poverty, was also given 'private correction' (i.e. whipping), and a
woman unable to pay her fine was put in the stocks.[6]

The many for whom payment of fines was out of the question received corporal punishment or short-term imprisonment.
Petty larceny was usually punished by whipping, which was also

[1] Forster, *East Riding Justices*, 41; Cockburn, *Hist. Eng. Assizes*, 97.
[2] Forster, *East Riding Justices*, 14–15; Barnes, *Somerset*, 53–5.      [3] Below, 1617A23.
[4] E.g. below, 1615A13, 1620C19, 1623C6, 1623D9. For misdemeanour procedure, *see* Barnes, *Somerset*, 54–5.
[5] Below, 1623C15.                    [6] Ibid. 1625C15, 1620A10, 1629C4.

prescribed for many other offences, sometimes when there was a
mere suspicion of crime.[1] In sentences there was a clear gradation
of severity, ranging from public whipping on market days, 'stripped
to the girdle' until 'all bloody', to private whipping in prison, or
discreet punishment in the lower Guildhall (probably reserved for
erring apprentices or freemen). Some offenders banished to their
alleged home parishes were whipped out of town 'at a cart's tail'.[2]
Among more imaginative humiliations was that for a rapist, who was
to be imprisoned, then pilloried for a day in the market place beneath
a paper denoting his crime, and at noon taken out and whipped. An
Abingdon man, guilty of abusing the city council, was to be similarly
labelled at the pillory, then whipped at a cart's tail from Northgate
to Southgate.[3] The stocks were much used to punish offences such as
drunkenness, and a spell in the stocks was occasionally offered as an
alternative to a fine.[4] Some men sent to the stocks had to wear labels
in their hats identifying their crime, and others were subjected to
a device, presumably restrictive and humiliating, called 'the devil's
yoke'; one drunkard, a notorious biter, was muzzled.[5] Women,
usually 'scolds' were sometimes exhibited in the 'cage', but more
frequently sent to the ducking stool.[6]

    Committal to the House of Correction for long terms or until
further order was sometimes the penalty for petty larceny, particularly when magistrates judged offenders to be 'idle rogues' or 'lewd
women'; one man, however, was sent there after persistent and
'barbarous' wife-beating.[7] Imprisonment in Bocardo was rarely used
as a long-term punishment: most sentences were for a few days only,
pending the payment of a fine, the production of sureties, submission
to the court or corporal punishment. Committal without bail until
the next sessions was reserved for the particularly intransigent, men
guilty of 'insufferable misdemeanours' or 'intolerable abuse'.[8] One
man was so unruly that the court prescribed three months in prison,
coupled with exposure in the stocks twice weekly on market days,
wearing 'the devil's yoke'; not surprisingly at the next sessions the
prisoner made an unreserved submission, and the magistrates expressed

[1] Ibid. 1623B8, 1628D1.
[2] Ibid. 1622A24.
[3] Ibid. 1617B19, 1623A18.
[4] Ibid. 1619A15, 1620C4.
[5] Ibid. 1617B23, 1623E8, 1623D14.
[6] Ibid. 1617C11, 1621E7, 1621C19, 1622B29.
[7] Ibid. 1620C22.
[8] Ibid. 1622B7, 1625A24.

hopes for his future behaviour.[1] A few other instances of long stays in Bocardo were caused by prisoners failing to find bail or awaiting trial at assizes.[2]

Executions were the responsibility of the city bailiffs,[3] but it is not clear from this order book whether they were carried out at the gallows at Green Ditch in the fields north of the city, or in the Castle (technically outside the city), where those condemned at assizes were hanged.[4] Of other punitive instruments the whipping post and pillory stood in Cornmarket Street, the cage, a roofed structure apparently with stocks within it, was at Carfax, and the ducking stool was at Castle Mill.[5] Other stocks stood in the Guildhall and outside St Michael's church, and indeed each parish was enjoined to provide a set.[6]

The overall impression of the court orders is that the Bench was indeed, as claimed in 1622, 'intending to do justice to all men indifferently',[7] but its patience was frequently tested. The order book illustrates the many tiresome problems associated with getting suspects into court – repeated warrants, reluctant constables, violently resisted arrests, prison escapes and, finally, in court, renewed violence and 'barbarous words' to the Bench.[8] One man, a persistent nuisance, was noted by the outraged clerk as 'above all other men unworthy to live in any well-governed place and should be spurned from this common-wealth'; his later abuse of the vice-chancellor caused a special meeting of senior justices to be convened to discuss the case.[9]

The impanelling of suitable juries was a recurrent problem in Oxford, as elsewhere. In 1621 and probably in most other years the customary sessions dinner for the grand jury was, significantly, to be paid for out of fines from those who had refused or evaded jury service.[10] Such fines, usually 3s. 4d. or 5s., could be as high as 20s., and similarly heavy fines and even imprisonment were imposed on jurors who misbehaved, for instance by being absent when their verdicts were given.[11] The jury room was evidently sacrosanct, guarded by a constable, and one man was disbarred from jury service for life after

[1] Ibid. 1625A21, 1625B1.
[2] Ibid. 1624E7, 1629D3 and index, s.v. Hussey, Joan, wid.
[3] Below, 1619B2.                           [4] V.C.H. Oxon. iv. 340.
[5] Ibid.; below, 1620b17, 1621A21.         [6] Below, 1629C4, 1625B12, 1617B26.
[7] Ibid. 1622C8.                           [8] Subject index, s.v. abusive behaviour.
[9] Below, 1622B7, 1625A24 and index, s.v. Gunn, Hen.    [10] Below, 1622B11.
[11] Ibid. 1616A6, 1622E19.

disclosing the grand jury's deliberations.[1] Yet the Bench felt quite able
to castigate juries for what it perceived to be mistaken verdicts: in
1617 a petty jury had 'not guided themselves well according to the
evidence' in acquitting a 'very lewd and light housewife', who was
then summarily dispatched to the House of Correction. In 1622 all
twelve jurymen were imprisoned when their 'most wrong' verdict
conflicted with the opinion of the court and 'plain evidence'.[2] On
several other occasions the justices simply ignored unacceptable
verdicts and sentenced the accused as they thought fit.[3]

### ADMINISTRATIVE TASKS

It has been remarked that it was as administrators that J.P.s made their
greatest contribution to local government.[4] This order book illustrates
the wide range of administrative tasks imposed by Tudor and early
Stuart legislation on justices both in and out of sessions. Although the
poor law Acts laid primary responsibility for poor-relief on the parish,
the Oxford justices closely supervised the work of parish officers,
granting warrants for the collection of rates, annually inspecting
overseers' accounts, and approving the election of new officers.[5] They
intervened frequently to support individual petitioners, instructing
parish officers to find lodging or provide relief in deserving cases,
such as a widow and children in Holywell in 1625 who had been
evicted by a 'hard landlord'.[6] The justices were arbitrators in many
cases of disputed responsibility between parishes, for instance when a
supported pauper in one parish had children known to have been born
in another; such cases were often complex, and one was even referred
to the assize judges for guidance.[7] Throughout this period the justices
had a special problem with St Peter-le-Bailey parish, where ratepayers
were too few to provide relief for the numerous poor. Frequently the
justices ordered wealthier parishes to lend financial support,[8] and in
1635 intervened directly, setting up a select vestry in St Peter-le-Bailey
to deal more efficiently with the poor.[9]

---

[1] Ibid. 1622E22, 1620D33.                    [2] Ibid. 1617D7, 1622A12.
[3] Ibid. 1618A16, 1620B39, 1624A28, 1628D2, 3.      [4] Barnes, *Somerset*, 58.
[5] E.g. below, 1618E23, 1619C6, 1626B11, 1627B15. For some lists of overseers and notes of
parochial taxes in this period, *see* O.R.O., Oxf. City Arch. QSC/A5/2, ff. 1–29.
[6] Ibid. 1625B14.                             [7] Ibid. 1631A1, 1632B1.
[8] Ibid. 1617A22, 1619C20, 1620A12, 1620B43.
[9] Ibid. 1634B1, 1635A1; *V.C.H. Oxon.* iv. 342.

Many sessions orders concern child maintenance, the justices
making *ad hoc* arrangements for foster care and apportioning
responsibility for payment as best they could, sometimes to relatives,
sometimes to more than one parish.[1] Contracts for long-term care
inevitably caused problems,[2] while in 1624 the justices were faced
with a general complaint from the city's child minders, presumably
over allowances.[3] In 1625 when five parishes were contributing to the
support of two orphans in St Peter-le-Bailey parish the total rate was
only 1s. 6d. a week. The maintenance demanded in 1621 from one
father of an illegitimate child was 6d. a week for seven years.[4] Paternity
allegations obliged justices, both in and out of sessions, to undertake
prolonged, and often fruitless, enquiries, as they puzzled over 'intricate'
details, testimony from midwives and even, in one case, a medical
report from three surgeons on a man's alleged incapacity to father a
child.[5] One suspected father, unable to provide the required sureties,
was left in Bocardo for six months.[6]

Vagrancy was regarded by both city and the university as a
particular problem in Oxford,[7] and certainly the justices dispatched
many wandering 'rogues' to the whipping post and to the House
of Correction, and thence with passports towards their alleged
home parishes.[8] For much of this period Oxford did not have its
own House of Correction but used one at Witney.[9] In 1617, determined to rid the city of 'the swarm and multitude of rogues,
vagrants and idle persons', the corporation and university agreed
to share the cost of a contract with Witney Bridewell (£22) to set
on work all vagrants sent there.[10] Nothing seems to have come of
a proposal in 1624 to open a House of Correction at Osney, but
in 1631 one was built at Northgate. In accordance with a general
recommendation of the Privy Council in that year it was adjacent
to the prison.[11]

---

[1] For typically complex arrangements, see below, 1622B3, 1625B5.
[2] Ibid. 1625B20, 1626A13.                               [3] Ibid. 1624E24.
[4] Ibid. 1625A28, 1621A20.
[5] Ibid. 1618C9, 1621B12, 1618A3. For procedures in bastardy cases, *see* Barnes, *Somerset*,
61–2; Forster, *East Riding Justices*, 47.
[6] Below, 1624B3, 1624C14, 1624E7.                       [7] *V.C.H. Oxon.* iv. 344.
[8] Subject index, s.v. expulsion; vagrants.
[9] *V.C.H. Oxon.* iv. 344; below, places index, s.v. House of Correction.
[10] *O.C.A. 1583–1626*, 267–8.
[11] Below, 1624E56; *V.C.H. Oxon.* iv. 344–5. For the Privy Council's Book of Orders,
circulated to justices in Jan. 1631, *see* Barnes, *Somerset*, 179 and *passim*.

A perhaps greater concern than vagrancy was the number of potential paupers actually settling in the city, in poorer tenements denigrated as 'cottages' or 'squab houses'.[1] The proliferation of such dwellings in a period of rapid population growth, and their occupation by dubious lodgers ('inmates'), was thought in 1624 to account for the 'great many poor people wandering the city and suburbs', begging and pilfering, and perhaps 'endangering the commonwealth' if plague came to the city.[2] Cottage-building became an issue between city and university, each blaming the other for what was clearly an irreversible trend.[3] The justices repeatedly demanded lists of all new tenements and the names of inmates and landlords.[4] Having taken advice from circuit judges they tried to enforce 'such orders as the law allows', chiefly obliging landlords on pain of imprisonment to secure parish officers against charges arising from their tenants.[5] In 1626 their position was strengthened by a Privy Council order giving the vice-chancellor and mayor the power, assisted by other J.P.s, to take harmless bonds from landlords and to forbid further cottage-building.[6] Yet in the 1630s the justices were still making rulings about slum tenements, still trying to make landlords responsible for their tenants, and insisting on monthly reviews of newcomers and 'strangers'.[7] By 1640 the university, convinced that cottage-building was out of control, again turned to the Privy Council, which ordered yet another survey.[8]

A similarly intractable problem, dividing the two communities and occupying a disproportionate amount of the justices' time, was that of alehouse licensing. Although this order book is replete with orders concerning alehouses, it was not in fact the principal record of the justices' licensing activity. From 1579 numbered lists of licensees were kept in a separate book, kept up fairly regularly until the 1650s, and containing memoranda of licensing sessions and associated material.[9] In the early 17th century, as in the mid 16th, it was customary for victuallers who were privileged persons to be licensed annually by the university registrar, and those who were citizens by the town clerk.[10] In 1605 there had been an agreement that the city should limit its licences

[1] E.g. below, 1620A13, 1624D1.    [2] Ibid. 1624E44.
[3] V.C.H. Oxon. iv. 89–90; Hist. Univ. Oxf. iv. 132–3.
[4] Below, 1618E27, 1620A13, 1624D1, 1624E53, 1626C5, 18.
[5] Ibid. 1618E10, 1623A3, 1626C5–9.    [6] Acts of P.C. 1625–6, 303–4.
[7] Below, 1633A1, 1631B1, 1632A1, 1634A1.
[8] V.C.H. Oxon. iv. 90.
[9] O.R.O., Oxf. City Arch. QSC/A5/1 (formerly N.4.1).
[10] Below, 1615A20; cf. V.C.H. Oxon. iv. 167.

to seventy and the university to twenty, and those limits were in force when the order book began.[1] Victuallers petitioning for licences were admitted only when a vacancy arose. They had to enter into a recognizance backed by two sureties to keep good order and observe the statutes; additional conditions, such as not to permit unlawful games or the dressing of meat on forbidden days were sometimes added.[2] The numerous unlicensed victuallers, presented by grand juries or ward constables, received a standard (statutory) punishment of three days imprisonment and a 20s. fine, and had to enter into a bond to refrain from victualling without licence.

In 1616, in the first of many concerted efforts to bring alehouses under control, the city and university J.P.s agreed to reduce the total number of licences to forty or fifty, and issued a series of restrictive orders which won the approval of the circuit judge: they included an obligation to identify all alehouses with a red post or lattice, and a ban on victualling in 'by-lanes'.[3] Later the number of licences increased, causing friction between city and university, both bodies alleging that the other issued too many licences: in 1622 the city J.P.s made their enforcement of statutory ale measures in alehouses dependent on the university enforcing the same rules with privileged victuallers; and in 1629 the city similarly refused to continue with the licensing and suppression of alehouses until the privileged persons 'be likewise dealt with'.[4] In the 1630s the university, with the backing of William Laud and the Privy Council, won theoretical control of licensing, but the city justices continued as before, and by 1635 they were approving sixty licences.[5] Throughout the period numerous orders reflect a determined, perhaps Puritanical, intent among Oxford justices to enforce statutory control of socially undesirable aspects of alehouse life, whether it be drinking on the Sabbath, playing cards, dice, skittles or bowls, or simply offering a haven to 'those who sleep by day and cause disorder by night'.[6]

Another regular administrative task carried out in quarter sessions was the operation of the fund, originating in a statute of 1593, to provide

[1] *V.C.H. Oxon.* iv. 167; below, 1615A29.
[2] O.R.O., Oxf. City Arch. QSC/A5/1, s.a. 1629. For an example of a licence, below, Appendix 3.
[3] Below, 1616E1–6, 1616F1–4.
[4] Ibid. 1622E27; O.R.O., Oxf. City Arch. QSC/A5/1, s.a.1629; *V.C.H. Oxon.* iv. 167.
[5] O.R.O., Oxf. City Arch. QSC/A5/1, 22 May 1635.    [6] E.g. below, 1616G1–9.

relief for deserving ex-soldiers. The Oxford justices appointed a treasurer and a collector for maimed soldiers annually in the Easter sessions, approved their accounts, and sometimes examined the soldiers who claimed benefit. The collection of the statutory rate in parishes was sometimes troublesome, and in 1627 Holywell was found to be twenty years in arrears.[1]

Throughout the period Roman Catholic recusants in Oxford were presented by grand juries at quarter sessions, their names certified to the Exchequer, and recognizances taken for their good behaviour; information about their activities was sometimes given to the court. They were expected to certify in writing their reasons for failing to attend church, and a statutory fine of 12d. for each absence was sometimes levied.[2] In 1618 the court removed an apprentice from his master to prevent his being 'seduced to popery'.[3]

The absence of sessions orders dealing with marketing offences reflects the unusual circumstance of the market in Oxford being controlled through the university chancellor's court.[4] Almost all matters of economic regulation coming before quarter sessions concerned apprenticeship, and even they were relatively few since most apprenticeship contracts were dealt with by the mayor and other J.P.s in the husting and other city courts. An action against a tailor for working without the statutory seven-year apprenticeship was something of a rarity,[5] and most of the apprenticeship contracts discussed in sessions involved masters or apprentices on criminal charges. Some routine complaints from masters or apprentices were dealt with, although many were referred back to the mayor.[6] Arbitration was sometimes successful, and continuation of some contracts was enforced where curtailment would have damaged the apprentice's interests.[7] When one of the parties was guilty of crime contracts were usually brought to an end,[8] and could be dissolved for other reasons, in one instance because a master did not 'use his trade', but more

---

[1] Ibid. 1627D22 and subject index, s.v. maimed soldiers. There is no mention of the related statutory fund for poor prisoners, although the two funds were administered together in this period: O.R.O., Oxf. City Arch. QSC/A5/2, ff. 30 sqq.

[2] Subject index, s.v. recusants.                        [3] Below, 1618A5.

[4] V.C.H. Oxon. iv. 165–6, 308. A few orders concerning ale-measures were made by the justices (including university J.P.s), presumably as an aspect of alehouse regulation: subject index, s.v. short measures.

[5] Below, 1628A3.                        [6] E.g. ibid. 1618A9, 1620B25, 1621B14, 1625C8.

[7] E.g. ibid. 1623A7, 1628A4.                        [8] E.g. ibid. 1620B16, 1622E13.

frequently after ill-treatment by the master or misbehaviour by the apprentice.[1] On two occasions the court considered wage disputes between masters and their journeymen.[2]

## THE CALENDAR

The title page and endpapers of the order book are transcribed in full. Elsewhere in the calendar some quotations have been retained because their meaning is not clear, or because in translation they would lose their flavour. It should be noted that the J.P.s listed at the head of each session are usually described as 'for the City, the suburbs, liberties and precincts of the same'. Those listed at the head of gaol delivery sessions are 'Commissioners assigned by his Majesty's Commission of Gaol Delivery to them directed'. Where alternative forms of a surname occur in the calendar, the first is taken from the main entry, the second from the marginalia. Editorial additions are enclosed in square brackets.

[1] Ibid. 1629B2, 1624B19, 1628C5.    [2] Ibid. 1618E1, 1629A3.

# OXFORD QUARTER
# SESSIONS ORDER BOOK

Civitas Oxon. A Book of all Orders made by the Kings highnes Justices of his Peace to be holden for the Citie of Oxon the liberties Suburbs and precints thereof from the xxiii<sup>th</sup> day of June Anno xii<sup>mo</sup> Jacobi Regis Annoque Domini 1614 and so forward:viz:

## CALENDAR

### [1614A]

Quarter Sessions Thurs. 23 June 1614. Thos. Singleton D.D., Vice- Chancellor, Hen. Toldervey esq., Mayor, Wm. Langton D.D., Thos. James D.D., Isaac Bartholmew ald., Thos. Harris gent., Wm. Potter gent., Wm. Wright gent., J.P.s.

1. Rog. Fouche (Foucher) of Oxf., fencer, to be discharged of his recogn. to keep the peace after he appeared and the court was not asked to continue it.

2. In the hope that Avis Wright, a convicted recusant, will conform by the next Q.S. she is not to be punished. She is to enter a new recogn. with good sureties to appear at the next Q.S., behave well and speak to Dr. Prideux of Exeter Coll., bringing a certificate of her conformity from him when she appears.

3. Rose Stacye, a convicted recusant, as in 1614A2, but to speak to Dr. James.

4. Rob. Dudley, a convicted recusant, as in 1614A3.

5. Wm. Badger, a convicted recusant, as in 1614A2, but to speak to Dr. Langton, President of Magdalen, despite having taken the Oath of Allegiance here.

6. Jn. Gill, Jn. Richardson, Nic. Allen and Dorothy Disson to be discharged from the House of Correction.

7. The court was told that Ric. Hales and Wm. Pemberton, boatmen, had abused Mr. Hollman, the master of Bridewell

(the House of Correction).[1] They are to be brought by warrant
before the next J.P. and bound with sufficient sureties to appear at the
next Q.S. and meanwhile behave well.

**8.** Jn. Mundy of the psh. of St. Nic. *alias* St. Thos., brewer, to enter recogn.
with good sureties not to victual or sell beer or ale in his house.

**9.** Ric. George of the psh. of St. Giles, labourer, to enter recogn. with
good sureties to appear at the next Q.S. and discharge his psh. of any
charge from his wife and children.

**10.** Rob. Davyes (Davies) of Oxf., cook, to enter recogn. not to victual
or sell ale or beer in his house without a licence from the court.

## [1614B]

p. 4   Quarter Sessions Thurs. 6 Oct. 1614. Wm. Goodwyne D.D., Vice-
Chancellor, Wm. Wrighte esq., Mayor, Rob. Abbott D.D., Thos.
James D.D., Jn. Hawley B.C.L., Wm. Ryves esq., Isaac Bartholmew
ald., Thos. Harris gent., Ric. Hannes ald., Hen. Toldervey gent.,
Wm. Potter gent., J.P.s.

**1.** Geo. Ryme's recogn., which the court considers forfeit, to be
estreated and Geo. to be imprisoned until he keeps the order made
at the Q.S. after last Easter for the maintenance of a bastard child
and brings forward its reputed father. Geo. is then to be discharged,
arrears of 8d. a week being paid.

[*Margin*] Mr. Ryves sent a writ of *supersedeas* to this order under his
hand 10 Oct. 1614.

**2.** Wm. Pemberton was bound by recogn. to appear on suspicion
of stealing a linen cloth from Mr. Fyndall who did not prosecute as
bound. Pemberton to be discharged but Mr. Fyndall to pay his fees.

**3.** Thos. Freeman's recogn. to be estreated as the court considers it
forfeit.

p. 5   **4.** Edw. Chittell (Chittle) imprisoned again for refusing to take the
Oath of Supremacy.

**5.** In the hope that Rose Stacy(e), a convicted recusant, will conform
by the next Q.S. she is not to be punished. She is to enter a new
recogn. with good sureties to appear at the next Q.S., behave well

---

[1] Holman (Hollman) was keeper of Witney Bridewell in 1617 (below, 1617D7), and
it seems likely that all references to the House of Correction at this period were to the
Witney house.

and speak to Dr. Prideux of Exeter Coll., bringing a certificate of her conformity from him when she appears.

**6.** Avis Wright, a convicted recusant, as in 1614B5 but to speak to Dr. James.

**7.** Rob. Dudley, a convicted recusant, as in 1614B6.

**8.** Rog. Moore, a convicted recusant, as in 1614B6.

**9.** A warrant to be issued for Thos. Freeman jun. according to the statute for unlicensed victualling. He is to be imprisoned in Bocardo for three days without bail or mainprise until he pays 20s. and enters recogn. with two sufficient sureties to appear at the next Q.S.

**10.** Wm. Hill and [*blank*] Browne, who appeared here, to be committed p. 6 to the House of Correction until Wm. brings the Mayor a certificate of his marriage to his wife, Margaret, and his good behaviour.

**11.** Hugh Edwardes to be committed to the House of Correction.

**12.** Ric. Hales to be committed to Bocardo for ten days for contempt and abusing Dr. James. Before his release he is to pay a fine of 20s. and find good and sufficient surety for his appearance at the next Q.S. and good behaviour in the meantime.

**13.** Wm. Badger, a convicted recusant, to enter a new recogn. with good and sufficient sureties to appear at the next Q.S. and obey the court's order if he has not conformed by then.

**14.** Wm. Wheeler to enter recogn. with sufficient sureties to appear at the next Q.S. to answer for hurting Susan Tayler's child.

**15.** Ric. Overton's son, [*named Ric. in margin*] who was born in the psh. of St. Peter-le-Bailey, to be apprenticed to a tradesman. The psh. of St. Peter to pay the psh. of St. Clement 20s. and be discharged from all further costs and charges for his upbringing, or the psh. of St. Clement to pay the psh. of St. Peter likewise and be discharged.

**16.** Thos. Crompton to have a licence to victual.

**17.** Wm. Hill, who was committed to the House of Correction, to remain in Bocardo until his wife brings a certificate of his good behaviour.[1]

---

[1] This might seem to imply that the House of Correction was at Bocardo, but probably that was not so: *see above*, 1614A7 and n.

3

# [1615A]

p. 7 Quarter Sessions 12 Jan. 1615. Rob. Abbotte, Pro-Vice-Chancellor, Wm. Wright esq., Mayor, Art. Lake D.D., Wm. Langton D.D., Thos. James D.D., Jn. Hawley D.C.L., Wm. Ryves esq., Isaac Bartholmew ald., Ric. Hannes ald., Thos. Harris gent., Hen. Toldervey gent., Wm. Potter gent., J.P.s.

1. Wm. Kensall to acknowledge his unjust accusation of Bart. Alder of Steventon of felony which caused him to be bound over to answer here. Kensall made his acknowledgement in court and to end further controversy, craved Alder's pardon and promised to pay the charges disbursed in this court and at the common law in Alder's prosecution of Kensall for slander. The court ordered that Alder should receive compensation of £5 for his disbursements and if Kensall refuses to pay or does not perform this order by 21 Jan. Alder shall be free to proceed at law.

2. Likewise Wm. Kensall to acknowledge his unjust accusation of Wm. Munday of Oxf., butcher, of felony. Kensall made his acknowledgement in open court and craved his pardon. Munday accepted this and agreed to relinquish any claim he might make by law if Kensall acknowledged the injury done to Munday before the Mayor and such friends as Munday should bring before him.

p. 8 3. Dr. Langton, President of Magdalen, to hear and determine the petition exhibited in court by Elias Archer against Jn. Thomlyns for detaining Beatrice, dau. of Thos. Wells of Headington, who had apprenticed herself to Archer.

4. Rose Stacy (Stacie) and the other convicted recusants bound by recogn. at the last Q.S. to appear here to enter new recogns. in the same sums with good sureties to appear at the next Q.S. and obey the court's order if they do not conform by then.

5. The dispute between Kath. Forrest and Eliz. Slye is to be referred to Mr. Potter after a petition was exhibited in court.

6. Mr. Thos. Harris and Ald. Bartholmew are to hear and determine the dispute between Susan Tayler (Taylor) and Wm. Wheeler about the injuring of her child. If they do so the party bound is to be dismissed, paying the fees for this and the last Q.S., or be bound over again.

7. Rose Jones to be committed until she finds good sureties for her appearance at the next Q.S. and good behaviour in the meantime.

**8.** A letter to be sent from the Bench to Sir Alex. Hampden asking p. 9
him to send his servant, Thos. White, husbandman, to be ordered
to provide for his wife and children, who are in great want and
complained that he was absent and did not support them.

**9.** Ric. Hales to be committed to prison until he finds sureties for his
good behaviour and appearance at the next Q.S.

**10.** Kath. Forrest and Eliz. Slye to be well ducked after the dispute
between them was heard and found to result from common strife and
scolding. Because of their repentance and humility in court the order
is not to be carried out unless notice of further quarrelling is given to
a J.P.

**11.** Jn. Wood(e) of the psh. of St. Ebbe to be committed until he enters
recogn. with good sureties to behave well and not victual and to secure
the psh. against any charge from his wife and children.

**12.** Wm. Gibbins and his wife to be committed to prison during the
pleasure of the court for abusing Rob. Bursey, the constable, when he
came to search for stolen goods.

**13.** Jn. Eastwood(e) and Wm. Hopton convicted as common wood
stealers on the oath and testimony of Mr. Yate. They are to be well
whipped at the post and committed to prison pending further consideration.

**14.** A warrant to be made out for the apprehension of Mrs. Freckleton p. 10
when she comes to the town so she can be examined by the next J.P.
for keeping an unlicensed alehouse and receiving stolen goods and
according to the truth of the matter sent to the House of Correction
or otherwise punished.

**15.** Ric. Symes to be well whipped for petty larceny.

**16.** Rob. Davys (Davis) and Wm. Coleman as in 1615A15.

**17.** Wm. Goolde (Goulde) *alias* Good(e) to be committed to the House of
Correction until the next Q.S. or G.D. for the county of Oxon.

**18.** Jn. Baldwyne to be discharged from victualling and bound for his
good behaviour.

**19.** Hen. Prickett to have a new licence to victual at Binsey, where he
lives, putting in sureties according to the statute.

**20.** All licensed alehouse keepers in the Univ. and City to report to
Mr. Jones, Registrar of the Univ. and the Town Clerk. Those that are
privileged are to receive notes of approval from Mr. Jones and the rest p. 11

from the Town Clerk, which are to be produced when required. The Registrar and Town Clerk are to keep a register in a book and take 2d. from each person registered and certified.[1] The constables are to warn all widows and other alehouse keepers in their wards to come before the Mayor and show their licences. The Mayor and another J.P. are to deal as the law requires with those who are not licensed.

**21.** Steph. (or Ric.) Ewen to be licensed to victual, entering recogn. with good sureties according to the statute.

**22.** Wm. Wolridge, fuller, was reported to the court for contempt for refusing to come when sent for. He is to enter recogn. with good sureties not to keep an alehouse.

**23.** Warrants to be made out according to the statute against unlicensed victuallers.

**24.** The constables petitioned for an allowance for charges disbursed for maimed, aged, impotent and lame people and other duties. From now on they should bring the bills for their expenses to the Q.S. to be rated and allowed.

p. 12  **25.** Ralph Oxley, a maimed soldier, to be allowed £3 a year and have a patent for this according to the statute.

**26.** Wm. Pope as in 1615A21.

**27.** Thos. Holte as in 1615A21.

**28.** Ric. Profitt as in 1615A21.

**29.** Those who petitioned at this Q.S. to be licensed victuallers to be admitted first as places become free, the number of licensed alehouses being limited to seventy.

## [1615B]

p. 13  Quarter Sessions 20 April 1615. Rob. Abbotte D.D., Pro-Vice-Chancellor, Wm. Wright esq., Mayor, Wm. Langton D.D., Thos. James D.D., Jn. Hawley D.C.L., Isaac Bartholomew ald., Wm. Potter gent., J.P.s.

**1.** Susan Taylor's complaint against Wm. Wheeler for injuring her child was renewed, but the order at the last Q.S. is to stand.

---

[1] The proposed register was begun, headed by a note that this Q.S. had agreed to limit city licences to seventy and requested that licences for privileged persons of the university be restricted to twenty: O.R.O., QSC/A5/1 (unfoliated), penultimate folio. The register was abandoned after a few entries, but recogs. taken at this Q.S. were also enrolled in the above MS. among licensing material covering the period 1578–1656.

**2.** Jn. Busby to be committed to prison for three days without bail or mainprise for unlicensed victualling and on release to pay 20s. and enter into recogn. not to victual.

**3.** A warrant to be made out for Jn. Ewen to be apprehended and brought before the next J.P. to be committed for unlicensed victualling according to the statute.

**4.** Rose, wife of Edw. Jones of Oxf., tailor, to be discharged of her recogn., paying her fees.

**5.** Ric. Hales committed to Bocardo until he obeys the order for his p. 13(2) submission on his knees for his abuse in open court at the last Q.S. or until further order.

[*Margin*] The day after the Q.S. Dr. James sent written consent to Hales' being bailed.

**6.** Wm. Woolridg(e) committed to prison and to pay 20s. for unlicensed victualling and enter recogn. with good sureties not to victual and to appear at the next Q.S.

**7.** Joan, wife of Ric. Payne, to be discharged from the peace requested against her by Eliz. Sheene, paying her fees.

**8.** Rob. Lovelace *alias* Oates and Nic. Chesheire, who were taken as lewd, idle vagrants and cannot give an account of where and how they live, to remain in prison until next market day and then be whipped and have passes.

**9.** Anne Freckleton, who appeared in court and is strongly suspected of being a lewd woman, to leave Oxf., its suburbs and liberties with bag and baggage by next Michaelmas. If she remains, on her apprehension by warrant the next J.P. is to commit her to prison until the next Q.S. for contempt or she is to put in very good sureties to leave.

**10.** Mary, wife of Jn. Ewen, to be discharged of the peace requested p. 14 against her by Joan, wife of Hen. Ingram, and of her recogn., paying her fees, no demand being made for it although the court examined the matter with both parties present.

**11.** Geo. Vaughan to be fined 40s. for contemptuous departure from the King's service after the court's command to attend and meanwhile to be committed during the court's pleasure.

**12.** Warrants to be made out for recusants presented by the jury and not yet bound to be brought before the two next J.P.s to enter recogns. to appear at the next Q.S. and meanwhile behave well.

**13.** Those presented by the jury for contempt for not coming to be bound not to dress meat in Lent according to the King's proclamation, to be attached by warrant and committed to prison during the J.P.'s pleasure and then to be bound not to victual.

**14.** Warrants to be made out against unlicensed victuallers presented by the jury and orders to be made according to the statute.

**15.** Dan Wright(e) to be whipped at the whipstock next Saturday.

**16.** Wm. Hopkins to be released from prison.

**17.** Edw. Wildgose (Wildgoose), glover, who appeared on his recogn., to be discharged paying his fees.

**18.** Eliz. Wyllyams (Williams) to be committed until she finds sureties for her appearance at the next G.D.

## [1615c]

p. 16　Quarter Sessions Thurs. 8 June 1615. Wm. Goodin D.D., Vice-Chancellor, Wm. Wright esq., Mayor, Art. Lake D.D., Wm. Langton D.D., Thos. James D.D., Jn. Hawley D.C.L., Isaac Bartholmew ald., Ric. Hannes ald., Thos. Harris gent., Wm. Potter gent., J.P.s.

**1.** Ric. Fowrd(e) was bound over to this Q.S. for abusing various parishioners of St. Thos., calling them cuckolds, and for other misdemeanours. Next Sunday, as soon after divine service as possible, he is to go to each person he abused and, in the presence of two or three honest neighbours, admit his offence and be reconciled with them. On notice to any J.P. that he has refused or failed to do so he is to be apprehended by warrant for contempt and a just order made.

**2.** Mr. Sam. Searle to be bound to keep the peace and appear at the next Q.S., on the oath of Mrs. Mallat.

**3.** The two next J.P.s to the psh. of St. John the Baptist are to make an order for lodging and relief to be provided for the poor woman who lies in the lane by Mr. Beeseley's corner on the way to Merton Coll.

p. 17　**4.** Jn. Fletcher, churchwarden of the psh. of St. Mic., sent a certificate that Rob. Dudley of the psh., carpenter, had attended the whole of divine service last Sunday and behaved himself. This was read and the Vice-Chancellor said he had seen him during divine service at Christ Church. His recogn. as a recusant for his good behaviour and appearance at this Q.S. is to be discharged and void.

**5.** The court examined Wal. Wilkins, goldsmith's, complaint that Joan, wife of Jn. New, tailor, had abused and scolded him. She confessed and apologised in open court for her offence and was discharged.

**6.** Augustine Gamon of the psh. of St. Peter-in-the-East petitioned to continue victualling. The full number of victuallers has been licensed but he is to be allowed to victual until further order without trouble from the bailiffs if he keeps order in his house. When a place becomes free he is to be licensed first.

## [1615D]

Gaol Delivery Mon. 5 June 1615. Wm. Wright esq., Mayor, Thos.   p. 18
Wentworth esq., Recorder, Jn. Hawley D.C.L., Wm. Rives esq., Isaac Bartholmew ald., Thos. Harris gent., Ric. Hannes ald., Hen. Toldervey gent., Wm. Potter gent., commissioners for G.D. and J.P.s.

**1.** Ric. Hales to be committed to Bocardo for contempt until he performs the order made at the last Q.S. or, before two J.P.s, penitently acknowledges his abuse of Dr. Hawley, who is to be given notice to attend. The court thinks he deserves worse punishment but makes this order because of the condition of his poor wife and children and in hope of his better behaviour.

**2.** Ric. Westley, who says he lives at Towcester and is Mr. Russell's tenant, Jn. King(e), Eliz. Wylliams (Willyams) and Abraham Blackleech to be discharged by proclamation paying their fees.

**3.** Those of the jury who appeared after being bound over for acquitting Jas. Bostock to be discharged if they pay their fees or be committed until they pay.

**4.** Jn. Huntscott took the Oath of a Suspect and is to be discharged   p. 19
from prison paying his fees.

**5.** Jn. Hayes not to be executed if he provides sufficient sureties to go to Bocardo when required until he obtains the King's pardon and to behave well ever after.

[*Margin*] His own recogn. was taken when the court rose.

**6.** Joan Huntley, who was sentenced to death for murdering Joan, wife of Francis Newbye, to have a stay of execution until the next G.D.

**7.** Nic. Lardner to be discharged paying his fees.

**8.** A warrant to be issued for the churchwardens of St. Peter-in-the-East to levy the statutory penalty for absence from church on four Sundays by distress from Wm. Badger.

**9.** Edw. Chittell (Chittle) to enter recogn. with two different sureties to appear at the next G.D. He took the Oath of Allegiance.

**10.** Adjourned until 19 Sept.

## [1615E]

p. 20  Gaol Delivery 19 Sept. 1615. Wm. Wright esq., Mayor, Thos. Wentworth esq., Recorder, commissioners with others for the delivery of Bocardo.

**1.** A certificate to be sent to the Lord Chancellor concerning the poverty of Jn. Haies, slater, and the truth of the matter for which he was found guilty.

**2.** Adjourned until the first day of the Q.S. for Oxon. after Easter unless the City's justices for G.D. meet on the first day of the Q.S. for the county of Oxon. after Christmas or the first day of the G.D. for the county gaol.

## [1615F]

p. 21  Quarter Sessions Thurs. 5 Oct. 1615. Wm. Goodwyn D.D., Vice-Chancellor, Jn. Byrd esq., Mayor, Jn. Hawley D.C.L., Thos. James D.D., Isaac Bartholmew ald., Hen. Toldervey gent., Wm. Wright gent., J.P.s.

**1.** All those who did not appear on the grand jury as summoned by the serjeant to be fined 10s., unless they have a good excuse.

**2.** A warrant to be made out for Edw. Chittle to be apprehended and committed to Bocardo until further order.

**3.** Sam. Searle appeared on his recogn. and tendered a writ of *supersedeas de pace* from the Crown office which was read publicly and allowed.

**4.** Rob. Charles to be committed to prison for lewd behaviour. Next market day he is to be whipped in public and sent by pass to Eynsham, where he lives, with a certificate that he has been punished.

p. 22  **5.** Geo. Fry and Jn. Wylliams, who were indicted and acquitted, are to be returned to Bocardo. Geo. Fry is to be well whipped next market day and sent with a certificate of his punishment by pass from constable to constable to Petworth, Sussex, where he says his master, Jn. Willyams, a fustian weaver, lives. If he has no such master he is to be delivered to the masters of Bridewell there and dealt with by the county justices. Jn. Willyams is to remain in prison until the Mayor receives a certificate of his good behaviour from Mr. Wm. Coles, a cook living at Pie Corner.[1] He is then to be released and sent by pass into the country.

**6.** The last warrants made against victuallers are to stand and the warrants now made are to order unlicensed victuallers to be brought before two J.P.s for an order under the statute.

**7.** Hen. Kenneston to remain in prison until he obtains a certificate of good behaviour from creditable persons or good sureties for his appearance at the next Q.S.

**8.** Warrants to be made out against persons presented by the jury: Joan Scott, widow, for disorder in her house at the time of divine service on Sunday; Mic. Foster and Mary Busby for not attending divine service; Nat. Waymacke (Waymake) as a common drunkard.

## [1616A]

Quarter Sessions Thurs. 11 Jan. 1616. Jn. Bird esq., Mayor, Jn. Hawley p. 23 D.C.L., Thos. James D.D., Wm. Rives esq., Isaac Bartholmew ald., Thos. Harris gent., Ric. Hannes ald., Wm. Potter gent., Hen. Toldervey gent., Wm. Wright gent., J.P.s.

**1.** The dispute between Hen. Samon (Sammon) and Jn. Browne to be referred to the next two J.P.s. to the psh. where they live and to the ald. of the ward. If not resolved both to be bound over to answer at the next Q.S.

**2.** A petition and articles sent from the J.P.s of the county. and presented by [*blank*] Okeley the father were considered and the circumstances fully heard and understood. Nic. Elliott was accused of being the father of the two bastards of Ockeley's daughter, Anne. Nic. produced a sealed testimonial from Dr. Blincoe that, before him, he had been acquitted of the charge and a gent. of good esteem confirmed this in open court.[2] The court is of the opinion that the Okeleys are

[1] Possibly at the junction of High Street and Oriel Street, where the city held Piebaker's Place: H. E. Salter, Survey of Oxf., i (O.H.S. N.s. xiv), 185.
[2] Ant. Blencowe (Blincoe), the bishop of Oxford's vicar-general or chancellor, presided over the local ecclesiastical courts: J. Howard-Drake, *Oxf. Church Courts, Depositions 1609–1616*, page v.

11

in the habit of laying a burden on Ellyott and trying to get money as
he is a man of good estate. The court acquitted Nic., thought Anne
worthy of double punishment and ordered her to reveal the true
father of her bastards.

p. 24  **3.** Thos. Fawcett (Faucet) having been indicted, arraigned and found
guilty of felony is allowed benefit of clergy and burnt on the hand.
Because of his lewd and evil disposition before he is set free Thos. to
put in a surety of £100 never to come within the City or Univ. or
their liberties, and to enter into a bond before Dr. Hawley and Mr.
Harris, or one of them, as they had previously examined him and
heard his confession.

**4.** By the next Q.S. Hen. Holmes, physician ('Professor of Physick'),
to give an account to the Regius Professor of Medicine of the physic
he has administered to Jn. Bentley and be bound to appear at the next
Q.S. and meanwhile be of good behaviour.

**5.** Jas. Feild and Thos. Pemerton to be fined £5 each for contempt in
leaving court without permission or doing their service.

**6.** Ric. Holby, one of the petty jury, fined 20s. and imprisoned for
four days for contempt in not being present for the delivery of their
verdict.

**7.** Jn. Brockhurst fined 20s. for leaving court without permission after
being summoned to serve on the petty jury.

**8.** Jn. Rowland's petition read in open court to be referred to the two
next J.P.s to where he lives.

p. 25  **9.** Geo. Smyth (Smith), porter of Brasenose Coll., found guilty of maliciously making false accusations against Wm. Willis of Oxf., brewer,
concerning the death of Jn. Smyth, keeper of the Swan inn, is ordered
to acknowledge his offence, make his submission in open court and ask
for pardon and forgiveness from Willis. He did so and was discharged
with Willis's consent, and Willis was discharged from his recogn.

**10.** Wm. and Laur. Maddox indicted and found not guilty of the felony
of stealing seven geese but, because of their disorderly and infamous
way of life, to be bound with good sureties before their release from
prison to behave well and appear at the next Q.S.

**11.** Thos. Harrington, having been indicted and convicted of stealing
linen cloths, to be well whipped in the open market next market day
and then be delivered.

**12.** Ric. Barnes, having been found guilty of the felony of stealing a ruff band, to be whipped in the open market on the next two market days (Saturday and Wednesday) and then be delivered.

**13.** Dan. Wright, having been indicted and convicted of stealing poultry, to be well whipped on the next two market days (Saturday and Wednesday).

**14.** Thos. Joyner *alias* Sumpton (Sunton), having been indicted and convicted of stealing poultry, to be well whipped next market day only.

**15.** Ellen Newman, having been indicted and convicted of petty p. 26 larceny and found to be 'a most lewd and cosening Queane', to be very well whipped on the next two market days and on the third market day to be whipped out of the town at a cart's tail.

**16.** Jn. Argo(e) to be hanged after being indicted, arraigned and convicted of burglary.

**17.** Thos. Fawcett, indicted, arraigned and convicted of felony, claimed benefit of clergy, read his book as a clerk, and was burnt on the hand. He is to remain in prison until he finds sureties for his good behaviour and to leave the city never to return.

**18.** Anne Steele, widow, to be bound with good sureties to appear at the next Q.S.

**19.** The petition of Margery Attwood, widow, was read, exhibited, and referred to the next two J.P.s, whose order is to rank as if made in open court.

**20.** The petition of the psh. of St. Mary was read. Those who take in inmates to be bound with good sureties to discharge their psh. of any future charge. Ric. Hodgkins, who harbours Wm. Gray, Geo. Smyth and Ric. Alligant, who were mentioned in the petition, are to be sent by warrant to a J.P. and bound as above or committed to prison.

**21.** The unlicensed victuallers presented by the grand jury are to be brought by warrant before J.P.s and bound with sufficient sureties not to victual and to obey the order under the statute of the next Q.S.

**22.** The constables requested the allowances ordered by the Q.S. p. 27 last Jan. The churchwardens are to levy the money from the pshs. in proportion to their liabilities.

**23.** Warrants to be made out for Ric. Robinson of the psh. of St. Mary, Wm. Jones of Canditch, Ewen Petty of the psh. of St. Mic., cobbler,

Ric. Hutchins of the psh. of St. Mic., Wm. Tavy of the psh. of St. Thos. and Geo. Flud of the psh. of St. Thos., sawyer, to be brought before the Mayor or a J.P. to be bound with good sureties to appear at the next Q.S. for common drunkenness and obey the court's order.

**24.** Ric. Ford of the psh. of St. Thos., [*blank*] Price jun. of the psh. of St. Mic. and Wm. Trindall of the psh. of St. Giles to be bound as in 1616A23 for playing skittle pins on the Sabbath.

## [1616B]

p. 28  Gaol Delivery 9 April 1616. Jn. Bird esq., Mayor, Thos. Wentworth esq., Recorder, Jn. Hawley D.C.L., Thos. Harris gent., Wm. Potter gent., Hen. Toldervey gent., Wm. Wright gent., commissioners for the delivery of Bocardo.

**1.** A warrant to be signed and sealed by a J.P. according to the statute of 3 James cap. 4 for the churchwardens of the psh. of St. Peter-in-the-East to distrain 3s. for Wm. Badger's absence from church on the last three Sundays as confessed in open court, and to distribute it to the poor according to the statute.

**2.** The recogn. of Francis Dixon to be certified into the Exchequer and a process to be obtained, and issued against him.

**3.** Edw. Chittle and Wm. Badger, convicted recusants who were bound to appear at this G.D., to be bound with good sureties to appear and answer at the Q.S. after Michaelmas and meanwhile to be of good behaviour, as Wm. confessed in open court that he had been married within the last three years by a Queen Mary seminary priest, and information was given against Edw. that mass had recently been said in his house.

**4.** Mary Higges, Hen. Higges and Ric. Owen as in 1616B2.

**5.** Oath of a suspect administered in court to Thos. Sunton.

## [1616c]

p. 29  Quarter Sessions Thurs. 11 April 1616. Jn. Bird esq., Mayor, Jn. Hawley D.C.L., Thos. James D.D., Thos. Harris gent., Ric. Hannes ald., Wm. Potter gent., Wm. Wright gent., J.P.s.

**1.** Wm. Sutton *alias* Robynson (Robinson) to be committed to Bocardo until a further order for abusing the constable sent to him and for rude behaviour to Mr. Harris before whom the constable brought him. On his release to be bound for his good behaviour.

14

**2.** Hen. Holmes appeared in court as bound and Dr. Clayton's certificate was read. Hen. to be discharged of his recogn. once he puts in good sureties not to practise as a physician or surgeon in the liberties of the City or Univ., as he is utterly unskilful, and to leave before Whitsun.

**3.** Agnes (Ann) Steele to be discharged of her recogn., paying her fees, after appearing with a certificate of good behaviour from the parson and several parishioners of her psh.

**4.** Ric. Fourd (Ford) who appeared on his recogn. after being presented at the last Q.S. confessed to playing unlawful games. Ric. to be committed to Bocardo until he pays 6s. 8d. and enters into recogn. with good sureties not to play unlawful games according to the statute.

**5.** A process of outlawry to be sent out against Mary Higgs (Higges) on the grand jury's indictment.

**6.** Agnes Huntmill discharged as no proof was shown when she appeared on her recogn., accused of stealing a pint pot from Mr. Gryse.

**7.** Joan, wife of Jn. Brookes, released from her recogn. with the p. 30 Mayor's consent despite her abuse to him.

**8.** Thos. Middleton, appearing on his recogn., and the court considering him, on the oath of Joan Elmes, worthy of punishment, is bound to appear at the next Q.S. and keep the peace.

**9.** Thos. Price jun., son of Art. Price (Pryce) as in 1616c4.

**10.** Warrants to be made for all unlicensed victuallers presented by the grand jury to be apprehended and dealt with according to the statute.

**11.** The unlicensed victuallers presented at the last Q.S. and appearing here, Joan Triplett, Eliz. Jones, Amy Teasler, Ric. Griffyn and Hugh Boseley, to be committed to Mr. Baylie's [? the bailiff's] custody to be imprisoned for three days and then to enter recogn. with sureties before a J.P. not to victual until licensed. Ordered likewise for others presented at this or the last Q.S.

**12.** Each alehouse keeper to paint his door and window posts or erect a lattice or sign to distinguish his house before the next Q.S. and to be stopped from victualling if certified to have failed to do so.

**13.** Those presented as common drunkards and those not performing their duties as churchwardens or collectors for the poor to be dealt with according to the statutes.

p. 31  **14.** Jn. Beamish(e) to be whipped for petty larceny and stealing Rob. Bursey's goods and to remain in prison until he satisfies him for the value of his yarn.

**15.** As no bill of indictment was brought when Nic. Lardner and Silvester Peirson appeared in court a public proclamation was made for them to be discharged of their recogn., paying their fees.

**16.** The forfeited recogns. of Thos. Roberts and Jn. Hutchins to be estreated and certified into the Exchequer.

**17.** Ric. Parker, having been indicted and found guilty of petty larceny, to be whipped in Bocardo in reasonable manner and then discharged, paying his fees.

**18.** Jn. Browne, cutter, to be fined 5s. on the indictment found at the last Q.S. and to be discharged on paying it and his fees.

[*Margin*] Paid it.

**19.** Jn. Ewen to be committed to and his wife released from Bocardo.

**20.** Ric. Evans to be bound to appear at the next Q.S. and meanwhile be of good behaviour.

**21.** Wm. Alverd's petition as a maimed soldier, which was exhibited in court, and his certificate to be considered by the court or the greater part of them by the next Q.S. when a final order shall be made according to the statute.

## [1616D]

p. 32  Quarter Sessions at the Guildhall 30 May 1616. Wm. Goodwyne, Dean of Christ Church, Vice-Chancellor, Jn. Byrd, Mayor, Isaac Bartholmewe ald., Thos. Harris ald., Wm. Wright gent., J.P.s.

**1.** Ric. Pope of the psh. of St. Thos. to enter recogn. with good surety to appear and answer at the next Q.S. and bring a certificate from the parson or vicar of the psh. where he lodges or works that meanwhile he has attended church for divine service and received communion.

**2.** Ric. Evans to be discharged of his recogn. as its continuation was not requested when he appeared.

**3.** Wm. Robynson, glazier, who appeared on his recogn., to be discharged paying his fees.

**4.** Rob. Robynson (Robinson), who appeared and was acquitted by proclamation, to be discharged, paying his fees.

**5.** On the evidence of Wm. Baylie (Bayly), baker, Hugh Dew(e) to be discharged from his apprenticeship with him. Hugh is to be given such clothes ('good apparrell') as he brought with him.

**6.** Since the late husband of Mary Yong(e), widow, living under the p. 33 Guildhall, had behaved well as a victualler and had died poor, leaving her no means of support, she entered recogn. and is licensed under the statute.

**7.** Sibyl Bayly(e) widow of Wm. Baylye of the psh. of St. Peter-le-Bailey as in 1616D6.

**8.** Jn. Pyme, shoemaker, and Widow Knapp, saddler, appearing as unlicensed victuallers after being convicted at the last Q.S., to be committed to Bocardo for three days, then to be bound with good sureties not to victual and to appear at the next Q.S. to be fined according to the statute.

**9.** Jn. Joyner *alias* Sumpton and Rob. Willes, having been found guilty on several indictments for petty larceny, to be well whipped at the whipstock and Jn. to put in sureties for his good behaviour before being discharged.

[*Margin, in another hand*] We desire to be forgiven.

**10.** Widow Knapp, who on the order above being made used very saucy words and ran away in contempt of court, to be committed to Bocardo until some of the J.P.s who saw this think fit to release her under suitable conditions. A warrant to be made out for her apprehension as she shut her doors against the constable and other officers who pursued her.

**11.** All recusants presented by the grand jury to be certified to the p. 34 Exchequer to be dealt with according to the law.

**12.** All common drunkards presented by the jury to be apprehended by warrant and dealt with according to the statute.

**13.** All those presented for playing unlawful games and working on the Sabbath to be prosecuted according to the law.

## [1616E]

p. 35  Orders 10 Aug. 1616 for suppressing alehouses and the disorder caused by them. Dr. Lake, Vice-Chancellor, Jn. Byrd esq., Mayor, Wm. Goodwyne D.D., Dean of Christ Church, Dr. Ayeray, Sir Hen. Savile, Dr. Langton, Dr. James, Dr. Hawley, Wm. Ryves esq., Thos. Harris ald., Wm. Potter gent., Wm. Wright gent., J.P.s.

**1.** Speedy proceedings to be taken against unlicensed victuallers and sellers of ale and beer, without waiting for the next Q.S.

**2.** The number of alehouses not to exceed forty or fifty, whether kept by privileged persons or not.

**3.** No one to be licensed who has another trade or can live by other means. Alehouse keepers to be able to control their houses and to bring a certificate from the minister of their psh. and their most substantial neighbours.

**4.** No one to sell ale or beer in a back lane, byway, corner or upper room. All alehouses to be distinguished by a lattice, coloured post or sign.

**5.** Dressing meat in alehouses, taverns, cooks' shops and so on on Fridays and other fast days contrary to law and proclamation to be enquired into and punished.

**6.** Idle sitting, drunkenness and other disorders in alehouses and tippling houses contrary to statutes of 1, 4 and 7 Jas. to be enquired into and severely punished.

Subscribed by Mr. Justice Croke: 'Theis orders are verie well Conceaved and are very meete to be observed and to be put in due execution. Jn. Croke'

Subscribed by the J.P.s listed above.

## [1616F]

p. 36  Orders for suppressing alehouses made at the Guildhall 10 Sept. 1616. Dr. Lake, Vice-Chancellor, Jn. Bird esq., Mayor, Dr. James, Dr. Hawley, Wm. Ryves esq., Wm. Potter gent., Hen. Toldervey gent., Wm. Wright gent. J.P.s.

**1.** Warrants to be sent telling the constables to present the names and dwelling places of all alehouse keepers and victuallers in their wards to the J.P.s and to warn them to appear before the J.P.s at the Guildhall on Tues come fortnight, 24 Sept. before 1 p.m.

18

**2.** All those who victual in by-lanes and obscure places to be suppressed, whether they are privileged or free.

**3.** Those with licences are to produce them. Even if approved by the J.P.s their licences will be void unless they put up a red painted lattice or post at their doors by the next Q.S.

**4.** The J.P.s to meet in a fortnight and then on the first Tuesday of each month when there is no Q.S. to make further orders for the punishment of disorderly alehouse keepers and victuallers on the basis of information and presentments.

Subscribed by the J.P.s.

## [1616G]

Orders made at the Guildhall 24 Sept. 1616. Dr. Ayeray, Pro-Vice- p. 37
Chancellor, Jn. Bird esq., Mayor, Dr. Prideux, Dr. James, Dr. Hawley, Isaac Bartholmew ald., Wm. Wright gent. J.P.s.

**1.** Widow Hankes questioned and found guilty of keeping an alehouse in a blind corner of Bear Lane known to be a haven for those who sleep by day and cause disorder by night. She is to move to a more open street by the Q.S. after Christmas next or be stopped from victualling.

**2.** Jn. Warrenner, cook (and his wife), who was found to keep a disorderly house, promised in open court to correct this and leave the house where he now victuals.

**3.** Hen. Gunne and Wal. Harding, who have been keeping unlicensed and disorderly alehouses in St. Michaels Lane, to be stopped from victualling and warrants to be made out against them.

**4.** Jn. Ewen, Humph. Jorden and Jn. Busby, who have been keeping alehouses in New Inn Lane, and Rob. Sargeant, who has been keeping an alehouse and lewd company in the lane by Broken Hays[1] to be stopped from doing so and if they continue to be dealt with according to the statute.

**5.** As in 1616G4 for Geo. Dalby and Rob. Dudley who have been victualling in Bentley's house near the Northgate, and are inmates, which this court 'utterly misliketh' and prohibits.

[1] The area later George Street and Gloucester Green.

p. 37 **6.** Jn. Stacy, musician, for keeping an inward alehouse, which the court much dislikes, to be stopped from selling ale or beer and, if he continues, to be dealt with according to the statute.

**7.** Wm. Rixon, barber, who has been victualling and selling ale inwardly, to satisfy the Dean of Christ Church and Dr. James within a month and either to be licensed and set up a red post or lattice at his door or window, or to be stopped from victualling.

**8.** Thos. Freman of the psh. of St. Thos. and Rob. Budd the bellman to be stopped from victualling and to be proceeded against as unlicensed victuallers if they continue, after a presentment against them for disorder and gaming in their houses.

**9.** Within the next six weeks every victualler or alehouse keeper to set up a red lattice at his window or a red post at his door so that it can be recognised. Anyone who fails to do so to be stopped from victualling, and if they continue to do so to be dealt with as unlicensed victuallers according to the statute.

## [1616H]

p. 39 Quarter Sessions at the Guildhall 3 Oct. 1616. Wm.Goodwyne, Vice-Chancellor, Ric. Smyth esq., Mayor, Dr. Langton D.D., Dr. Prideux D.D., Dr. James D.D., Jn. Hawley D.C.L., Isaac Bartholmew ald., Thos. Harris ald., Ric. Hannes ald., Wm. Potter, Wm. Wright, J.P.s.

**1.** Wm. Jenings, tailor, who appeared and was not prosecuted, to be discharged of his recogn.

**2.** Writs of *certiorari* for removing the recogns. of Jn. Leighford *alias* Heighlorde and Wal. Meares, skinners of London, to be allowed and the recogns. certified.

**3.** Joan, wife of Jn. Copperthwait(e), who appeared in court, to be discharged.

**4.** Rob. Needle, carpenter, to be discharged of his recogn. if he pays his fees or to be taken by warrant and bound over to appear at the next Q.S.

**5.** Wal. Hardwell of Great Milton, Oxon., agreed in court to take charge of Jn. Smyth, aged about six and a half, son of the late Jn. Smyth, innkeeper of the Swan at Oxf. The psh. of St. Mary to pay Wal. 12d. per week until Jn. is of sufficient age and stature to be

apprenticed or until the psh. orders otherwise. Mr. Jn. Garbrand paid
a month's allowance of 4s. to Wal. in court and Wal. is to be paid
monthly in advance as long as the boy is well looked after.

**6.** Hen. Aykers to be discharged of his recogn. paying his fees.

**7.** Abraham Shawe to be discharged of his recogn.                    p. 40

**8.** Anne Freeman (Freman), widow, of the psh. of St. Ebbe entered
recogn. in open court to prosecute Margery Morgan(e) for receiving
stolen goods.

**9.** Jn. Phillips, shoemaker, to be discharged of his recogn.

**10.** Jn. Came to be bound with good sureties for his good behaviour
and meanwhile to be committed to Bocardo. A certificate of his case
and behaviour to be sent to the Lord Chief Justice with his Lord-
ship's warrant which was taken on Came on his apprehension.

**11.** Jn. Kerke (Kirke) to remain in prison to await the opinion of the
judges of the circuit on his feloniously having two wives at once.

**12.** Ric. Parsons, Cyprian Godfrey and Chris. Barbor to be
committed to Bocardo until the court orders further and Cyprian not
to be discharged until he finds good sureties to be bound for his good
behaviour.

**13.** Thos. Chollerick the younger, Rob. Budd, Eliz. Budd and Mary
Smyth to be discharged of their recogns. Old Mr. Chollerick of
Choursden [? Churchdown], Gloucs., gave his word in court that he
will bring his son to court if before the next Q.S. anything new comes
to light concerning the death of Sir Hen. Savell's (Savile's) man and his
son is to appear in person.

**14.** Thos. Smyth(e) of Oxf., cordwainer, to be discharged paying his
fees.

**15.** Ralph Oxley to retain his patent for an allowance as a maimed soldier
of £3 per year from the city payable by the Treasurer. Wm. Alverd, a
maimed soldier pressed in Oxf., who was sent with the King's order    p. 41
certified by one of the Masters of Requests and Sir Wm. Wood, Chief
Muster Master, to have an allowance of 40s. per year with the first
payment at the next Q.S. A patent of this was signed by the J.P.s,
sealed and delivered to him.

**16.** Thos. Noble, indicted here, to be discharged after the jury did not
find the bill against him.

**17.** Edw. Hutchins to be committed to Bocardo until he asks for the public forgiveness of Wal. Wilkins the constable to whom, as was proved on oath, he was violent and lewd when he was commanded in the King's name to keep the peace and go home when he was drunk and disorderly at 11 p.m. Edw. to pay a fine of 20s. before being released. Edw. and his brother Ric. Hutchins, who is considered a worse offender, to put in good sureties for their behaviour and a warrant to be made for the apprehension of Ric. until he performs the same order as Edw. If the Mayor is satisfied with their submission he may remit the fine.

**18.** Thos. Taylor, who appeared on submission of stealing pewter found on him clipped, cut and battered to be put in the stocks for two hours next market day with the pewter hung up for people to see. He shall remain in prison until the next Wednesday in case any further evidence is found. If not, he shall be well whipped as a vagrant rogue and sent, with a pass and certificate of his behaviour and punishment, to Cricklade where he says he was born.

p. 42 **19.** Jn. Studley to be well whipped for stealing three pewter dishes.

**20.** Mary Butcher to be well whipped on three market days for robbing her master, Mr. Steph. Fayerbeard.

**21.** Wal. Fysher (Fisher), who was found guilty of stealing a silver gilt salt cellar from Mr. Wright, allowed benefit of clergy and before being discharged was burnt on the hand.

**22.** Rob. Warde the baker, his wife Jane and son Edw., to be fined 20s. each after being indicted and found guilty of assaulting and maiming Jn. Knapp and to be imprisoned until they pay. They were present in court and on request were admitted to their traverses, each separately traversing the indictment.

**23.** Jas. Wilson to be bound with good sureties to appear at the next Q.S.

**24.** Rob. Ward(e) the baker to be committed to Bocardo for a day and a night for abusing Dr. James, refusing to appear on his warrant and for contempt in open court. Rob. to remain there until he submits to Dr. James and acknowledges his offence.

**25.** The dispute between Wm. Davyes (Davies) and Eliz., wife of Thos. Clarke, to be examined by Dr. Prideux, Dr. James and Dr. Hawley or any two of them and dealt with at the next Q.S. according to their report. Wm. to enter recogn. to appear before them at a day's notice left at Thos.'s house or, if he does not, at the next Q.S.

**26.** Ric. Parsons, surgeon, to be discharged of his recogn. <sub>p. 43</sub>

**27.** Chris. Barbor to be discharged of his recogn.

**28.** Rose Stacy, Rob. Dudley, Rog. Moore, Avis Wright and Edw. Chittle to be bound to their good behaviour and to appear at the next Q.S. and warrants to be made for other recusants presented by the grand jury to appear before a J.P. to be bound in the same way.

**29.** The pshs. in the note attached to the file of this Q.S. to be taxed quarterly for relief of the maimed soldiers, Ralph Oxley and Wm. Alverd, as follows: St. Martin 3s. 6d.; All Saints 3s. 6d.; St. Aldate 3s.; St. Mary 3s.; St. Peter-in-the-East 2s. 6d.; St. Mic. 2s.; St. Mary Magdalen 2s. 6d.; St. Peter-le-Bailey 2s.; St. Ebbe 2s.; St. Giles 2s.; St. Thos. 2s.; Binsey 2s.; total 30s.

**30.** Warrants to be made for all those who were bound to appear for breach of the peace and were to be discharged paying their fees, but who left without doing so, to be brought before a J.P. to be bound to appear at the next Q.S. to answer for their contempt.

## [1616I]

Orders Tues. 10 Dec. 1616. Sebastian Benfeild, Pro-Vice-Chancellor, <sub>p. 44</sub> Ric. Smyth esq., Mayor, Dr. Prideux, Dr. James, Thos. Harris ald., Wm. Potter gent., Hen. Toldervey gent., Wm. Wright gent., Ralph Flexney gent., J.P.s.

**1.** Hen. Gunne and Wal. Harding to be attached by warrant and proceeded against according to the statute as unlicensed victuallers.

**2.** Jn. Ewen, Jn. Busby, Humph. Jorden and Rob. Sargeant as in 1616II.

**3.** Geo. Dalby and Rob. Dudley as in 1616II.

**4.** Jn. Stacy, musician, to be allowed until the Q.S. after Easter to find a more suitable house to victual at and meanwhile to paint his door post or window towards the street so his house can be recognised.

**5.** Wm. Rixon, barber, to comply with order 1616G7 by the next Q.S. or be stopped from victualling.

**6.** Thos. Freman (jun.) of the psh. of St. Thos., who was presented for allowing disorder, to comply with order 1616G8. Rob. Budd the bellman to receive a similar notice from the constable and both to appear at the next Q.S. for a further order.

p. 45   **7.** Jn. Plaisted, miller, to set up a red lattice or post by Christmas or be stopped from victualling.

**8.** Jn. Woods, carpenter (psh. St. Ebbe), to be stopped from victualling and to take down his red lattice by the next Q.S. or be attached by warrant and brought before the J.P.s to be dealt with according to the statute as an unlicensed victualler.

**9.** Wm. Rose, being neither privileged nor free, to be apprehended by warrant as an unlicensed victualler to appear at the next Q.S. for a further order.

**10.** The constables to give a notice in their wards to each unlicensed victualler, of whom they have a note from the office, telling them to get tickets from the Town Clerk if they are freemen or from Mr. Jones the Registrar, if privileged, and to set up a red lattice or door post by the next Q.S. or be stopped from victualling.

## [1617A]

p. 46   Quarter Sessions at the Guildhall 9 Jan. 1617. Rt. Revd. Art. Lake, Bp. of Bath and Wells, Ric. Smyth esq., Mayor, Jn. Prideux D.D., Thos. James D.D., Jn. Hawley D.C.L., Wm. Ryves esq., Thos. Harris ald., Ric. Hannes ald., Wm. Potter gent., Hen. Toldervey gent., Wm. Wright gent., J.P.s.

**1.** Edw. Wyrdnam (Wirdnam), apprentice to Mr. Jn. Byrd, mercer, was well whipped in the lower hall, by order of the court, for lewd words and behaviour towards Dr. James and on his knees acknowledged his offence and asked for Dr. James's forgiveness. He asked for his master's forgiveness for misdemeanours against him before all the J.P.s at a meeting on the same day at Mr. Freer's house.

**2.** Thos. Freman (jun.) of the psh. of St. Thos. to be committed to Bocardo for three days without bail or mainprise as an unlicensed victualler and on his release to put in sureties for his good behaviour and not to victual without licence and to pay a fine of 20s.

**3.** Geo. Vaughan, cutler, to be committed to Bocardo for abusing the constable until he enters recogn. with good sureties for his good behaviour.

**4.** Edw. Bythell to be committed to Bocardo until he enters recogn. with good sureties to behave well, appear at the next Q.S. and answer the suspicion that he helped to steal the gelding from All Souls College.

24

**5.** Ric. Hutchins to be committed to Bocardo until he enters recogn. p. 47
with good sureties to behave well and appear at the next Q.S.

**6.** Edw. Hart, who was found guilty by the grand jury on an indictment for assault and battery of Thos. Dodge, to be committed to
Bocardo until he pays a fine of 10s. and his fees.

**7.** Margery Morgan to be discharged and pay her fees after a proclamation was made in open court and no prosecution was brought.

**8.** Jn. Willyams, who was found guilty of being a common hedge
breaker and wood stealer by the oath in court of Ant. Hore, to be
committed to Bocardo until he finds good sureties for his good
behaviour and appearance at the next Q.S.

**9.** Margaret Dudley to be committed until she enters recogn. with
sureties to behave well and appear at the next Q.S.

**10.** Helen Davyes (Davies) as in 1617A7.

**11.** Thos. Neale to be discharged paying his fees.

**12.** Cyprian Godfrey's recogn. to be postponed to the next Q.S. and
the clerk of the court to make out a warrant for his re-arrest. Cyprian
then to be bound by good sureties to appear at the next Q.S. and
meanwhile behave well.

**13.** The convicted recusants Rose Stacy, Rog. Moore, Wm. Badger
and Edw. Chittle bound by recogn. to appear at the next Q.S. and
meanwhile behave well.

**14.** If no complaint is made against her at the next Q.S. Rose Stacy p. 48
to be discharged as she was first committed by Mr. Justice Williams
and ever since has been bound over from Q.S. to Q.S. without any
complaint being made against her.

**15.** Jas. Wilson to be discharged paying his fees.

**16.** Jn. Pyme of Oxf., cordwainer, who was proved often to have
been in contempt of the court's orders and to have victualled without
licence, to be stopped from doing so and to be committed to Bocardo
for three days according to the statute. On his release to enter recogn.
with good sureties not to victual without licence and to pay a fine
of 20s.

**17.** Ric. Jones and his wife Margaret to be well whipped as
wandering rogues and sent with a pass and a certificate of this to their
birthplace.

25

**18.** Wm. Wyatt to be committed to Bocardo until further order because of his disorderly way of life.

**19.** Jn. Busby to be committed to Bocardo for three days as an unlicensed victualler and on his release to enter recogn. with good sureties not to victual without licence and to be fined 20s.

**20.** Edw. Wyldgoose (Wildgoose), glover, to be licensed to victual, putting in good sureties to keep order, for as long as he cannot work because of poor eyesight.

p. 49   **21.** Francis Allen for unlicensed victualling as in 1617A19.

**22.** Eliz. Greene (Grene) claimed 21s. from the psh. of St. Peter-le-Bailey for keeping a poor child left on the psh. by its parents who died leaving nothing. It is to be collected there and paid to her but because of the smallness and poverty of the psh. the churchwardens of the pshs. of St. Aldate, St. Martin, All Saints and St. Mary to collect 3d. per week each and of the psh. of St. Peter-in-the-East 2d. per week and pay it to Eliz. until the court orders otherwise.

**23.** Warrants to be made out against everyone presented by the grand jury for any misdemeanours punishable by statute.

**24.** And. Symes asked for allowance from the court as a maimed soldier. If the Recorder finds on searching that he was pressed into the wars 'out of this body' and maimed as he claims, the Treasurer[1] of Oxf. to pay him an allowance of 20s. in return for a covenant not to claim a further allowance.

p. 50   **25.** Chas. Raynesford (Raynsford) to be stopped from victualling because of complaints in open court that there is great disorder in his house every day and, if he continues, to be dealt with according to the statute as an unlicensed victualler.

**26.** The psh. of St. Aldate to provide a house for goodwife Mathew within the next fortnight or be fined 40s. for her use and the rest of the poor of the psh., her allowance being decided by the majority of J.P.s at the next Q.S.

## [1617B]

p. 51   Quarter Sessions at the Guildhall Wed. 30 April 1617. Rt. Revd. Bp. of Bath and Wells [Art. Lake], Ric. Smyth esq., Mayor, Dr. Langton, Dr. Prideux, Dr. James, Dr. Hawley, Wm. Ryves esq.,

---

[1] i.e. the treasurer for maimed soldiers.

Thos. Harris ald., Ric. Hannes ald., Wm. Potter gent., Hen. Toldervey gent., Wm. Wright gent., J.P.s.

**1.** Alice, dau. of Eliz. Rackton, who behaves in a lewd way and is strongly suspected of being a cutpurse, to be committed to Bocardo as she cannot find sureties and to be well whipped by Mrs. Brushe and sent home to her mother.

**2.** Thos. Whyte (White) to be put in the stocks for four hours for being drunk in court.

**3.** Wm. Mabbs, who appeared on his recogn., to be committed to Bocardo until he finds sureties for his appearance at the next county of Oxon. sessions unless the Lord Chief Justice, who has previously examined him, orders otherwise.

**4.** Mr. Wm. Bosswell to be discharged after he appeared on the recogn. taken by the Mayor, to answer concerning his former servant Jn. Mathew.

**5.** Wm. Steevenson (Stevenson), apprentice to Mr. Fulke Emerson, to be committed to Bocardo during the pleasure of the court, for being one of the 'disguised' actors in the riding company who passed the Guildhall during open sessions on May Day in contempt of the court and the Mayor's order.

**6.** Wm. Rawlynson *alias* Rauson of Woodstock and his companion Rob. Howell to be discharged by proclamation after they appeared on their recogn. and no prosecution was brought.

**7.** The churchwardens of the psh. of St. Martin to pay Wm. Waspe by p. 52 Ascension Day the arrears of £5 claimed for keeping a poor boy as his apprentice. The Mayor and Mr. Potter to make a further order if the churchwardens show reasons for not paying.

**8.** Thos. Alcock, who appeared on his recogn., to be discharged as Mary Bursey could not show why it should be continued.

**9.** Warrants to be made out against Wm. Stapler, [blank] Frost the cobbler, Peter Short the cutler, [blank] Tilcock the painter and [blank] Pigeon the chimney sweep, for being among the unruly May Day riders in contempt of the Mayor's order. On their apprehension to be brought before some of the J.P.s to be punished.

**10.** Thos. Fuller, cook, being bound for abusing and beating the constable sent to apprehend him by warrant from Dr. James, to be committed to Bocardo until Saturday, then to be put in the stocks at market time from 10 a.m. to 2 p.m. and then find good sureties for the peace or remain in prison.

**11.** Hen. Harbert, who appeared on his recogn., to be discharged. Elias Archer to be fined 8s. for troubling Hen. without cause and then not prosecuting him.

**12.** Mary Ewen to be discharged but she and her husband to be sent to the House of Correction on proof that she harbours guests or sells drink or victuals in the future.

p. 53 **13.** Jn. Mathew(e), former apprentice of Mr. Bosswell, to be discharged.

**14.** Edw. Bythell to be bound by recogn. to appear at the next Q.S. and to be discharged by proclamation if no evidence is brought against him.

**15.** Rob. Ward, his wife Jane and son Edw., to be fined 6s. 8d. each and be discharged paying their fees after submitting to the court for breach of the peace and beating Jn. Knapp.

**16.** Thos. Deane to be fined 6s. 8d. after being indicted for assault and breach of the peace. Thos. and Hen. Rounsevall (Rounsevale), who prosecuted him, submitted to the court. Thos. to pay 20s. compensation to Hen., both parties to release each other, and Thos. to be discharged on payment.

**17.** Jn. Pyme to be discharged after appearing in court as no information was given that he had kept disorder in his house or sold ale or beer since he was ordered to stop victualling.

**18.** Edw. Stubbs, Jn. Mathew(e) and all others bound to appear at this Q.S. after Mr. Bosswell's complaint to be newly bound to appear at the next Q.S. and to come to the clerk of the court with sureties.

**19.** Rog. Foushe *alias* Barnard to be committed to Bocardo for ravishing Denise Wright as proved in open court. Next market day to be set on the pillory with a paper showing his offence from 10 a.m. to 2 p.m., being taken down and whipped at noon, then to put in sureties for his good behaviour and appearance at the next Q.S.

p. 54 **20.** Edw. Pyme to be put in the stocks for petty larceny from 10 a.m. to noon and then to be whipped on the next three market days and then to go to the House of Correction as ordered by the Bp. of Bath and Wells.

28

**21.** Geo. Bannester to be discharged after the grand jury did not find the bill of indictment for felony.

**22.** The churchwardens of each psh. to levy 12d. from each recusant for each Sunday they do not attend church and distrain for it according to the statute. Rog. Moore, Edw. Chittle, Wm. Badger, Rose Stacey and Margaret Dudley who have often been convicted as recusants are to be discharged of their recogns. and be subject to the 12d. penalty from the next Q.S. At that time they should deliver their reasons in writing for absence from church and the churchwardens should warn all recusants to attend the next Q.S. to give their reasons for absence.

**23.** The riders [cf. 1617B9] to be put in the stocks for two hours next market day with papers in their hats giving the reason for their punishment.

**24.** The Mayor, Dr. James, Dr. Hawley and Ald. Harris to take the account of the poor and name overseers.

**25.** The recogn. of Hen. Holmes (the surgeon) to be estreated.

**26.** Warrants to be made out for each psh. to provide a pair of stocks.

## [1617c]

Quarter Sessions at the Guildhall 19 June 1617. Rt. Revd. Bp. of Bath   p. 55
and Wells, Ric. Smyth esq., Mayor, Wm. Langton D.D., Jn. Prideux D.D., Thos. James D.D., Jn. Hawley D.C.L., Thos. Harris ald., Ric. Hannes ald., Wm. Potter, Wm. Wright, J.P.s.

**1.** Wm. Mabbs of Drury Lane [? London] and his sureties to be discharged of the recogn. taken at the last Q.S. a certificate having been received from the Lord Chief Justice that he has taken a recogn. from Wm. to appear before him to answer the same charges.

**2.** Edw. Stubbs bound by recogn. to appear at the next Q.S. and warrants to be made out against his confederates.

**3.** Hen. Samon, who appeared on his recogn. to answer for himself and his wife, to be discharged, since the prosecutor, Rog. Hill, does not ask or show that he should be bound over.

**4.** Mary, wife of Wm. Wilks, to be fined 5s. after being indicted and found guilty by the jury of assault and battery on Eliz., wife of Ralph Oxley.

**5.** Martin Knowles, who was indicted on three charges, to be fined 3s.   p. 56
4d. for assault and battery on Evan Petty and 20s. for assault and battery

29

on Edw. Bythell, one of the serjeants-at-mace to the city bailiffs, and, on the charge of being a common barrator, to be bound to his good behaviour and be committed until he performs this order.

**6.** Rowland Owen to find good sureties for his recogn. to be of good behaviour and appear at the next Q.S.

**7.** Thos. Lewis allowed to put in his traverse to the indictment found against him and entered recogn. in the sum of £20 to prosecute it.

**8.** Warrants to be made out under the statute against the church-wardens of Binsey and the psh. of St. Mic. for not paying the money for maimed soldiers.

**9.** Ric. Williams *alias* Symes *alias* Vynall and Phil. Norgrove to be hanged after being found guilty on indictments for stealing 120lb. of wool and yarn and a grey nag taken with them at Oxf.

**10.** Thos. Sunton *alias* Joyner to be hanged after being found guilty on indictments for felony and burglary.

**11.** Mary Hill to be publicly whipped on the next three market days and to stand in the cage for an hour before and an hour afterwards after the jury found her guilty on several indictments but only of petty larceny.

p. 57 **12.** Rog. Hill to be committed to Bocardo for three days according to the statute as an unlicensed victualler and to be bound to appear at the next Q.S. and meanwhile to be stopped from victualling.

**13.** Edw. Bythell (Bithell) discharged by proclamation after being bound over for several sessions without proof made or evidence being brought against him.

**14.** Edw. Chittle bound by recogn. of £40 to appear and answer at the next Q.S. and meanwhile be of good behaviour. Sureties of £20 each: Wal. Jones of Oxf., glover, and Jn. Ryme of Oxf., cutler.

**15.** Edw. Stubbs, former servant and apprentice to Mr. Wm. Bosswell, bound by recogn. of £40 to appear at the next Q.S. and meanwhile be of good behaviour. Sureties of £20 each: Thos. Penn of Oxf., chandler, and Ric. Astell of Oxf., tailor.

## [1617D]

p. 58 Quarter Sessions 2 Oct. 1617. Wm. Goodwyne, Dean of Christ Church and Vice-Chancellor, Wal. Payne esq., Mayor, Jn. Prideux D.D., Thos. James D.D., Jn. Hawley D.C.L., Thos. Wentworthe esq., Recorder,

Thos. Harris ald., Ric. Hannes ald., Wm. Potter gent., Wm. Wright gent., Ralph Flexney gent., Jn. Byrd gent., Ric. Smythe gent., J.P.s.

**1.** Hen. Gunne to be discharged paying his fees after he appeared on his recogn. and Widow Wright, who was prosecuting him, did not ask for it to be continued.

**2.** Edw. Stubbs, former servant of Mr. Wm. Bosswell, to be bound by recogn. with good sureties to appear at the next Q.S. and meanwhile be of good behaviour. Dr. James, Dr. Hawley and Ald. Harris to consider whether those who have been questioned here as receivers of the money, goods and wares stolen from Mr. Bosswell should be bound over.

**3.** Kath. Shury, who appeared on her recogn., to be discharged.

**4.** Judith, wife of Dominic Pynnart, to be bound with good sureties to appear at the next Q.S.

**5.** Rog. Moore, Edw. Chittle and Martin Knowles, who appeared in court, to be discharged of their recogns., paying their fees. p. 59

**6.** Jas. Bonham (Bonnam) to be committed to Bocardo for three days for unlicensed victualling and before release to pay a fine of 20s. and be bound not to victual.

**7.** The petty jury had acquitted Anne Nurse when she was indicted and arraigned under statute of 1 Jas. for having two husbands at once, Hen. Nurse and Edm. Tynker. The court considered the jury not to have guided themselves well according to the evidence and thought her a very lewd and 'light housewife' who deserved the rigour of the law. She is to be committed to the custody of Mr. Holman, the keeper of the House of Correction at Witney for one year, and only to be discharged then by order in open court there.

**8.** Ric. Mumford to be committed to the House of Correction at Witney for one year and only to be discharged then by order in open court.

**9.** The bailiffs at the time to be fined following the recent escape of the seminary priest from Bocardo and they shall be given notice to attend the next Q.S. to answer so the fine can be set.

**10.** On further consideration, Judith, wife of Dominic Pynnart, bookbinder, to be discharged of her recogn.

**11.** After full evidence the jury empanelled to try Wm. Wyatt after he was admitted to his traverse found him not guilty. He is to be discharged of his recogn. p. 60

**12.** Simon Callis to be discharged paying his fees, after he appeared on his recogn. and nothing was objected against him.

**13.** Wm. Page as in 1617D12.

**14.** Thos. Lewis, maltster, indicted for assault and battery on [*blank*], was admitted to his traverse and pleaded not guilty. Issue was then taken for the King and the jury empanelled and sworn, finding him guilty after full evidence. He was fined 6s. 8d.

**15.** After full evidence the jury found Jerome Veale guilty on an indictment for felony. He is to be proceeded against by process of outlawry as he has fled.

p. 61 **16.** Jurors who were empanelled and did not attend at all to be fined 3s. 4d. each and jurors who were sworn but left and were not ready when called to be fined 6s. 8d. each as their negligence had delayed the court.

## [1618A]

p. 62 Quarter Sessions at the Guildhall 15 Jan. 1618. Wal. Payne esq., Mayor, Wm. Langton D.D., Jn. Prideux D.D., Thos. James D.D., Thos. Wentworth esq., Recorder, Jn. Hawley D.C.L., Wm. Ryves esq., Thos. Harris ald., Wm. Potter gent., Wm. Wright gent., Ralph Flexney gent., Jn. Byrd gent., Ric. Smythe gent., J.P.s.

**1.** Art. Welbeck to be committed to Bocardo without bail or mainprise until the next Q.S. for wilful refusal to take the Oath of Allegiance in open court and only to be discharged by order of the court.

**2.** Jn. Lucas, who confessed to whoredom committed with Dorothy Kaye, to be bound with good sureties to be of good behaviour and appear at the next Q.S. for a further order.

**3.** Wm. Reason *alias* Hucks to be examined by three surgeons, Mr. Jas. Van Otten, Mr. Jn. Cantwell and Mr. Toby Toms, assisted by a physician as he claims to be broken-bodied and unable to father a child as he is accused. The court to order further after the surgeons give a certificate of their opinion.

p. 63 **4.** Edw. Chittle and Wm. Badger, two often convicted recusants, appeared in court and confessed that they had been absent from church on the last three Sundays. Warrants to be made out for the churchwardens of their pshs. to distrain their goods for the sum of 12d. each for each absence according to the statute. If Edw. and Wm. do not pay, the churchwardens to sell the goods and return any surplus to the owners.

**5.** Wm. Badger's apprentice, Lawr. Smale, to be taken from him to prevent his being seduced to popery and to be bound to another master. Wm. to have such compensation for the remaining service in Lawr.'s indenture as the Mayor thinks fit.

**6.** Ralph Hodges to be fined 13s. 4d. and be committed until he pays, after being indicted and found guilty of and confessing to assaulting and wounding Thos. Stone. He paid.

**7.** Following Edw. Mayler's complaint against Wm. Bushell, Wm. to be discharged and Edw. to pay him 10s. and all molestation between them to cease.

**8.** Likewise Thos. Lockton (Locton) to be absolutely discharged.

**9.** The Mayor to consider the complaint on behalf of Dan. Janes, p. 64 apprentice to Mr. Hen. Samon, against his master and settle their dispute.

**10.** Hen. Gunne to be discharged after he appeared on his recogn. and no complaint was made.

**11.** Jn. Blackshaw to enter a new recogn. to appear at the next Q.S. or be committed if he refuses.

**12.** Edw. Chittle and Wm. Badger, who appeared on their recogns., to be discharged but still to be distrained of their goods for absence from church contrary to the statute.

**13.** Eliz. Swyfte (Swifte), who appeared on her recogn., to be discharged.

**14.** Wm. Hucks to be committed to Bocardo until the court orders his release.

**15.** Frances Sheppard *alias* Hore indicted under the statute for having two husbands and acquitted by the petty jury. Shepparde claimed at the bar to be her husband but she said Ant. Hore was her only husband. The court, who consider her to be a very lewd woman who they have grounds to suspect, and order that she be sent from Bocardo to the House of Correction until further order. The Assize Judges to be notified of the case and directions obtained from them.

**16.** Thos. Swayne indicted for feloniously stealing seven yards of p. 65 linsey-woolsey from Jn. Pownall, mercer, and acquitted by the jury.

The court, however, considers Thos. to be a common pilferer and idle vagrant, and commits him to the House of Correction until he is discharged by warrant from two J.P.s.

**17.** The Mayor to examine and punish Hugh Lewis, a lewd fellow, for running away from his master and stealing small trifles.

**18.** Because of his age and infirmity old Jn. Brushe to be licensed to carry on victualling and to enter recogn. according to the statute.

**19.** Mr. Holman, the keeper of the Bridewell at Witney, complained in open court that he had hired Jn. Stapler and [*blank*] Humfreis, a glover, to convey one Mrs. Newbery there and had given them food ('diet') and 5s., but they had wilfully allowed her to escape. Stapler and Humfreis to be apprehended by warrant and brought before a J.P. to be committed until they repay the sum paid by Mr. Holman.

**20.** Warrants to be made out by the clerk of the court for the church-wardens of the pshs. which have refused to meet the charge for paying Eliz. Grene for keeping a poor child left on the psh. of St. Peter-le-Bailey as ordered by this court. The churchwardens to be brought before the next J.P. and ordered to pay.

p. 66 **21.** Warrants to be made out by the clerk of the court for the apprehension of Thos. Irons and [*blank*] Conny(e) the victualler. Then to be brought before the Mayor and Ald. Harris for orders concerning Irons's breach of the peace and Conny's allowing him to be drunk in his house.

**22.** The Mayor and Ald. Harris to consider the information given to the court concerning one of the children of Jn. Hartley supposedly born in the psh. of St. Martin and order according to the truth of the matter.

**23.** Many questions and doubts arise concerning the complaint of Mr. Bosswell against Edw. Stubbs, Jn. Mathew and others on the point of law of apprentices over the age of eighteen taking away their masters' money and goods which had been entrusted to them. A majority of the court to state a case for the opinion of the Judges at the next Assizes and their final direction. Edw., Jn. and the others to be bound over with good sureties to appear at the next Q.S. and meanwhile to be of good behaviour.

Edw. Stubbs, mercer, recogn. of £40. Sureties of £20 each: Thos. Penn and Rob. Nickolls.

Jn. Mathew jun., mercer, recogn. of £40. Sureties of £20 each: Jn. Mathew sen. and Luke Eaton.

Chas. Grene, cutler, recogn. of £40. Surety of £20: Thos. Penn, chandler.

Wm. Huett, cutler, recogn. of £40. Sureties of £20 each: Luke Eaton and Ric. Good.

**24.** Unlicensed victuallers presented by the jury: Thos. Richardson; Jn. Barsdale, shoemaker; Widow Acton in Catte Street; Thos. Sylly in Canditch; Jn. Evans, cook, at the Turl; Jn. Richmont at the Turl; Wm. Gray, hatter; Widow Norland; Rob. Dudley.  p. 67

**25.** Recusants presented by the jury:

Psh. of All Saints: Mrs. Harrison; Widow Hitchman and Eleanor Hitchman.

St. Peter-le-Bailey: Mrs. Shepreve and her maid; Wm. Tredwell and her [sic] maid; Rose Stacy, widow and Susan Pitts.

St. Martin: Mrs. Bowne.

St. Aldate: Widow Wright.

St. Mary Magdalen: Mrs. Barbor.

St. Mic.: Rob. Dudley's wife and dau. Ellen.

St. Peter-in-the-East: Edw. Chittle and his wife Ellen; Wm. Badger and his wife Eliz.

St. Thos.: Rog. Moore, painter.

# [1618B]

Quarter Sessions at the Guildhall 16 April 1618. Wm. Godwyn D.D.,  p. 68
Vice-Chancellor, Wal. Payne esq., Mayor, Jn. Prideux D.D., Thos. James D.D., Thos. Wentworth esq., Recorder, Jn. Hawley D.C.L., Thos. Harris ald., Wm. Wright ald., Jn. Bird gent., J.P.s.

**1.** Hen. Samon to be discharged after he appeared on his recogn.

**2.** Jn. Leverett as in 1618B1.

**3.** Wm. Hobbes (Hobbs) as in 1618B1.

**4.** Thos. Harbert, who was committed to prison by order of the court for bastardy with Eliz. Hughes and Isobel Robins, to be released, putting in good sureties to appear at the next Q.S.

**5.** Ald. Wright was asked to be treasurer for maimed soldiers for the year and Jn. Chillingworth is appointed collector.

**6.** Thos. Jarns to submit to the constable for the offence committed against him when enforcing a warrant and then to be discharged of his recogn.

**7.** Eliz., wife of Sheene Selwood, to find sureties not to victual any more.

p. 69 **8.** Ald. Harris and Ald. Wright to consider the complaint about the many inmates in the psh. of St. Peter-le-Bailey.

**9.** Mr. Boswell's case against Wm. [*sic*] Stubbs and others to be examined and the Town Clerk and Mr. Jas. Chesterman to attend the Recorder who is asked to refer the matter to the Judges next term. If their opinion is that it is not a felony the parties to be absolutely discharged. If it is a felony they are to appear at the next Q.S. or G.D.

**10.** Dr. Hawley, Ald. Harris and Ald. Wright to make orders concerning the woman got with child by Hen. Cotton.

**11.** Anne Nurse to be discharged from the House of Correction and have a pass.

**12.** At the next meeting for choosing overseers for the poor a way to be agreed to assist the psh. of St. Peter-le-Bailey with the matters complained about by Mr. Munday and Mr. Fisher on behalf of the psh.

**13.** Wm. Hincks, who is accused of getting Dorothy Studly (Studley) with child, to bring a certificate from a surgeon to be confirmed by Ald. Harris and Ald. Wright. Dorothy to be committed to the House of Correction for a year if she can be taken.
[*Margin*] Sentence against Dorothy to be mitigated and referred to the J.P.s if she is sent for at Jn. Chillingworth's suit.

**14.** Eliz. Robins to be sent to the House of Correction until further notice.

p. 70 **15.** Jn. Rosterne gent. of Brasenose to be discharged by proclamation after he appeared and Thos. Stapleton did not appear on his recogn. to prosecute and no evidence was brought against him.

**16.** Thos. Harbert to be released if he puts in sureties to appear at the next Q.S.

**17.** Edw. Stubbes (Stubbs), mercer of Oxon., recogn. of £40. Sureties of £20 each; Rob. and Thos. Nicholls, tailors of Oxon. The condition of the recogn. is that if, before the next Q.S. or G.D., the Assize Judges for the county of Oxon. declare in writing that the offence for which Edw. was bound over on the prosecution of Mr. Wm. Boswell, mercer, is a felony and he appears at the next Q.S. or G.D., then this recogn. to be void and otherwise to stand. The recogn. likewise to be void if the Judges do not think the case is a felony.

**18.** Jn. Mathewe (Mathew) jun., mercer of Oxon., recogn. of £40. Sureties of £20 each: Jn. Mathew sen., yeoman of Water [*blank*] and Jn. Chillingworth of Oxf., yeoman.

Conditions as in 1618B17.

**19.** Chas. Greene and Wm. Hewett to find new sureties as the two others have done.

**20.** Recogn. of Jn. Lucas to be estreated.

**21.** Art. Welbecke (Welbeck) to be remanded to Bocardo without bail or mainprise after repeated refusal to take the Oath of Allegiance. To be dealt with as a person convicted of *Praemunire*.

## [1618c]

Quarter Sessions at the Guildhall 4 June 1618. Wm. Goodwyne, p. 71 Vice-Chancellor, Wal. Payne esq., Mayor, Jn. Prideux D.D., Thos. James D.D., Jn. Hawley D.C.L., Thos. Harris ald., Wm. Wright ald., Jn. Bird gent., J.P.s.

**1.** Jn. Durrant, who appeared on his recogn., to be fined 20s. for unlicensed victualling and not to be released until he pays and then to await a further order.

**2.** Valentine Fulks to be discharged after he appeared on his recogn. and was not prosecuted.

**3.** Kath. Misson, Kath. Dryver and Alice Readinge and Edw., Eliz. and Frideswide Hinde to be discharged after they appeared on their recogns. and were reconciled in open court.

**4.** Wm. Pemberton and Ric. Hales to be bound by recogn. not to use a boat after 9 p.m. nor to carry any scholars or apprentices at such unseasonable hours. If any scholars make them stay longer they must on the following morning tell the Vice-Chancellor in the case of scholars or the Mayor in the case of apprentices.

p. 72  **5.** Wm. Coleman to be fined 12d. after appearing on a process issued after the indictment found against him at the Michaelmas Q.S.

**6.** Wm. Pemberton and Ric. Hales to be attached by warrant to be committed until they pay the fees for their discharge and recogn.

**7.** Jn. Durrant (Durant) and Jn. Barksdale to be licensed to victual putting in recogns. with good sureties according to the statute.

**8.** Jn. Norreis (Norris), who appeared on his recogn., to be fined 20s. for unlicensed victualling and enter recogn. with good sureties not to victual without special licence.

**9.** Dr. Hawley, Ald. Harris and Ald. Wright reported on the accusation, referrred to them at the last Q.S., that Hen. Cotton (Cotten) had got a woman with child. The woman claimed that her first acquaintance with him had been last Sept. but it appeared that she had given birth privately without the help of any woman the Feb. before so they did not think Hen. was the father. He is to be discharged paying his fees.

**10.** Wm. Beale to be sent to the House of Correction until an order from two J.P.s after he confessed before Dr. Hawley to stealing a hat.

p. 73  **11.** Ric. Poole to pay Eliz. the wife of [*blank*] Hart 2s. 6d. for injuring her hand with his knife and to be discharged. A final settlement to be made between them that neither shall bring an action.

**12.** Jn. Sunton indicted and discharged, paying a fine of 2s. 6d. for battery of Simon Cockerman and his fees after the jury acquitted him of another indictment of burglary.

**13.** The G.D. adjourned until 8 o'clock the day after the next county Assizes, unless it is a festival day.

**14.** Thos. Herbert to find better sureties before a J.P. and be brought by warrant before Ald. Harris and Ald. Wright.

## [1618D]

Gaol Delivery Mon. 6 July 1618. Wal. Payne esq., Mayor, Jn. Hawley D.C.L., Thos. Harrys ald., Wm. Wright ald., Jn. Birde, J.P.s.

**1.** Sam. Bagnoll and Thos. Kendall condemned to death after being found guilty on five indictments at the last sessions. Judgement pronounced by Dr. Hawley in the absence of the Recorder and Mr. Ryves.

**2.** Wm. Parks, apprehended last Tuesday in the psh. of St. Giles on suspicion of the felony of stealing a gown from a dau. of Ric. Proffitt, is convicted. As he could give no account of how he lives he is to be committed to the House of Correction as an idle vagrant and to remain there until the court orders or two J.P.s issue a warrant to release him.

**3.** Abraham Glascock to pay Jn. Partridg(e) of Beckley 6s. 8d. compen-    p. 74
sation for a pair of breeches and two pairs of stockings stolen from Jn. by a lewd fellow, Vaughan, who left them at Glascock's house. The court thought Glascock knew how Vaughan had come by them but this time he is to be discharged of his recogn.

**4.** Alice Styles to be sent by warrant to the House of Correction, for leaving a bastard child on the psh. of St. Peter-le-Bailey, and to remain there until the court orders or two J.P.s discharge her by warrant.

**5.** The court adjourned to the end of the next city Q.S.

## [1618E]

Quarter Sessions at the Guildhall 8 Oct. 1618. Wm. Potter esq., Mayor,    p. 75
Wm. Langton D.D., Jn. Prideux D.D., Thos. James D.D., Jn. Hawley D.C.L., Thos. Harris ald., Wm. Wright ald., Jn. Bird gent., J.P.s.

**1.** Jn. Seaman's complaint against his master Jn. Dowghty about unpaid wages was heard at length. Dowghty to pay Seaman 40s. next St. Luke's Day, which he promised to do. If he does not, to be sent for by some of the J.P.s and bound over to answer at the next Q.S. Also for his heinous contempt to Dr. Hawley, Dowghty to find good sureties for his appearance at the next Q.S. and his good behaviour in the meantime.

**2.** Thos. Header to be committed to Bocardo until further order after confessing in court to abuse and irreverence to Dr. James and the constable sent for him which he blamed on great drunkenness. Also Jonas Clench, who was complained about here for not assisting the constable, Thos. Kettle, is to warn a petty constable for him.

**3.** Maurice Heath to be committed to Bocardo for three days for abusing the bailiffs and then to find good sureties for his appearance at the next Q.S. and good behaviour in the meantime and to be bound to stop gaming.

p. 76 **4.** The case of Aldred Bassill (Basill) to be heard by Dr. James, Dr. Hawley and Ald. Harris and Bassill to put in new sureties for his appearance at the next Q.S.

**5.** Wm. Waspe's petition against Martin Knowles, which was exhibited in court, to be referred to Ald. Harris and Ald. Wright to determine if they can. If not the parties to be bound to answer at the next Q.S.

**6.** Wm. Wilks to be committed to Bocardo for three days and then to be discharged paying his fees, after he appeared in court, was accused by Isabel Harbert, and was proved to have used very barbarous violence and uncivil and inhumane words against her.

**7.** Jn. Powell, who appeared in court on his recogn. and made his submission with the consent of Mr. Radclyff [Town Clerk], to be discharged.

**8.** Hen. Symonds and his wife, Eliz., to be discharged paying their fees after the grand jury did not find the indictment against them for feloniously stealing two gold rings from Mr. Toby Clutterbuck.

**9.** A warrant to be made out for Wal. Crofte to be appear before Dr. Hawley and be examined.

**10.** A letter to be sent to the Judges for directions concerning those who take in inmates within the city and liberties.

p. 77 **11.** A certificate and a stated case to be sent on behalf of the Bench in answer to the petition of Jn. Mathewe sen. to the Assize Judges for the county of Oxon., Sir Peter Warberton and Sir Jn. Crooke, concerning the dispute between Mr. Boswell and his apprentices. The Judges to give their opinion to the J.P.s. Meanwhile the parties previously bound by recogn. to be bound with new sureties to appear at the next Q.S.

**12.** Thos. Metcalf's case to be referred to Dr. Prideux and Dr. James for determination.

**13.** Edw. Stubbs and his brother, Wm., to be bound in the sum of £40 for Edw.'s appearance before the J.P.s at ten days' notice left at Wm.'s shop in Oxf.

**14.** Warrants to be made out against Chas. Greene and Wm. Hewett for the court's fees.

**15.** Hen. Rownsefall to be committed to Bocardo during the pleasure of the court for making the court wait for him after he was sworn as a member of the petty jury.

**16.** Jn. Tyllyard (Tylliard) to be sent to the House of Correction until further order or a warrant from Dr. James and Dr. Hawley.

**17.** Edw. Hutchings to be fined 3s. and committed to Bocardo for three days for assaulting and abusing Mr. Arnold, the keeper of Bocardo, and rescuing his brother, who had been committed there by warrant.

**18.** Warrants to be made out against those presented for non-attendance at church who are to pay according to the statute.

**19.** Warrants to be made out against those presented for drunkenness who are to be censured according to the statute.

**20.** Jn. Snell who was presented by the grand jury for drunkenness, to p. 78 be put in the psh. stocks for three hours unless he pays 5s. according to the statute.

**21.** Thos. Alcock and his wife, Frances, who appeared in court on their recogns., to be discharged paying their fees.

**22.** Mary Ewen to find sureties for her good behaviour or be committed.

**23.** Warrants to be sent to all churchwardens and overseers of the poor to make the collections in their pshs. allowed by statute.

**24.** Eliz. Selwood to find good sureties for her good behaviour and pay the fees of Alcock, who complained against and had received injury from her, or to be committed until further notice.

**25.** The recogns. of Edw. Day and Thos. Manford *alias* Manthorpe to be estreated.

**26.** Emmot Violl to leave Oxf. before St. Luke's Day and to be sent to the House of Correction if found living here after that. If she is unable to leave because of her alleged infirmity the next two J.P.s may at their discretion allow a longer time.

**27.** Warrants to be sent to the constables to make a diligent search and bring a written certificate of the inmates in their wards and by whom they are received and to tell the overseers to bring a note of the number of their poor and by whom and how they are relieved.

**28.** Rob. Whittmore and Jn. Tyllyard (Tilliard) to be sent to the House of Correction until further notice.

## [1619A]

Quarter Sessions at the Guildhall 14 Jan. 1619. Wm. Godwyne D.D., p. 79
Vice-Chancellor, Wm. Potter esq., Mayor, Wm. Lanckton D.D., Jn.

Prideux D.D., Thos. James D.D., Thos. Wentworth esq., Recorder,
Jn. Hawley D.C.L., Wm. Rives esq., Thos. Harris ald., Wm. Wright
ald., Ralph Flexney gent., Jn. Byrd gent., J.P.s.

**1.** Jn. Woolly (Woolley) to be bound with sureties for his good behaviour and appearance at the next Q.S.

**2.** Thos. Munson to be put in the stocks for two hours next market day for hiding the top of a beadle's staff which he found.

**3.** Joan Smith's (Smyth's) recogn. to be estreated.

**4.** Ric. Musgrave's recogn. to be estreated after he did not appear.

**5.** Wm. Rainfford to be discharged of his recogn. paying his fees.

**6.** Wal. Craft's recogn. to be estreated and warrants to be made out for his apprehension so he can be committed until he finds very good sureties for his appearance at the next Q.S. and his good behaviour.

**7.** Wm. Wheeler to be discharged of his recogn. after he appeared in court and nothing was objected against him.

p. 80 **8.** Wm. Coleman as in 1619A7.

**9.** Ric. Yeomans to be discharged as a victualler and to find sureties for his good behaviour until the court makes a further order after he was accused and proved guilty in open court of much disorder.

**10.** Thos. Freeman (Freman), after confessing in open court to selling three pints of drink at less than a full pint for a penny, is fined 10s.

**11.** Ric. Musgrave to be stopped from victualling and be committed to prison until he finds good sureties for his good behaviour.

**12.** Dr. James, Dr. Hawley and Ald. Harris to examine Mary Ewin (Ewen) and if they find just cause she shall be sent to the House of Correction unless she leaves Oxf. She is to be bound for her good behaviour and committed to prison until she finds new sureties.

**13.** Jas. Clarke to be committed to prison for interrupting the jury for life and death, while they were being sworn in open court.

**14.** Thos. Pritchard, who is suspected of felony but was not prosecuted, to be discharged paying his fees and not be released without the warrant of some of the J.P.s.

**15.** Jn. Richardson to be fined 5s. or sit in the stocks for six hours according to the statute for often being drunk and to be fined 3s. for common barratry.

**16.** Thos. More (Moore), servant to Hen. Bonner, to be discharged  p. 81
after he submitted on his knees in open court and asked his master's
forgiveness for his disobedience and violence to him.

**17.** Dr. James, Dr. Hawley and Ald. Harris to examine Sheene Sellwood (Selwood) and his wife and if they find just cause they shall be
sent to the House of Correction unless they leave the city, and they
are to be bound for their good behaviour.

**18.** Rob. Neale's petition concerning the keeping of the child to be
considered.

**19.** Dr. Hawley to consider Joyce More's (Moore) petition.

**20.** Warrants to be made out against recusants for 12d. levied for the
poor according to the statute.

**21.** All gamblers, unlicensed victuallers and drunkards presented by
the jury to be proceeded against according to the statute.

**22.** Alice Read(e) to put in sureties for her appearance at the next Q.S.
and then to be discharged if no further cause is brought against her.

**23.** Wm. Wood to be sent to the House of Correction until further
order of the court.

**24.** Wm. Tylcock (Tilcock) and his wife, Mary, to be fined 6s. 8d.  p. 82
after being found guilty by the jury of common barratry.

**25.** Thos. Freeman (Freman) to be discharged of his fees and fine of
10s.

**26.** Wal. Osborne to be bound to appear and answer at the next Q.S.
and to pay Rob. Oates 5s.

**27.** Thos. Smith (Smyth), brazier, to be discharged after he appeared
on suspicion of being a receiver of stolen goods and no direct proof
was found.

**28.** Jn. Baldwyn(e) and Edw. Peake to be discharged of their recogns.
paying their fees.

**29.** Anne, wife of Wm. Gray, to be bound with sureties to answer at
the next Q.S.

## [1619B]

Gaol Delivery Fri. 15 Jan. 1619. Wm. Goodwyne D.D., Vice-Chancellor,  p. 83
Wm. Potter esq., Mayor, Thos. Wentworth esq., Recorder, Jn. Hawley

D.C.L., Wm. Rives esq., Thos. Harris ald., Wm. Wright ald., Ralph Flexney gent., Jn. Byrd gent., J.P.s.[1]

**1.** The jury did not find the indictment against the prisoner Hugh Lloyd (Lloyde), and proclamation was made and no further prosecution brought. He is to be discharged but not released without a further order of the court, which considers him a lewd fellow.

**2.** Thos. Sunton *alias* Joyner, Sam. Bagnoll and Thos. Kendall, who had been condemned for felony and reprieved, were asked in court why execution of the law should not proceed. They could say nothing and submitted themselves to the law. The bailiffs of the city were required to see to their execution.

**3.** Joan Browne for the murder of her child, Chris. Lister for burglary, Thos. Andrewes and Jas. Goodwyn for several burglaries and Jn. Frowde as a cutpurse indicted, arraigned, found guilty, condemned and committed to the bailiffs to be put to death.

p. 84    **4.** Ric. James and Mark Grene discharged by proclamation of the charge of felony but not to be released from prison without further order from the court.

**5.** Thos. Burtofte and Chris. Baker to be sent to the House of Correction during the pleasure of the court as vagrants and incorrigible rogues.

**6.** Mic. Buffett, Jn. Horden, Wm. Francklyn (Franklyn) and Wm. Wood to be discharged after proclamation was made and no prosecution was brought but not to be released without special direction of the court. Francklyn to be sent by *mittimus* from the Vice-Chancellor into Berkshire to be prosecuted by Bailiff Willis.

**7.** Nic. Creiton (Creyton) *alias* Sandy who appeared for vile outrages, breach of the peace and daily drunkenness of which he is widely accused, to find sureties for his appearance at the next Q.S. and his good behaviour in the meantime. Since nobody would be a surety for such a lewd fellow, the court took his own recogn. for £20 in hope of his future behaviour.

**8.** The commission of G.D. having a few days longer to run, the court was adjourned until 16 Feb.[2] There being no further business

---

[1] The names of Drs. Lanckton, Prideux, and James, entered after the Mayor, are struck through, presumably because this second day of sessions had been turned into a gaol delivery, for which they were not on the commission.

[2] The commission had been issued for one year on 19 Feb. 1618: TNA, C181/2.

the commission became void and was dissolved. [*Signed*] Radclyffe [Town Clerk].

## [1619c]

Quarter Sessions at the Guildhall Thurs. 8 April 1619. Wm. Potter  p. 85
esq., Mayor, Thos. James D.D., Jn. Hawley D.C.L., Thos. Harris ald.,
Wm. Wright ald., Jn. Bird gent., J.P.s.

**1.** Jonas Clench sworn as high constable and Martin Bedwell petty constable of Northgate ward.

**2.** Dan. Warwick appeared on his recogn. on suspicion of taking a 'reytish' [? rattish][1] roan coloured nag from Mat. Leach, cook. In open court he brought forward Hen. Stephens, fisherman, of Eaton Hastings, Berks., who brought a letter claimed to be from Sir Jn. Hungerford, kt., of Down Ampney, Gloucs., saying that he bought the horse from Jn. Elborowe of Purton, Wilts., at the last St. John's Bridge fair [at Lechlade, Gloucs.] but did not pay toll for him. Elborowe is not known to the court and they require further satisfaction from Stephens, who is to find sureties for his appearance at the next Q.S. The court will order as is just if he can clear himself of suspicion by producing Elborrowe or otherwise. Leach to be bound to prosecute  p. 86
Steevens at the next Q.S. The bailiffs, who have seized the horse are to return it to Leach as long as he undertakes to give it back if he fails to prosecute. [*Margin*] Dan. Warwick discharged.

**3.** Ric. Yeomans discharged after he appeared on his recogn. and nothing further was alleged against him.

**4.** A process of outlawry to be made out against Denise Wright after she was indicted for felony and found guilty by the grand jury of taking a purse and 50s. 6d. of goods from Ric. Glover.

**5.** A process of outlawry to be made out against Wm. Stapler after he was found guilty on an indictment for feloniously stealing a riding coat from Josiah Guye the carrier.

**6.** The overseers of the poor for the psh. of St. Martin to have a warrant to make a collection for next year and next Easter to present accounts of this and the arrears of the past year when they had no warrant to collect.

---

[1] 'Rattish' seems to have been used in the 17th century to describe horses with rat-like tails: *N.E.D.*

**7.** A certificate to be made of the popish recusants convicted before and now presented again.

**8.** Thos. Kettle, who was indicted and found guilty by the grand and petty juries of having two wives, claimed benefit of clergy and was burnt on the hand. He was discharged on recogn. to leave Oxf. within three days and not return to live here, to discharge the city of any children of Alice Dudley, his recently married wife, if she is with child, and to be of good behaviour.

p. 87   **9.** Rob. Bell discharged after the petty jury did not find the indictment for stealing a lamb.

**10.** Anne Gray to be bound with good sureties to appear at the next Q.S. or be committed.

**11.** Ric. Evans appeared on the testimony of the churchwardens of All Saints psh., Thos. Wells and Steph. Gunn, that when they went to his house to collect the money for maimed soldiers, he said he had heard that he had been presented at the Q.S. and spoke passionately and disgracefully, saying that the foreman and the rest of the grand jury were knaves, thus discouraging others from serving. He is to acknowledge his error to the jurors and be bound for his appearance at the next Q.S. and his good behaviour.

**12.** Jn., son of Ric. Spurr, to be sent to St. Mary Magdalen psh. where he was born, and be kept there.

**13.** Likewise Eliz., dau. of Ric. Spurr, to be sent to and kept by the psh. of St. Mic. where she was born.

**14.** Ald. Harris to be treasurer for maimed soldiers for the year.

**15.** Jn. Chillingworth to be collector for maimed soldiers for the year.

p. 88   **16.** Frances Shepherd *alias* Hore to be committed to prison for three days unless she finds good sureties for the peace on the oath and complaint of Jane Hore and Mary Veazie. If she fails to do so by the third day, she is to be committed to the House of Correction until further order. In the meantime to behave well and leave Oxf.

**17.** The judges' opinion to be obtained concerning Aldred Basill and Joan Hussey, the dumb wench got with child.

**18.** Anne, wife of Wm. Gray, hatter, to find good sureties for her behaviour or be committed to Bocardo.

46

**19.** Jn. Longe, baker, to be apprehended by warrant and brought before a J.P. to be committed until he finds sureties for his good behaviour and appearance at the next Q.S.

**20.** The pshs. of St. Martin, St. Aldate and All Saints each to pay 5s. per quarter to assist the psh. of St. Peter-le-Bailey with the relief of its poor unless they show reasons not to do so.

## [1619D]

Quarter Sessions at the Guildhall Thurs. 27 May 1619. Wm. Potter esq., p. 89 Mayor, Wm. Lancton D.D., Thos. James D.D., Jn. Hawley D.C.L., Thos. Harris ald., Ralph Flexney gent., Jn. Bird gent., J.P.s.

**1.** Each of the grand jurors who were called and did not appear to be fined 5s. for contempt.

**2.** The order of King's Bench discharging the conviction of Joan Huntly (Huntley) for insufficient evidence ('insufficency') and for her appearance to answer at this Q.S. was seen. Since she attended throughout the Q.S. and no prosecution was brought after three proclamations, she is to be discharged.

**3.** Certificates to be made of all popish recusants.

**4.** Ric. Evans discharged after submitting to the court and admitting speaking disgracefully of the jury at the last Q.S.

**5.** Christian Cumber (Comber) to be bound to keep the peace and p. 90 to appear at the next Q.S. on the oaths of Anne Howse and Alice Pemberton.

**6.** Jn. Alley of Arncott, Oxon., to be sent to prison after unjustly claiming that the wife of Thos. Cooke and dau. of Mr. Staynoe of Oxf. was his betrothed. As he promised to leave Oxf. he is to be discharged paying his fees to the keeper.

**7.** Jn. Redding(e), gent., suspected of very bad behaviour and lately committed to Bocardo, is to remain there until he obtains a certificate of his good behaviour from the two next J.P.s to Little Missenden, Bucks., where he says he lives, or finds good sureties for his appearance at the next Q.S. He used ill-mannered and scornful words to the Bench, but was released on his submission and apology for his contempt.

**8.** Rob. Dudley to enter recogn. not to victual or sell ale and his former recogn. to be estreated against him and his sureties as he sold ale contrary to its conditions.

p. 91 **9.** The indictment on which Thos. Androwes was condemned on the prosecution of Christian Bust was delivered to the grand jury so that they could investigate an accessory, Paris Mustowe, and afterwards returned to the file.

**10.** The indictment on which Thos. Androwes was condemned on the prosecution of Steph. Gunne was delivered to the grand jury to make enquiries of an accessory, Anne Gray, and afterwards returned to the file.

**11.** Wm. Hynde (Hynd) to be discharged of his recogn. paying his fees after he was indicted for felony and found not guilty by the petty jury.

**12.** Hen. Stephens (Stevens) and his sureties to be discharged of their recogn. after he appeared and was not proved to have stolen a horse alleged to belong to Mat. Leech of Oxf., cook. To avoid further trouble and expense Hen. and Mat. agreed that the question of the
p. 92 ownership of the horse should be referred to Mr. Rob. Myton and Mr. Geo. Chambers, two grave citizens of Oxf., and if they cannot decide Dr. Hawley to be umpire. The arbitrators declared in open court in the presence of both parties that if Mat. kept the horse he should pay Hen. 40s., or if he refused the horse Hen. should have it and pay Mat. 30s. Mat. paid the 40s. in public and they left as friends.

**13.** A writ of *habeas corpus* was granted in open court for the removal of Paris Mustowe from Bocardo to the Guildhall where he was indicted to be tried there for felony.

**14.** Mary, wife of Edm. Slayman, bound by recogn. for her good behaviour.

p. 93 **15.** Hen. Hiorns (Hyorns), who was indicted and found guilty of felony to the value of 12d., to be whipped in the market place next market day and remain in prison until he finds sureties for his good behaviour.

**16.** Wm. Beale, indicted and found guilty of felony to the value of 10d. He has been indicted previously and is a 'person of very lewd and evil fame'. He is to be whipped on the next two market days and have a pass.

**17.** Peter Romane *alias* Thos. Earlsman, who was taken with a counterfeit pass, to be whipped as a vagrant and sent to his birthplace.

**18.** Wm. Jones to be whipped next market day and sent by pass to his birthplace.

**19.** Paris Mustowe (Musto) to be discharged paying his fees after being indicted for felony and found not guilty.

## [1619E]

Quarter Sessions at the Guildhall Thurs. 19 Aug. 1619. Jn. Prideaux, p. 94
Vice-Chancellor, Wm. Potter esq., Mayor, Thos. James D.D., Jn. Hawley D.C.L., Thos. Harris ald., J.P.s.

**1.** All constables who failed to bring in their warrants and attend the session to be committed to Bocardo for twenty-four hours.

**2.** Benet James, who says he is a tinker and is a vagrant and suspected rogue, to be taken to the post and thoroughly whipped and sent by pass to his birthplace.

**3.** Jn. Jackson, a ratcatcher, who is taken to be a juggler and lewd person and has already been imprisoned, to be discharged after promising to leave Oxf.

**4.** Mr. Dawson of the Blue Boar to make sure Paris Mustowe is paid p. 95
10s. by next week ('this day senight') for his efforts in finding the goods stolen from Mr. Dawson's house.

**5.** Edm. Slayman to be imprisoned for three days and fined according to the statute for unlicensed victualling and then to enter recogn. with sufficient sureties not to victual any more without a licence.

**6.** Thos. Crompton as in 1619E5.

**7.** Edw. Kellam, glassman, and Ric. Swifte, his supposed servant, to leave Oxf. by Michaelmas day and to live there no longer.

**8.** Moses Browne for contempt in not assisting the constable in the King's service when so ordered. is to be put for two hours in those stocks before his own door.

## [1619F]

Gaol Delivery 30 June 1619. Wm. Potter esq., Mayor, Thos. Wentworth p. 96
esq., Recorder, Thos. James D.D., Jn. Hawley D.C.L., Thos. Harris ald., Wm. Wright ald., Jn. Byrd, Ralph Flaxney, justices for G.D.

**1.** Hen. Herbert, Jn. Hurst and Ric. Profett[1] to be fined 6s. 8d. each for contempt after Rob. Needle, constable of St. Giles, swore he had warned them and they did not attend.

---

[1] Described in the margin as constables.

**2.** All who failed to appear to serve on the grand jury to be fined 3s.

**3.** A writ of *habeas corpus* from the Assize Judges in respect of Wm. Wyse, who is in Bocardo after the coroner's inquest found him guilty of his wife's manslaughter, was delivered into court by Mr. Symondson, sub-Warden of Merton. The writ was allowed and a return delivered to Mr. Justice Warburton, then Assize Judge, in open court, saying that the justices of Gaol Delivery could try the case as the prisoner was here for an act committed within the liberties of Oxf. Mr. Justice Warburton accepted this as he said it was a matter of jurisdiction which was at issue between the college and the town.

**4.** Court adjourned until 1 p.m. on Fri. 2 July, when the above J.P.s came.

**5.** Alice Wylmott and Jane Garland, arrested on suspicion of purse cutting at the time Mrs. Willis of Rewley had her purse cut near Carfax on 30 June, appeared in court having been examined earlier when nothing was said on the basis of which they could be charged. After giving contradictory answers on their re-examination in open p. 97 court, they are thought to be very lewd, wild and badly behaved women, and are committed to the House of Correction. Jane is to remain there until she provides a certificate of her good behaviour from Sir Simon Weston, kt., of Staffs., where she says she lives, and from another gent. of note there. Alice to provide a similar certificate from the minister of Kettering psh., Northants., and the next J.P. there.

**6.** Wm. Walter had been held in prison since the Q.S. on 27 May when he was indicted, arraigned and confessed to stealing two oxen worth £20 belonging to Sir Ric. Mollineux. He claimed benefit of clergy, read the book as a clerk and was burnt on the hand and released by proclamation.

**7.** Hen. Hyorne *alias* Iornes to be discharged by proclamation, paying his fees.

**8.** Wm. Fyndall to be discharged after proclamation, nothing further being objected against him.

**9.** Alice Wylmott and Jane Garland likewise discharged by proclamation 'as for the matter of felony'.

**10.** Anne, wife of Wm. Graye of Oxf., hatter, indicted and arraigned as an accessory of Thos. Androwes, who had been found guilty of burglary and stealing Ric. Hannds's cloak from the house of Mrs. Edith Hands in Grampoole (Grandpont), was acquitted by the petty jury and now is discharged by proclamation.

**11.** Court adjourned until 23 Sept.

## [1619G]

Gaol Delivery at the Guildhall Thurs. 23 Sept. 1619. Jn. Prideaux　p. 98 D.D., Vice-Chancellor, Wm. Potter esq., Mayor, Thos. James D.D., Jn. Hawley D.C.L., Thos. Harris ald., Wm. Wright ald., Ralph Flexney gent., justices for G.D.

**1.** The trial of Wm. Wyse and Wm. Findall, felons held in Bocardo, to be adjourned until Wed. 6 Oct.

**2.** Wm. Hopkins, the prisoner at the bar, found by the oaths of several men in open court to have committed barbarous and gross outrages and misdemeanours against various persons. He is to be returned to Bocardo and remain there without bail until next Saturday, then to be put in the stocks in the open market from 1 p.m. until 3 p.m. As he has no sureties for his good behaviour he is to remain in Bocardo until the next G.D. and then if he still has no sureties be sent to the House of Correction.

**3.** Thos. Harrison of Derbs., arrested in Oxf., gave unsatisfactory answers (was 'found in divers Tales') when questioned about felonies, the theft of a bushel of wheat in a sack, and his journey here. He is to remain in prison until the next Q.S. unless he finds good sureties　p. 99 for a recogn. for his good behaviour and appearance to answer at the next Q.S.

**4.** Ric. Mumford to be apprehended by warrant and sent to the House of Correction for threatening to murder his wife and child.

**5.** Court adjourned until Wed. 6 Oct.

**6.** On 6 Oct. adjourned until Tues. 14 Dec.

## [1619H]

Quarter Sessions at the Guildhall Thurs. 17 Oct. 1619.[1] Jn. Prideaux, Vice-Chancellor, Oliver Smyth esq., Mayor, Thos. James D.D., Jn. Hawley D.C.L., Thos. Harris ald., Jn. Bird gent., J.P.s.

---

[1] Evidently a clerical error: 17 Oct. 1619 was a Sunday, and probably 7 Oct. was the correct date.

**1.** The constable of North and South Osney to be fined 5s. for not appearing and returning his precept.

p. 100 **2.** Edw. Tilliard, Wm. Fletcher, Jn. Browne and the others warned by the serjeants who did not appear to serve on the grand jury to be fined 5s. each for contempt.

**3.** Christian Comber to be discharged of her recogn. with a warning that she will be bound again if she misbehaves towards Goodwife Howse and Goodwife Pemberton.

**4.** Alex. Horne to be committed to Bocardo for three days and pay 20s. according to the statute for unlicensed victualling.

**5.** Wm. Willis, Jn. Pryce, Wm. Thompson and Ric. Horne appointed supervisors of highways and bridges.

**6.** Margaret Slayman to be bound again to appear at the next Q.S. and be of good behaviour and as she did not attend while the court was sitting her recogn. to be estreated.

**7.** Ellen Webb, who appeared on her recogn., is to ask forgiveness next Sun. after the service after dinner at St. Peter-le-Bailey from Goodwife Humfreyes, Joyce Towne, widow and Rob. Coate's dau. for her abuse of them and to pay her fees and meanwhile remain upon her recogn.

**8.** Rob. Dudley to confer with Mr. Carpenter, sub-Rector of Exeter Coll., within the next fortnight and to be absolutely discharged if he then conforms and brings a certificate to the Mayor to that effect; otherwise to be apprehended by warrant.

p. 101 **9.** Geo. Vaughan's recogn. to be estreated.

**10.** Martin Knowles to be committed to Bocardo for a night and sent in safe custody to the House of Correction for using barbarous words to the Bench, threatening and abusing Ald. Harris in open court and at other times, and also abusing the constable. He is to remain there until the next Q.S. and not be released without sureties satisfactory to the court for his good behaviour.

**11.** Hen. Greene's recogn. to be estreated.

**12.** Thos. Harrison to sit in the stocks in the open market from 1 p.m. until 4 p.m. next Saturday and then to be discharged paying his fees, meanwhile remaining in prison.

**13.** Jn. Peade, who appeared on his recogn., to be discharged paying his fees.

**14.** Wm. Findall, who was indicted and found not guilty of the felony of taking 2s. 4d. and two pairs of gloves worth 12d. from Wm. Alley *alias* Leveret, to be discharged.

## [1619I]

Gaol Delivery at the Guildhall 14 Dec. 1619. Jn. Prideaux D.D.,   p. 102
Vice-Chancellor, Oliver Smyth esq., Mayor, Thos. Wentworth esq., Recorder, Thos. James D.D., Thos. Harris ald., Wm. Wright ald., Wm. Potter ald., Ralph Flexney gent., Jn. Bird gent., justices for G.D.

**1.** Ric. Belcher, although indicted and found not guilty of stealing or consenting to the theft of nine pairs of gloves from Hen. Holloway, glover, is to remain in prison until he finds good sureties for his behaviour.

**2.** Ric. Heddy, apprentice of Hen. Holloway, indicted for the same offence as above and found not guilty by the jury, is by order of the whole court to be punished at the Mayor's discretion.

**3.** Ric. Belcher and Ric. Heddie discharged of felony by proclamation.

**4.** Wm. Wyse, indicted and arraigned for felony and the murder of his wife, Mary, and found guilty only of manslaughter, claimed benefit of clergy, was burnt on the hand, and ordered to find sureties for his good behaviour.

**5.** Court adjourned until 13 Jan.

**6.** Adjourned again until Fri. 28 April.

## [1620A]

Quarter Sessions at the Guildhall Thurs. 13 Jan. 1620. Jn. Prideaux,   p. 103
Vice-Chancellor, Oliver Smyth esq., Mayor, Wm. Langton D.D., Thos. James D.D., Jn. Hawley D.C.L., Wm. Wright ald., Wm. Potter ald., Ralph Flaxney gent., Jn. Byrde gent., J.P.s.

**1.** Martin Knowles, who appeared on his recogn., to be discharged from the House of Correction where he was committed after misbehaving to Ald. Harris at the last Q.S. as he submitted and Ald. Harris made no further complaint.

**2.** Leonard Gryndon, who appeared on his recogn. on suspicion of getting Jane Pawle with child, to be discharged as the child is now dead and nothing was proved against him.

**3.** Chris. Wytell, a licensed victualler, who confessed to disorder in his house, to be bound with sureties for his good behaviour and to appear on 1 April or when the J.P.s next sit to license victuallers according to the King's proclamation.

p. 104 **4.** Wm. Singleton, constable of Osney, to be apprehended by warrant and brought before a J.P. to be committed to Bocardo until he pays a fine of 5s. for not attending court.

**5.** Estreats to be made for the bailiffs to levy 5s. from those who did not appear as grand jurors after being empanelled and warned for the last Q.S.

**6.** Further to an order at the last Q.S., Rob. Dudley to be apprehended by warrant and brought before a J.P. to be bound to appear and answer at the next Q.S.

**7.** Edw. Slye to be fined 5s. for being drunk and very disorderly. He is discharged, but will be imprisoned and bound according to the statute if, in future, he is proved before any of the Bench to have been drunk.

**8.** Isobel Harbert and goodwife Mawdytt (Mawditt), wife of Moses Mawdytt, reconciled in open court and Isobel to pay goodwife Mawdytt 12d. for breaking her head and be absolutely discharged.

p. 105 **9.** Process of outlawry to be made out against Thos. Rogers for not prosecuting Wm. Blackett according to his recogn.

**10.** Humph. Hill, indicted and found guilty of misdemeanour and battery against Edw. Bowell, because of his confession, submission and poverty to be fined only 2s. 6d. but also to 'have private correction' in the Guildhall.

**11.** Thos. Willyams (Williams), who was present in court, to be committed to the House of Correction for his proven gross contempt, abuse and misbehaviour towards Dr. Langton. He is to remain there until further order or his discharge by some of the Bench after he submits and after Dr. Langton certifies that he has acknowledged his offence.

**12.** A letter from the Bench to be sent to Rt. Hon. Lord Norreis of Rycote to tell him that the four children of his former servant, Paris Mustow (Musto), are to be sent to the psh. of Beckley where they were born as their mother is dead and Paris very poor. This is so they shall not be a charge on the psh. of St. Peter-le-Bailey which is very poor and has had to seek the help of other pshs. by order of this court because of charges beyond its means.

**13.** The court to choose a time to view all 'squabd' houses[1] and cottages in the city and suburbs and order as appropriate. Warrants to be made for the churchwardens of pshs. with such houses, cottages and lean-tos from time to time to notify a J.P. of any new inhabitants of such new buildings so steps can be taken for the common welfare.

**14.** Thos. Preist has recently come from the country with many children and taken a part of the house of Wm. Smyth, the chandler, in the psh. of St. Martin but has no trade or known livelihood. He is to put in sufficient sureties on or before Candlemas before Ald. Harris and Ald. Wright to be bound with him in the penal sum of £200 that he, his wife and children will not be a charge on the psh. of St. Martin. Otherwise they shall leave the psh., Oxf. and its vicinity. Thos. humbly submitted in open court and accepted the order.  p. 106

**15.** Warrants to be sent out within three days of the Q.S. to the wards of the city and parts of the suburbs against victuallers presented as unlicensed. The names of privileged persons to be sent to the Vice-Chancellor, those who live in the pshs. of St. Mary Magdalen, St. Giles and St. Thos. to Dr. James and Dr. Hawley, and the rest to the Mayor and the other city J.P.s to be dealt with according to the statute.

**16.** The aldermen to enquire in their wards what each householder would give per quarter to maintain a scavenger to carry away the soil from the streets. The results to be sent to the Mayor and Vice-Chancellor to consider if enough can be raised to hire a fit and able man.

**17.** Nic. Berry to be discharged of his recogn.

**18.** Hugh James to find sureties within six days to discharge the psh. of St. Mary Magdalen of any future charge or trouble from himself, his wife or children. Otherwise to be sent in safe custody to the House of Correction to work until the court or two J.P.s order further.  p. 107

**19.** Joan Symonds to have lodgings as before with Thos. Willyams and his wife until Lady Day as she has always paid her rent and the court do not think she should be turned out suddenly.

---

[1] Squab (or squabbed), used repeatedly in Oxf. sources of this period to denote unsatisfactory, probably makeshift, dwellings, is not noted in *N.E.D.*

**20.** [*blank*] Owen to be committed to Bocardo during the pleasure of the court for refusing to assist the constable when called.

**21.** Rob. Ewen was found guilty on a bill presented for battery of Alice Woodams, confessed, submitted and was fined 2s. 6d. Both agreed to obey a final resolution of their dispute to be given by Dr. James.

**22.** Ald. Harris as alderman of the ward to hear and determine the dispute between Alice Wilcocks and Thos. Freman 'for putting her away within the year'.[1]

**23.** Warrants to be sent out to all constables to warn all victuallers, vintners, innkeepers, cooks and butchers, following the King's proclamation, to appear at the Guildhall next Tuesday before the Vice-Chancellor, the Mayor and the rest of the J.P.s and to find sureties to be bound by recogn. not to eat, dress or sell any flesh in Lent or on other prohibited days. The warrants to be made out under the hands and seals of the Vice-Chancellor and the Mayor.

## [1620B]

p. 108  Quarter Sessions at the Guildhall Thurs. 27 April 1620. Jn. Prideaux, Vice-Chancellor, Oliver Smyth esq., Mayor, Thos. James D.D., Jn. Hawley D.C.L., Thos. Flexney esq., Thos. Harris ald., Wm. Wright ald., Wm. Potter ald., Ralph Flexney gent., Jn. Byrd gent., J.P.s.

**1.** Jn. Adams (Addams) to be bound with good sureties for his appearance at the next Q.S. and meanwhile be of good behaviour. In the interim he stands committed.

**2.** Bernard Hawe discharged of his recogn., paying his fees.

**3.** Jn. Clark's recogn. to be estreated.

**4.** Edw. Daye to be fined 20s. and imprisoned for three days for unlicensed victualling. He is to be stopped from victualling, enter a new recogn. not to do so, and be detained until he pays his fine.

**5.** Thos. Bland discharged paying his fees.

**6.** Steph. Skevington to be released from the recogn. entered at the suit of Edw. Morris as they are now good friends, and to pay his fees.

**7.** Rob. Carpenter for unlicensed victualling as in 1620B4.

p. 109  **8.** Thos. Cantyn (Cantin) for unlicensed victualling as in 1620B4.

**9.** Jn. Stacy to have a licence to victual if he puts in sufficient sureties and pays his fine according to the statute for contempt.

[1] Perhaps meaning the dismissal of a covenanted servant within her year's contract.

**10.** Thos. Keene to be licensed as in 1620B9.

**11.** Wm. Pope to be licensed as in 1620B9.

**12.** Jn. Younge to be find 20s. and imprisoned for three days according to the statute for unlicensed victualling and to be stopped from victualling until he enters a new recogn. with good sureties on obtaining a new licence.

**13.** Jas. Godfrey discharged from victualling.

**14.** Wm. Umbles for unlicensed victualling as in 1620B4.

**15.** Ric. Hucks and Wm. Smyth committed to prison until they pay their fees.

**16.** Jn. Hutchins to be bound to appear at the next Q.S., meanwhile to be of good behaviour and be discharged from his office of constable. His apprentices Nic. Maris and Jn. Combes to be discharged from their indentures as it was proved in court that he had persuaded them to commit lewd and felonious acts. At the next Q.S. he is to pay Nic. 50s. and Jn. 20s. out of the money he received with them.

**17.** Ric. Chambers was suspected of felony but nothing was proved against him. He confessed to being drunk and was ordered to sit in the stocks in the cage for three hours and drink nothing but water until he is repentant and sober. p. 110

**18.** Wm. London and Jn. Harris committed until they find sureties for their good behaviour and appearance at the next Q.S.

**19.** Jn. Browne committed to Bocardo for three days and to pay his fine and enter recogn. under the statute for unlicensed victualling.

**20.** Thos. Almond to be discharged of his recogn. as nothing material was objected against him in respect of the death of Jn. Day.

**21.** The said Thos. Almond for unlicensed victualling as in 1620B19.

**22.** Wm. Owram and Wm. Gardner discharged of their recogns. paying their fees.

**23.** Ant. Crooke indicted and fined 5s.

**24.** Kath. Androwes discharged of her recogn. paying her fees.

**25.** The Mayor to end the controversy between Plott and his apprentice.

**26.** Bernard Boulton to be sent to the House of Correction until the next Q.S. and then to enter recogn. with good sureties for the peace.

**27.** Thos. Lane to be whipped in public next market day and be sent by pass to his birthplace.

p. 111  **28.** The recogns. of Jn. Clarke and Ric. Hucks to be estreated.

**29.** Kath. Androwes discharged of her recogn.

**30.** Edw. Davis discharged of his recogn.

**31.** Jn. Thomas to be whipped in public for bringing a false pass and sent by pass to his birthplace, which he says is Glascwm (Glascome), Radnorshire.

**32.** If Ric. Edney's recogn. is not removed by 10 May by Jn. Striblehill *alias* Striplinge, Ric. to be discharged and Jn. to be bound to prosecute.

**33.** Ric. Edney indicted *per pro* Jn. Striblehill and discharged by the jury.

**34.** The constables of the four wards in the city to be fined 10s. each for not attending when judgement was given on Saturday morning.

**35.** Chris. Wytell, Rob. Bursey, Wm. Coleman, Thos. Combe *alias* Hamlett, Wm. Bushell and Rog. Bradshawe, who were indicted and found guilty, to be hanged.

**36.** Mr. Jn. Bird and Mr. Jn. Chillingworth chosen as treasurer and collector for maimed soldiers respectively.

**37.** Thos. Rogers, who was indicted and found guilty at the last Q.S. of stealing a pair of shoes from Wm. Blackett, was arraigned again after escaping and being recaptured, claimed benefit of clergy, was burnt on the hand and discharged.

p. 112  **38.** Ric. Chambers, who was indicted and confessed to a small felony, claimed benefit of clergy, was burnt on the hand and discharged.

**39.** Jn. Hyat(t) had been committed on suspicion of burglary but the jury did not find the indictment against him for lack of proof. His carriage, behaviour and the account given of him show him to be a very lewd and sturdy rogue and he is to be committed to the House of Correction until he obtains a certificate of his good behaviour from Broadway [Worcs.] which he says is his birthplace.

**40.** Martha Myles committed to the House of Correction until the next Q.S.

**41.** Hugh Floyd to be banished from Oxf. and, if he ever returns, to be sent to the House of Correction for a year.

**42.** Jn. ap Thomas, a vagrant, to be whipped.

**43.** At the Q.S. last April the pshs. of St. Martin, St. Aldate and All Saints were ordered to pay 5s. each per quarter to assist the psh. of St. Peter-le-Bailey with the relief of its poor unless they showed a good reason not to. No such reason has been shown but, in contempt of the court, the churchwardens of All Saints have refused to pay, so warrants are to be made out for them to be brought before a J.P. and committed to prison until they pay the arrears.

## [1620c]

Quarter Sessions Thurs. 15 June 1620. Oliver Smyth, Mayor, Thos. James    p. 113
D.D., Jn. Hawly D.C.L., Thos. Flexney esq., Thos. Harris ald. J.P.s.

**1.** Wm. Porter appeared on his recogn. to prosecute Francis Freeman. He had been put to great charge in pursuing Francis to recover a mare which was borrowed for a day but taken away and kept for a long time. He has now got the mare and the court granted his request to be discharged from his recogn. and allowed to seek a remedy by law.

**2.** Hen. Gunn(e), who was proved to be an unlicensed victualler, to be committed to Bocardo for three days and fined 20s. according to the statute and to be bound not to victual.

**3.** A warrant to be made out for the speedy apprehension of Humph. Williams, labourer, of the psh. of St. Peter-le-Bailey, for barbarously beating his wife who was present in court and seen by all.

**4.** Edw. Sly(e) to be fined 5s. or go to the stocks for being drunk and if he does not pay to be committed until he pays his fine and his fees and to be bound for his good behaviour. He did pay, was discharged and the fine given to Mr. Ric. Wardell, a churchwarden of Sly's psh. of St. Peter-in-the-East.

**5.** Hen. Barefoot(e) discharged of his recogn., paying his fees.

**6.** Thos. Almond was committed during the pleasure of the court for    p. 114
rash and ill-mannered words to Dr. James but was discharged when he submitted and confessed in public and Dr. James accepted this.

**7.** Joan, wife of Ric. Browne, was dismissed after penitently submitting in open court to Mr. Thos. Almond and asking his forgiveness for her injury and abuse of him and promising to behave soberly and well towards him in future, which he accepted.

**8.** Hen. Argoll discharged after appearing on his recogn.

**9.** In a dispute between Jn. Davies and Steph. Wilks the court decides that Jn. should give to Steph. all the goods due to him under the will of old Mr. Wilks, glover, decd., and that Steph. should discharge Jn. in law. Both were present in court and agreed to this, were discharged of their recogns. and were told to be good friends as they are brothers-in-law.

[*Margin*] Memo. that £5 was left to Hen. Wilks by the will of old Mr. Wilks; Jn. Davies has agreed to pay it and the court orders him to do so.

**10.** Jas. Feild bound by recogn. in the sum of £40 that his son, Jas. will appear to answer before any two J.P.s at reasonable summons and not leave without licence.

**11.** Jn. Addams discharged after appearing on his recogn.

**12.** Julian, wife of Chris. Wytell, who was recently executed for felony, appeared in court after being bound over on suspicion of similar offences but nothing was objected against her and she is discharged.

**13.** Thos. Edwards, who had been bound over for the peace, discharged of his recogn. as nothing was objected against him.

p. 115 **14.** Nic. Maris and Jn. Combs, former apprentices of Jn. Hutchins, slater, for filching odd pieces of laths, rafters, coals and timbers from several colleges where Hutchins worked, to be whipped in the Guildhall, although they had been encouraged by Hutchins.

**15.** Jn. Hutchins, Wm. London and Jn. Harris, slaters, discharged of their recogns. by the court's favour, in hope of their better behaviour in future.

**16.** Christian, wife of Wm. Bushell, who was recently executed, appeared on the recogn. by which she was bound on suspicion of felony and pilfering and was discharged as no prosecution was brought.

**17.** Wm. Fyndall to be sent to the House of Correction and to remain there until information is given by Mr. Arnold that he has been reformed in his opinion on the deity, which he denied. He may then be discharged by two J.P.s.

**18.** Dorothy Rogers, suspected but discharged as in 1620c12 and 1620c16, is also informed against in open court over suspected witchcraft. She is to find sureties for her good behaviour and appearance at the next Q.S, and those with knowledge of the suspected matter to be brought before some of the court and bound to prosecute.

**19.** On credible testimony in court that Mary, wife of Ric. Parsons, is a very badly behaved woman she is to find sureties for her good behaviour and appearance at the next Q.S. Her husband entered into recogn. of £20.

**20.** Anne Woodely (Woodleye), wife of Jn. Foach(e), labourer, of Newbury, Berks., was questioned concerning misbehaviour and it appeared that Foache has another wife and three children. She is to go to Newbury and enter recogn. before a J.P. to prosecute Foache and bring a certificate of this to the Mayor or a J.P. If she does not, to be apprehended by warrant and dealt with.

**21.** Margaret, wife of Edm. Slayman, to be kept in safe custody until  p. 116 she can be safely carried to the ducking stool after many misdemeanours, daily disorders, abuse of officers and drunkenness were proved in court.

**22.** Bernard Bolton to be sent to the House of Correction for barbarously beating his wife for a third time and his recogn. and sureties to be estreated.

**23.** Ant. Crook(e), the constable, to pay his fine to the bailiffs and his fees to the clerk of the court and be discharged.

## [1620D]

Quarter Sessions at the Guildhall Thurs. 5 Oct. 1620 Jn. Prideaux D.D., Vice-Chancellor, Ant. Fyndall esq., Mayor, Thos. James D.D., Jn. Hawley D.C.L., Thos. Flexny esq., Thos. Harris ald., Wm. Wright ald., Wm. Potter ald., Ralph Flexny gent., Jn. Byrd gent., J.P.s.

**1.** Ric. Durbridge, tithingman of North Osney, fined 10s. for contempt for not attending court after being ordered by warrant.

**2.** Each juror who failed to attend to be fined 20s.

**3.** Ant. Ives, who had victualled without licence and had bowling and  p. 117 disorder in his house despite being warned, to be proceeded against according to the statute if he victuals in future. In the meantime to be discharged of his recogn.

**4.** Chris. Toms, husbandman, of Beckley, Oxon., entered into recogn. that at the next Q.S. he and Humph. Jorden, freemason, of Oxf., would bring Wm. Toms, suspected father of the child of Mary Tucky *alias* Alnutt, to answer and not depart without leave.

**5.** Thos. Robynson to be whipped for abusing Dr. James.

**6.** Edw. Bethell to be licensed to victual and discharged of his recogn. by proclamation as no prosecution was brought against him.

**7.** Hen. Nicholls entered recogn. to appear at the next Q.S. and meanwhile be of good behaviour.

**8.** Hen. Seamon *alias* Symon, an unlicensed victualler, to be committed to prison, fined according to the statute and stopped from victualling.

**9.** Hen. Pedgelye (Pedgly) to go to prison for unlicensed victualling, be fined 20s. and find surety not to victual until licensed.

**10.** Frances, wife of Edw. Shawe, entered recogn. to appear at the next Q.S. and meanwhile be of good behaviour.

p. 118 **11.** Bernard Boulton (Bolton) discharged of his recogn. paying his fees.

**12.** Sibyl Carter to be released from her recogn. paying her fees as no prosecution was brought.

**13.** Ann Willyams committed to prison until she finds sureties for her appearance at the next Q.S. and to be bound for her good behaviour in the meantime.

**14.** Wm. Wirdnam who appeared on his recogn. discharged of it as nothing was objected against him.

**15.** Wm. Prickett, who appeared as bound, discharged of his recogn. paying his fees.

**16.** Jn. Addams discharged of his recogn. paying his fees.

**17.** Ric. Glover discharged of his recogn., no prosecution being brought.

**18.** Dan. Davis ordered to be publicly whipped but quit by proclamation on his humble submission in hope of his better behaviour.

**19.** Wm. Eelye (Eely) ordered to be whipped but quit by proclamation.

**20.** Jn. Daniell discharged of his recogn. paying his fees.

**21.** Thos. Cantyn is committed to prison as an unlicensed victualler and be fined 20s. according to the statute, and not to victual without licence.

**22.** Jn. Playsteed for unlicensed victualling as in 1620D21, and to put in sureties not to victual without licence.

**23.** Geo. Hudson, who appeared on his recogn., discharged as no p. 119 further prosecution was brought.

**24.** Ric. Willyams quit by proclamation from his recogn. paying his fees.

**25.** Agnes and Jessop Noake discharged after appearing on their recogns.

**26.** Wm. Pickeringe (Pickringe) found sureties for his appearance at the next Q.S. so was not committed to prison.

**27.** Wm. Willmott indicted and arraigned for felony, is acquitted by the petty jury and discharged.

**28.** Thos. Poole and Wm. Barton entered recogn. to bring Ric. Lovesaye to the next Q.S. and the court granted a special warrant for his apprehension.

**29.** Jas. Hall to be committed to Bocardo for using audacious, scornful and lewd words to a J.P., not fit to be recorded or remembered. Next Saturday he is to sit in the stocks in the open market from 2 p.m. to 4 p.m. and then be released.

**30.** Vincent Ranckle discharged of his recogn.

**31.** Eliz. Noake, widow, found Jessop Noake and Ric. Weste as sureties for her appearance at the next Q.S.

**32.** Humph. Hill to be committed to the House of Correction for pilfering.

**33.** Ric. Whetstone, one of the grand jury, for revealing a present- p. 120 ment agreed on by the jury which he had sworn to keep secret, is bound for his good behaviour on the surety of Phil. Dodwell and Rob. Barton, and is discharged from ever being a juror.

**34.** Thos. Wells to be bound for his good behaviour and on his recogn. until the next Q.S. Ant. Crooke and Jerome Poole bound for him.

**35.** Nic. Plott committed to Bocardo for saucy words to officers sent to summon him before the Mayor and Ald. Harris. Since he is decayed and unable to keep his apprentices on work, Francis Beesely and Wm. Blissett are discharged from their apprenticeship.

**36.** Eliz. Plott discharged of her recogn.

**37.** Mary Parsons and Christian Bushell to be discharged by proclamation paying their fees.

**38.** Wm. Jennings bound by the recogn. of Thos. Bolt and Wm. Applebye to appear at the next Q.S. and keep the peace.

**39.** If Ellis, wife of Jn. Sunton, against whom the jury found an indictment of forcible entry, does not pray to be admitted to a traverse within a month then it may be demanded, or at the next Q.S. such restitution shall be granted as the law will allow, after good advice has been taken.

**40.** Jn. Tew's petition against Wm. Kendall, servant of Mrs. Clare, to be referred to Mr. Byrd, the next J.P. to her house.

**41.** Dorothy Rogers to be acquitted by proclamation, notwithstanding the scandalous words of Joan Egby.[1]

**42.** All former orders concerning the poor of the psh. of St. Peter to be considered by Dr. Hawly and Mr. Thos. Flexnye.

p. 121   **43.** Jn. Peade and Thos. Pare bound to appear at the next Q.S.

**44.** Warrants to be sent out for all who refuse to pay their fees.

# [1621A]

Quarter Sessions Thurs. 11 Jan. 1621. Jn. Prideaux, Vice-Chancellor, Ant. Fyndall esq., Mayor, Wm. Langton D.D., Thos. James D.D., Thos. Flexney esq., Thos. Harris ald., Wm. Wright ald., Jn. Byrd gent., J.P.s.

**1.** Hen. Nicholls to be discharged after he appeared on his recogn. and no further complaint was made.

**2.** Ric. Whetstone to enter into a new recogn. to be of good behaviour. His former recogn. to behave well and appear at the next Q.S. to be estreated as he broke its conditions. Wm. Bland and Steph. Gunn to be sureties.

**3.** Thos. Wells as in 1621A1.

p. 122   **4.** Wm. Jennings, tailor, as in 1621A1.

**5.** Rob. Needle to be discharged of his recogn. if he pays his fees, otherwise to be committed to Bocardo and his recogn. to be estreated.

**6.** Jeremy Poole to be discharged after appearing on his recogn. at the prosecution of Margery Newe, as the court found no cause for the prosecution 'but rather spleene of the woman'.

**7.** Thos. Peare discharged of his recogn. as no prosecution was brought.

---

[1] Rogers had been accused of witchcraft; above, 1620c18.

**8.** Eliz. Noake as in 1621A1.

**9.** Jn. Pead(e), who appeared on his recogn., is discharged.

**10.** Wm. Toms, who had been bound over as the suspected father of a child to be born to Mary Tucky *alias* Allnutt, is discharged as he has married her.

**11.** Wm. Pickring(e) bound on the surety of his master, Thos. Penn of Oxf., chandler, and his father, Jas. Pickringe, for his attendance during the court's pleasure at the next Q.S.

**12.** Francis Burnham, who appeared on his recogn. as the father of Frances Pearce's child, to be discharged as the child died after delivery, and he has married the woman.

**13.** Thos. Tayler as in 1621A1.

**14.** Wm. Kensall the younger appeared on the recogn. by which he was p. 123 bound over by Mr. Byrd J.P. after Jn. Tew's complaint was referred to him at the last Q.S. He is discharged after Mr. Byrd's report as no further prosecution was brought.

**15.** Edw. Sansome had complained to Thos. Flexney J.P. that Jn. Bostall of Barton in Headington psh., freemason, had feloniously taken his ruler and Bostall had been bound to appear and answer at the next Q.S. and Sansome bound to prosecute. Sansome appeared and presented a bill of indictment but the grand jury decided that he had 'dissembled his knowledge', which the court considered an abuse and a hindrance to justice. Fearing an order against him for contempt, Sansome left without permission, so a warrant is to be made out for him to be brought before a J.P. and be imprisoned until he finds good sureties for his appearance at the next Q.S.; in the meantime to be of good behaviour.

**16.** Ric. Lovesey (Lovesaye) discharged of the recogn. prayed against him by Wm. Howse and his wife.

**17.** Wm. Ryce (Rice), who appeared on the recogn. prayed against him by his wife, Eliz., to be discharged as Dr. Hawly certified that in his presence she had been reconciled to Wm.

**18.** Jn. Lloyde, tailor, who appeared after being bound over on suspicion of an affray against a young gentleman, a scholar of Exeter Coll., was discharged of his recogn., no further prosecution being brought.

**19.** Ann Nixon to be discharged of her recogn., provided she leaves Oxf. by Easter Day and does not return on pain of further order of

p. 124 the court and in the meantime behaves so that no further complaint is made. If she does return the next J.P. to send for her and bind her over for her good behaviour.

**20.** Edw. Jones committed to Bocardo for not paying 6d. a week and the arrears of this to Penelope White, who bore his child. The matter had been referred to Dr. James and Dr. Hawley who ordered him to pay this for seven years if the child lives so long.

**21.** Examination of the complaint of Jn. Weaver and his wife against goodwife Thackham was referred to the Mayor. She was carted and ducked in the cucking stool at the Castle mills.

**22.** Jn. Bostall to pay a fine of 5s. according to the statute for being drunk and the fine to be distributed to the poor of the psh. of St. Peter-le-Bailey. His recogn. to be estreated if the fine and his fees are not paid by Saturday.

**23.** Playstead (Playsted) and Cantyn to be bound not to victual and to be sent for by warrant.

**24.** Wm. Smyth and Wm. Plott (Platt) bound for their appearance at the next Q.S. and good behaviour in the meantime for deceiving Jn. Wolly by bargaining with him for half the value of nineteen sheep supposedly stolen from Wolly.[1] Ric. Edens, butcher, and Wm. Mundy, butcher, are sureties for Wm. Smyth's appearance and Francis Pusy, tailor, and Jas. Clarke, haberdasher, for Wm. Plott's appearance.

**25.** Warrants to be made out against all unlicensed victuallers presented by the grand jury.

p. 125 **26.** Jn. Johnson, who had been committed by Mr. Byrd as a wandering soldier and for abusing Dr. James, to be discharged on his humble submission and with the consent of Dr. James and to leave the city tomorrow morning, 12 Jan.

**27.** Dan. Davyes (Davis) to be publicly whipped at a post next Friday and to be sent to the House of Correction during the pleasure of the court.

**28.** Nic. Raynsford to be punished as in 1621A27.

**29.** Hen. Rownsevall and Ric. Crooke to be sent for by strict warrant and brought before Ald. Harris to be examined and dealt with.

---

[1] The meaning of the entry is unclear, but perhaps the accused had sought payment for returning cattle which had not in fact been stolen.

**30.** The recogn. of Francis Shawe to be estreated.

## [1621B]

Quarter Sessions Thurs. 12 April 1621. Jn. Prideaux D.D., Vice-Chan- p. 126
cellor, Ant. Fyndall esq., Mayor, Thos. Wentworth esq., Recorder,
Thos. James D.D., Jn. Hawly D.C.L., Thos. Flexney esq., Thos.
Harris ald., Wm. Wright ald., Wm. Potter ald., Ralph Flexney gent.,
Jn. Byrd gent., J.P.s.

**1.** Jas. Feild of the psh. of St. Thos. fined 3s. 4d. after failing to appear
and serve at this Q.S. after being warned in person last Tuesday. For
the same offence Humph. Bewe and Rob. Paynter fined 2s. each on
the oath of Edw. Thorneton, constable, that he had warned them at
their houses to attend.

**2.** Ric. Wardell, bound over for misdemeanour and abusing Mr.
Boswell, on the proof under oath of Edw. Tomlyns, is committed to
Bocardo during the pleasure of the court. Afterwards he submitted to
Mr. Boswell and was discharged in hope of his good behaviour.

**3.** Jn. Biggins had been committed according to the statute for unlicensed victualling on the certificate of Dr. James and Thos. Flexney
esq. He is to enter recogn. with good sureties not to victual without
licence and to pay a fine of 20s. or be imprisoned.

**4.** Thos. Preston, tailor, to be sent to Mr. Russell, Master of the
Tailors, to be well whipped, after being found guilty of a foul offence
and being a pander between a young gent. and a maid of Mr. Flexney,
'bringing them together to committ lewdness'.

**5.** Geo. Box discharged after Ald. Harris accepted his apology for
abusing him.

**6.** Jas. Hall to be committed to Bocardo pending further order for p. 127
abusing the J.P.s with words too foul to be recorded.

**7.** Wm. Pope to pay half the fees of Edm. Hart, who was then
discharged of his recogn. Pope appeared and paid.

**8.** Mart. Knowles fined 6s. 8d. after he appeared in court and the
jury found an indictment against him for assault and battery of Eliz.
Powell, widow.

**9.** Edw. Badger, the constable of North-West ward, was found guilty
by the grand jury on an indictment for flinging to the ground the
Mayor's warrant brought to him by Jn. Burgyn, one of the beadles,

and for beating the beadle. As he is unfit to hold office he is to be replaced by his petty constable, Thos. Wells, the joiner. He paid a fine of 20s. and was discharged.

**10.** Warrants to be made out against all unlicensed victuallers, and against Jn. Twin, Mary Holness and her husband.

**11.** Ralph Hodges was found guilty by the jury on an indictment for battery of Edw. Carter the constable. He paid a fine of 6s. 8d. for this and 5s. for being presented as a drunkard which was given to Mr. Gough for the poor of the psh. of St. Ebbe.

**12.** Isaac Copperthwayte was questioned about getting Joan Newman pregnant, but on the evidence of various women the particulars seemed 'intricate'. The matter is referred to Dr. Hawley and Ald. Harris and in the meantime Copperthwayte to remain in prison until he can put in sureties to abide their order.

p. 128    **13.** Thos. Rogers had previously been indicted, arraigned and burnt on the hand and was bound over to appear here for many misdemeanours and on suspicion of pilfering. If he does not leave Oxf. within eight days or if he returns he is to be sent to the House of Correction.

**14.** Following a complaint against Jn. Wolly he shall put in sureties within a fortnight to keep and treat his apprentice, Jn. Kersill, properly. Otherwise the Mayor and Ald. Harris to make an order and the apprentice to be discharged.

**15.** Jn. Prytchard (Prychard) and Wm. Hynd(e) were found guilty by the petty jury on an indictment for felony and taking 37s. 6d. from Peter Omellallowe, an Irishman. They each claimed benefit of clergy and were burnt on the hand.

**16.** Frideswide Pemerton discharged paying her fees after the jury found her not guilty on an indictment concerning two silver bowls belonging to Mr. Harris.

**17.** Ric. Claxton was found not guilty by the jury of stealing a Bible from Mr. Jas. Robynson of Magdalen Hall, although the evidence was 'very pregnant' and he was admonished by the Recorder. He is discharged of this offence paying his fees but is to answer on suspicion of stealing pewter.

**18.** Edw. Baylie to be whipped and sent away with a pass after the jury found him guilty to the value of 11d. of stealing a sheet worth 6s. from Hen. Harbert.

**19.** Wm. Tilcock to be whipped and discharged after being found guilty by the petty jury of petty larceny to the value of 8d.

**20.** The jury did not find the indictment against Jn. Addams for stealing four books called Burton's Works from Jn. Allam despite strong suspicions. He is to be discharged paying his fees.

**21.** Thos. Peare to be bound for his good behaviour for a year for his ill-mannered conduct in open court.

**22.** Marg. Slayman fined 20s. for unlicensed victualling.

**23.** Dr. Hawley, Mr. Thos. Flexney, Ald. Harris and Ald. Wright to p. 129 view the bridge at the Castle mills next to Mr. Bosworth's house, estimate the cost of repairing it and give their opinion on how it should be raised. The money is to be raised accordingly.

**24.** Ric. Claxton to be whipped in the open market next Saturday, 14 April, and to be sent to the House of Correction if he is found in or about Oxf. after five days.

**25.** Jn. Addams to be sent to the House of Correction.

**26.** Jn. Younge to be discharged from keeping an alehouse as he is an idle and lewd fellow.

**27.** Maurice Heath, who was bound to appear here, to be discharged by proclamation as no prosecution was brought.

**28.** Toby White to find sureties for his good behaviour for abusing Mr. Flexney in open court and falsely accusing him of binding him to prosecute Jn. Beard without his consent. In the absence of sureties to be committed.

**29.** Jn. Beard to be fined 5s. to be paid at 3d. per week to the poor of the psh. of St. Peter-le-Bailey for being drunk. As it was his first offence known to the court he is to be dealt with leniently in hope of his better behaviour.

**30.** Nic. Edmonds, who appeared on his recogn., is to await the opinion and 'doome' of the Vice-Chancellor concerning his misuse of young Mr. Leake of St. John's Coll.

**31.** By May Day Art. Nicholls is to take Hen. Weekes, son of Steph. Weekes, glover, as his apprentice for twelve years from Lady Day 1621. Jn. Davies (Davis), executor of old Hen. Weekes, decd., is to pay 56s. to make the 44s. formerly lent to Nicholls up to £5 and also give him a suit of apparel. This shall discharge Davies of the legacy of £5 from old Hen. to young Hen. Weekes.[1] After twelve years Nicholls shall give him a cloak and double apparel or 30s. and double apparel.

p. 130 **32.** Ric. Aldam, bound to appear on suspicion of felony, is discharged by proclamation as no further prosecution was brought.

**33.** Jas. Hall's own recogn. taken for his appearance at the next Q.S. and good behaviour in the meantime. He is to go to the House of Correction if he does not provide a certificate of his good behaviour at the next Q.S.

**34.** Wm. Forrest to be brought before Mr. Byrde to be told to give Joan Symonds houseroom or be committed until he performs the last order made.

**35.** Mr. Jn. Byrd to be treasurer and Mr. Wm. Fletcher collector for maimed soldiers.

**36.** Thos. Burneham and Thos. Watts allowed to be victuallers.

**37.** A warrant to be made out for Francis Shawe's appearance at the next Q.S.

## [1621C]

Quarter Sessions at the Guildhall Thurs. 31 May 1621. Jn. Prideaux, Vice-Chancellor, Ant. Fyndall esq., Mayor, Thos. James D.D., Jn. Hawley D.C.L., Thos. Flexney esq., Thos. Harris ald., Wm. Wright ald., Jn. Byrd gent., J.P.s.

**1.** Thos. Preston to be whipped in the Town Hall during the session for not obeying the order of the last Q.S.

**2.** In future all warrants against unlicensed victuallers to be made out within three days of the end of each session and to require the offender to appear before the convenient J.P. for that division. Those presented at the former sessions to be dealt with according to this order.

p. 131 **3.** Various parishioners of St. Peter-le-Bailey had given certificates on behalf of Margaret Slayman and she had penitently confessed and acknowledged her past offences. Although she had formerly been punished, in hope of her future behaviour she is to be allowed to victual as long as she behaves well and puts in good sureties.

**4.** Thos. Wheatland, who appeared on his recogn. for unlicensed victualling, committed for three days according to the statute, fined 20s. and allowed to victual.

----

[1] See above, 1620c9.

**5.** Thos. Richardson, who had been imprisoned for contempt for unlicensed victualling, paid his fine of 20s. in court.

**6.** Jn. Evans fined 20s. for unlicensed victualling but not to be imprisoned at present.

**7.** Thos. Smyth committed to Bocardo for three days paying his fine, for unlicensed victualling and using contemptuous words in court.

**8.** Margaret Slayman, widow, to be allowed to victual if she keeps good order. Peter Fishe of Holton, Oxon., yeoman and Geo. Watkins of Oxf., labourer, entered into recogn.

**9.** Steph. Ashley (Ashly) appeared on his recogn. and his former prosecutors, Jn. Hurst, carpenter, and Rob. Needle, carpenter, were examined in court. It appears that their complaint arises from spleen and not just cause. Ashley to be discharged and to keep the peace, but not to be bound.

**10.** Hen. Higgs to pay fines of 40s. for allowing unlawful games and 10s. for allowing Rog. Moore, apprentice of Ant. Toms the barber, to drink in his house contrary to the statute between 11 and 12 o'clock and stay there beyond 1 o'clock. He is to be committed until he pays 10s. to the poor. By grace of the court quit on paying 5s. to the poor.

**11.** Sandy, a prisoner in Bocardo, to be put in the dungeon on information that he is too unruly and dangerous to be kept 'at large as other prisoners'. p. 132

**12.** Thos. Jellyman of St. Giles presented for great disorder in his house, selling 'strong water', and putting up the sign of the Still without warrant. He is also complained of for unlicensed victualling but that was not proved. He is not to sell ale or beer, and is to take down his sign and keep good order in his house.

**13.** Jas. Hall to show a certificate of his good behaviour to the Vice-Chancellor, the Mayor and at least two J.P.s by next Saturday. If he does so he is to be discharged. If not, to be sent to the House of Correction as ordered at the last Q.S.

**14.** Jn. Knapp, who had been imprisoned as an unlicensed victualler according to the statute and appeared on his recogn., is fined 20s. and is to remain committed until he pays the officers' fees and 2s. to the justices' clerk who took his recogn.

**15.** Alex. Cooke, Jn. Clarke and Thos. Wheatland licensed to victual by the court and Thos. Richardson by the Mayor and Vice-Chancellor.

**16.** Hen. Gunn(e) discharged of his recogn. of the peace as no prosecution was brought but after three days' imprisonment for unlicensed victualling is committed on another recogn. until he pays a fine of 20s. and the fees of the court and the justices' clerk. Jonas Clinch, glazier, who caused Gunn to be bound over and did not prosecute, to be apprehended by warrant and imprisoned until he pays Gunn's costs and charges. Mr. Palmer and Mr. Samon to repay a fine of 20s. taken from Gunn without being levied by the court or be brought before a J.P. to be committed until they do so.

p. 133 **17.** Thos Corbett *alias* Smyth, who was indicted for stealing a cloak from Ric. Saintesbury at Christ Church and found guilty of felony to the value of 9d., to be stripped to his girdle and whipped at the post and to have a pass.

**18.** Jn. Misson discharged by proclamation paying his fees after being arraigned on an indictment on the sessions file of last Oct. for stealing a parcel of silk lace from Thos. Cooper the mercer and being acquitted by the petty jury.

**19.** Margaret Atwood to be put in the ducking stool at a time to be named for horrible scolding and base and scandalous words to Agnes Lee, and for various other misdemeanours.

**20.** Hugh Shawe, imprisoned for three days for unlicensed victualling appeared on his recogn., and is to pay a fine of 20s. and the fees of the court and the justices' clerk.

**21.** Warrants to be made out against Joan Horne and Margery Atwood for not paying their fees.

**22.** Jn. Hicks to be punished as a vagrant and sent by pass to Worcester where he says his wife lives.

**23.** Margery Gunne committed to Mr. Arnold[1] for not paying the fees of the court and the justices' clerk.

**24.** Jn. Knowles appeared on his recogn. for the peace and for abusing the serjeant, and because he was not prosecuted he was discharged, paying his fees to the court and to the clerks of Mr. Justice Hawley.

**25.** The next two J.P.s are to enquire how much Rob. Warde is in arrears to the poor and to deal with him. In the meantime his recogn. to be estreated. The recogns. of Ric. Wardell, Hen. Nicholls and Chris. Poulter to be estreated.

[1] Wm. Arnold was keeper of Bocardo, appointed in Nov. 1617: *O.C.A. 1583–1626*, 273.

**26.** Chris. Poulter to be apprehended by warrant and brought before   p. 134
the next J.P. to be committed until he pays his fine of 20s. and the fees
of the court and the justices' clerks.

**27.** All recusants presented by the grand jury at this Q.S. to surrender
to the bailiffs by the next Q.S. or 'to stand convicted'. Then to be
certified into the Exchequer.

**28.** Jn. Blunt, constable of the Senior ward,[1] fined 3s. 4d. for not
attending his alderman and to be committed until he pays.

## [1621D]

Special Sessions at the Guildhall Thurs. 13 Sept. 1621. Wm. Peirse,
Vice-Chancellor, Ant. Fyndall esq., Mayor, Thos. Harris ald., Ralph
Flexney gent., Jn. Byrd gent., J.P.s.

**1.** All those called to be jurors and not attending to be fined 3s. 4d.

**2.** Widow Willmott to be committed for three days for unlicensed
victualling and fined 20s. according to the statute.

**3.** Edw. Daye to be suspended as a victualler until he brings a certificate of his good behaviour to the Vice-Chancellor.

**4.** Ralph Oxley, Thos. Price, Hen. Pedgly and Jn. Pyme to be stopped
from victualling as they have good trades by which they can maintain
themselves.

**5.** Jn. Slatford, Jas. Toldervey, Thos. Dodge and Gideon Turner to be   p. 135
stopped from victualling.

**6.** On his petition to the court Jas. Hall allowed to victual if he keeps
good order.

**7.** Thos. Richardson and Jn. Wood to be stopped from victualling as
unfit persons.

**8.** Thos. Smyth to be imprisoned for three days for unlicensed victualling and fined 20s.

**9.** Rob. March *alias* Thatcher to be allowed to victual if he puts in
sureties and keeps order in his house on his petition that he is no
longer fit to make his living.

**10.** All those who did not attend this session after being warned to be
stopped from victualling until the court grants them a licence.

---

[1] Perhaps the ward of the senior alderman, Thomas Harris. Blunt, however, was not
one of the four ward constables appointed for this municipal year: *O.C.A. 1583–1626*, 295.

**11.** Joan Tomlins committed for unlicensed victualling but afterwards granted a licence.

**12.** Prudence Umbles, widow, Cicely Francklyn, widow, Ann Till-yard, widow, and widow Playsted to be licensed to victual, entering into recogn.

**13.** Warrants to be made out against unlicensed victuallers.

**14.** Thos Dodge and Rob. Budd allowed to victual, putting in good sureties.

## [1621E]

p. 136 Quarter Sessions at the Guildhall Thurs. 4 Oct. 1621. Wm. Peirse, Vice-Chancellor, Jn. Davenante esq., Mayor, Jn. Prideaux D.D., Thos. James D.D., Jn. Hawley D.C.L., Thos. Flexney esq., Thos. Harris ald., Wm. Potter ald., Ralph Flexney gent., Jn. Bird gent., J.P.s.

**1.** Wm. Jennings (Jenings), tailor, to be bound for his good behaviour and meanwhile be committed to prison for saucy and contemptuous words to the court. Afterwards he was bound in the sum of £40 for his good behaviour especially to Mr. Chas. Russaile and Mr. Mic. Cox and Edw. Tomlinson were bound for him in the sum of £20 each.

**2.** Jn. Gosse, who had been bound to prosecute Hen. Higgs from whom he had hired a white nag, which had been stolen from one [*blank*] Saltmarshe of Westm.,[1] is absolutely discharged. On examination it appeared that the horse had been left with Higgs by its pretended owner 'as a pawn for his charges'. Higgs to be indicted for stealing the horse, and for contempt and misbehaviour to the bailiffs when they enquired about the horse at his house. He was bound to appear at the next Q.S. on the recogn. of Thos. Byrd sen. and Wm. Wells, saddler.

**3.** Ant. Crooke, cutler, discharged by proclamation after he appeared on his recogn. and no further prosecution was brought.

**4.** Jn. Maris, who had been committed to prison according to the statute for unlicensed victualling, to remain there until he pays a fine of 20s.

p. 137 **5.** Jn. Gardner discharged after he appeared on his recogn. and no further prosecution was brought.

**6.** The Vice-Chancellor to examine and determine the dispute between Toby Lugg and his wife and Jn. Dale, furrier.

---

[1] Probably Westminster is meant.

7. Isabel Harbert to stand in the cage for an hour next market day as a notorious scold.

8. Alice Short(e) and Ambrose Newberry discharged after being indicted and acquitted by the jury.

9. Simon Foxe and Joan Spratley discharged after being indicted and acquitted by the jury on a charge of felony.

10. Owen Warland had been bound by recogn. to bring his wife, Joan, on the prosecution of Joan, wife of Thos. Sympson. She appeared, was indicted as a common scold, but acquitted by the jury because of insufficient evidence. She is absolutely discharged.

11. Edith, wife of Thos. Collins of Oxf., whitebaker, to be discharged after being indicted for felony and acquitted by the grand jury.

12. Jas. Steeles to be bound for his good behaviour for insufferable abuse of his wife and their dispute to be referred to Dr. Hawley for resolution.

13. Ann Netherway(e) entered recogn. in open court of £40 to prosecute Jn. Wells, a prisoner in Bocardo, at the next county Assizes. A writ to be sought from the judge to remove him to the county jail.

14. Rob. and Thos. Lovesey to be whipped in the Guildhall during the session and then be discharged. They had tried to bury alive a child of Ann, wife of Hugh Harte of the psh. of St. Peter-in-the-East and strained and forced him so that he bled almost a pottle [two quarts] and was in danger of dying.

15. Thos. Peare discharged on his humble submission after slighting p. 138 and not obeying Mr. Flexney's warrant brought to him by the constable.

16. Mary Townesend to enter recogn. to appear and answer at the next Assizes. Jn. Fisher of Abingdon, gent., and Jn. Bancks of Oxf., cordwainer, bound for her.

17. Nic. Church, who appeared on his recogn., committed for three days for unlicensed victualling, to put in sureties not to victual and pay 6s. to the bailiffs to make the 14s. he has already paid up to his fine of 20s. according to the statute.

18. Thos. Noble, Wm. Tawney, Edm. Wise, Edw. Warde, Jos. Warde and Hen. Graves to be discharged after they appeared on their recogns. and no further prosecution was brought.

**19.** A process of outlawry to be made out against Edw. Jones.

**20.** The former Q.S. order for Jonas Clinch (Clynch) to pay Hen. Gunne's charges is cancelled after re-examination found no cause for it.

**21.** Joan, wife of Thos. Sympson, indicted and found to be a common scold and disturber of the peace among her neighbours. She was present in court and was admitted to her traverse. She is to have until four o'clock in the afternoon to consider whether to put in her traverse or pay her fine and meanwhile to stand on her recogn.

**22.** Ann Holloway(e) paid her fine of 6s. 8d. for unlicensed victualling and was discharged having already been imprisoned for three days.

**23.** Helen Rancklyn and Ann Smyth were found guilty of a wicked conspiracy against Jn. Tipper, falsely accusing him of ravishing Ann Smyth. The jury convicted on the basis of evidence and their public confession. They are to be carted through the High Street from East-gate to Northgate or *vice versa* between 2 p.m. and 3 p.m. next market day and then released from prison. A warrant is to be made out for Vincent Rancklyn, a principal agent in this matter, to be bound for his good behaviour.

p. 139 **24.** Jn. Newman, who appeared on his recogn. for the peace on the prosecution of Ric. Wardell, is discharged as they have been reconciled. Jn. Astell is also discharged, having made his peace with the bailiffs. Griffin likewise discharged.

**25.** Thos. Price referred to the bailiff to be fined up to the limit of the statute for allowing unlawful games in his house and discharged.

**26.** Julian Willmott, widow, and Rob. Wolley, cordwainer, allowed to victual and entered recogn. with sufficient sureties to keep good order.

**27.** The dispute between Thos. Sympson and his wife Joan and Owen Warland and his wife to be referred to Mr. Thos. Flexney and Ald. Harris to make an order if they can or report to the court at the next Q.S. In the meantime Joan Sympson, having been indicted and found guilty, was fined 2s. 6d., paid it and was discharged.

**28.** Jn. Woodward indicted and found guilty of assault and battery and fined 2s. 6d.

**29.** Geo. Scott indicted for a felony, found not guilty and discharged.

**30.** Wm. Gough(e) indicted for battery and found guilty by the jury. He paid his fine of 6s. 8d. and is discharged.

**31.** Felix Swadling(e) to take down the sign of the Labour in Vain in St. Giles as formerly ordered by the Assize Judges. He undertook in court to do so and was discharged.

**32.** Simon Perrott, a stranger in Oxf. with no trade or livelihood, has victualled under cover of a licence 'which was procured but is utterly misliked' because of many complaints of daily disorder in his house. He is to be stopped from victualling for ever and he and his wife are to secure the psh. of St. Peter-in-the-East where they live against any future charge from their children or else leave Oxf.

**33.** Jn. Hales indicted and found guilty by the grand jury but discharged by the petty jury on the charge of stealing two white swans.

**34.** Mart. Knowles indicted and found guilty of battery, fined 5s. and p. 140 discharged.

**35.** Hen. Clarke in court asked his master, Chas. Russaile (Russell), to forgive him for misbehaviour, and was discharged.

**36.** The court think the bridge outside Westgate, near Castle mills, should be repaired as quickly as possible according to the statute as it is in a state of ruin and decay and a great danger to travellers, horse-drawn carts and cattle. Mr. Ric. Paynter, Mr. Phil. Dodwell, Mr. Hen. Bosworth and Mr. Alex. Hill appointed as overseers to levy and collect money for the work and recruit workmen. The Mayor is asked to encourage the citizens to contribute.

**37.** 'Little' Jn. Byrd to be committed to prison for rude words and behaviour in court and elsewhere and abuse of Jn. Blunt the constable. To find sureties for his appearance at the next Q.S. and good behaviour in the meantime.

**38.** Jn. Cumber and his wife, Edith, indicted and found guilty of trespass by the jury and fined 20d. each.

**39.** Wm. Misson and Nat. Bethwyn indicted and found guilty of allowing unlawful games, are fined according to the statute and left to the discretion of the bailiffs.

**40.** Hen. Pidgly and Jn. Hayles to be stopped from victualling for ever.

**41.** Thos. Smyth, Chris Gibbins, Julian Willmott, widow, and Rob. Wolly allowed to continue victualling and have entered into recogn. with sufficient sureties. Jn. Crutch, miller, allowed to continue victualling.

# [1622A]

p. 141  Quarter Sessions at the Guildhall Thurs. 10 Jan. 1622. Wm. Peirs, Vice-Chancellor, Jn. Davenant esq., Mayor, Wm. Langton D.D., Thos. James D.D., Thos. Wentworth esq., Recorder, Jn. Hawley D.C.L., Thos. Flexney esq., Thos. Harris ald., Wm. Potter ald., Wm. Wright ald., J.P.s.

**1.** Hen. Higgs discharged after he appeared on his recogn. and no further prosecution was brought.

**2.** Jn. Byrd the younger as in 1622A1.

**3.** Thos. Taylor to be committed until Sunday night and be bound for his good behaviour for lewd words about Thos. Sympson's wife causing discord with her husband and, as certified in court, for trying to persuade one Lloyd to knock his master on the head.

**4.** The matter pursued against Ant. Edwards by Mr. Thos. Breeze is referred to the Vice-Chancellor and Ant. is discharged of his recogn.

**5.** Wm. Jennings, who had been bound to appear at this Q.S., discharged of his recogn. as no one came to prosecute.

**6.** Mary Peesely fined 20s. according to the statute for unlicensed victualling and bound not to victual.

**7.** Jn. Woodward discharged of his recogn. but committed until he pays his fees. A warrant to be made out following his escape out of court.

**8.** Humph. Worly undertook by recogn. to bring his son Wm. Worly to the next Q.S.

**9.** Thos. Steevens to pay 3s. 4d., and Wm. Bullocke, Wm. Leverett and Rob. Rudland to pay 10s. each for contempt in leaving after being warned for the petty jury.

p. 142  **10.** Art. Hughes appeared on his recogn. and an indictment was found against him. The constable made a presentment against him on oath for very bad misdemeanours. He is to be committed until he pays a fine of 13s. 4d.

**11.** Wm. King(e) to be fined 5s. and be imprisoned until Monday night after an indictment for battery and abuse of Hore, the constable of St. Giles, was proved in open court.

**12.** Wm. Barton, Thos. Steevens, Jn. Randall, Wal. Bonner, Jn. Parsons, Wm. Bullock, Nat. Miller, Thos. Roberts, Nic. Berry, Edw.

Wildgoose, Thos. Wildgoose and Ric. Lea who had been empanelled and sworn as a petty jury brought in a 'most wronge' verdict contrary to the opinion of the court despite plain evidence. As an example to all other jurors they are to be committed until they find good sureties to be bound for their good behaviour. Warrants to be made out if they escape.

**13.** Jn. Baldwyn the elder keeps a house called The Blue Bell in the psh. of St. Mary Magdalen which is a known resort of thieves, lewd and disorderly persons to the disquiet of the Univ. and city. The sign to be taken down and the house not to be allowed to be either an inn or an alehouse any more. Jn. Baldwyn bound to appear at the next Q.S. and meanwhile be of good behaviour on the surety of Jn. Stacy, musician, and Sampson Stronge.

**14.** Geo. Scott discharged after he appeared on his recogn. and no prosecution was brought.

**15.** A warrant to be made out against Vincent Ranckle for various misdemeanours.

**16.** Rob. Haynes, who was indicted, arraigned and found guilty of stealing a pair of sheets and a waistcoat from Mr. Ric. Paynter, claimed benefit of clergy and having read was burnt on the hand.

**17.** Edw. Cox, who was indicted and found guilty of assaulting Peter p. 143 Omellallowe, an Irishman, during the night and taking 37s. 6d. from his pocket, claimed benefit of clergy and was burnt on the hand.

**18.** Rob. Mason and Wal. Prior discharged of their recogns. as no further prosecution was brought.

**19.** Rob. Bannister claimed benefit of clergy and was burnt on the hand after being indicted, arraigned and confessing to stealing two pewter dishes belonging to Mat. Leech and one belonging to Martin Stacy from New College kitchen.

**20.** Thos. Rogers, who had formerly been burnt on the hand twice in the county, was indicted and found guilty of felony in respect of things of small value. Judgement is reserved until the next Q.S.

**21.** Ann Worley (Worly), who was found guilty of petty larceny, to be whipped at the post and sent from Oxf. with a pass.

**22.** Jn. Potter to be stripped from the shoulders to the girdle and whipped at the post until he bleeds, then to be sent by pass to Derby, where he says he was born.

**23.** Jn. Ashton, who was indicted for stealing a pair of sheets and acquitted by the petty jury, is nevertheless to be well whipped at the post and sent away by pass as he is an idle vagrant.

**24.** Thos. Warland to be whipped out of town at a cart's tail as a wandering rogue towards Eling, Hants., where he recently lived.

**25.** Judgement of Gregory Bland is reserved until the next Q.S.

## [1622B]

p. 144   Quarter Sessions at the Guildhall Thurs. 2 May 1622. Thos. Harris esq., Mayor, Jn. Prideaux D.D., Thos. James D.D., Jn. Hawley D.C.L., Thos. Flexney esq., Wm. Potter ald., Wm. Wright ald., Oliver Smyth ald., Jn. Byrd gent., J.P.s.

**1.** Jn. Baldwyn (Baldwin), Jn. Creeke and Jn. *alias* Cyprian Godfrey discharged after they appeared on their recogns. and no further prosecution was brought.

**2.** Jn. Vaughan to be fined 40s. for breach of the statute and be committed until he pays, for entertaining Thos. Harris, saddler, Hen. Nickolls, cutler, and Ric. Bradshawe, glover, in his master's house for two days and a night when they played dice and other unlawful games, and for supplying them with food and drink and lending them more than £6.

**3.** The maintenance of a child of Jn. Smith, shoemaker, of Oxf., was considered. The child was left with Thos. Maisters, labourer, of the psh. of St. Ebbe, by the wife of And. Marton of Warborough, Oxon. Jn. Smyth of Warborough was the child's father's grandfather and the consanguinity between them was considered. According to the deposition of witnesses in open court Mr. Jn. Smyth, tailor, of the psh. of St. Martin, promised to maintain the child in return for 43s. 4d. which one Wm. Bartlett agreed to pay him. This Mr. Jn. Smyth shall either pay £5 or keep the child according to the law, or the poor man who has the child and his psh. shall make the true father keep the child.

[*Margin*] Mr. Jn. Smyth paid 40s. and was discharged of the child.

**4.** Jn. Coley, Ric. Billingsly and Thos. Preston, who had been accused of going with guns and pieces ('peecs') and killing poor men's poultry, are discharged as they have satisfied the aggrieved parties and no further prosecution is brought.

**5.** Hen. Nicholls, cutler, and Ric. Bradshawe to be fined 20s. each and   p. 145
be imprisoned until they pay, after being convicted on evidence of
playing dice and other unlawful games and being strongly suspected
of using false dice and cheating Thos. Harris, saddler. They are to be
bound according to the statute not to play, and to pay 3s. 4d. each
for the poor of the psh. where they played for tippling in an inn and
neglecting their trades and occupations.

**6.** Hen. Rownsefall appeared on his recogn. for the peace sworn
against him by Wm. Ewen, cobbler, before the Mayor. He is discharged
paying his fees as no further prosecution was brought but it is noted
that he is a very quarrelsome fellow.

**7.** Hen. Gunne (Gunn) is, above all other men, unworthy to live in any
well-governed place and should be spurned from this commonwealth.
He has uttered many scandalous and false words against various J.P.s
of this Bench, and committed insufferable misdemeanours not fit
to be recorded. He is to be committed to Bocardo and remain there
without bail or mainprise until a further order shall set an example to
such barbarous and notorious men. He shall not be released in haste
without careful consideration and shall be bound by recogn. to the
king's use for at least £5 each from two good and sufficient sureties,
known to be worthy men, and obey the conditions of the recogn.

[*Margin*] Convicted by witnesses and his own confession.

**8.** Nic. Larner, indicted for an alleged burglary, was acquitted by the
petty jury for life and death and discharged.

**9.** Thos. Bowton to be whipped next market day and sent by pass to
his birthplace after he confessed to stealing pewter and other things.

**10.** Francis Whitby was indicted and arraigned for the death of Thos.   p. 146
Barnett, a fellow servant of Mrs. Iverye of Oxf., and after full evidence
at the bar it was found to be in self-defence by the jury of life and
death. He is to be absolutely discharged and enter into recogn. to be
of good behaviour until he obtains the pardon usual in such cases, and
brings it to be pleaded in this court. Thos. Whitbye of Buckingham,
clerk, and Jas. Fisher, gent., were present in court and entered into
recogn. in the sum of £40 for Francis' appearance at the next Q.S.

**11.** At a Special Sessions on 13 Sept. 1621 many men were fined 3s. 4d.
each after failing to attend when called to serve on the jury. It was
ordered that the grand jury's dinner taken at Mr. Jn. Smyth's house

should be paid for out of the fines but the bailiffs for that year who were to receive the fines have not paid the bill. After a complaint about this each man who was fined is to be distrained unless he pays or the bailiffs themselves are to be distrained so Mr. Smyth can be paid.

**12.** A process (*venire facias*) to be made out on the traverse of Mr. Palmer and Mr. Samon.

**13.** Thos. Streete and Thos. Teasler discharged of their recogns. and Thos. Streete to find sureties not to victual without licence or be committed.

**14.** Processes of outlawry to be made out against Stukely, Gillard, Edw. Farland and Margaret Farland.

**15.** Francis Radborne *alias* Ewer, who was indicted for the trespass of taking a gold ring from Mary Bursye and found guilty by the grand jury, to be fined 3s. 4d. and discharged.

**16.** Ant. Pitman and Chris. Guy discharged paying their fees after appearing on their recogns.

**17.** Jn. Vaughan discharged after being indicted, prosecuted and acquitted by the grand jury.

p. 147   **18.** Hen. le Raynsford (Rainsford), gent., who was bound over to answer for assaulting and wounding Francis Gregory the younger, gent., absolutely discharged after Francis here acknowledged an agreement between them and released Hen. from any further prosecution.

**19.** Dan. Byton appeared on his recogn. and confessed to keeping a threepenny drinking ordinary[1] which was likely to cause scandal. On his promise of good behaviour in future the court agreed to discharge him this time and not send him to prison.

**20.** Margaret Slayman *alias* Stokes discharged of her recogn. Jn. Stokes, who has married her, is well thought of by the court and in hope of his good behaviour he is to come before the next two J.P.s to enter recogn. with good sureties to victual according to the statute and be licensed until the next Q.S. The court will then consider the continuation of the licence if there has been no complaint of disorder or misdemeanour.

**21.** Jas. Clarke, Jn. Pyme, Jn. Willyams and Ellen Poole discharged after they appeared on their recogns. and no further prosecution was brought.

---

[1] An eating house or tavern where meals were provided at a fixed price, often associated with gaming: *N.E.D.*

**22.** A process of outlawry to be made out against Thos. Kellam *alias* Hardly who was indicted and found guilty.

**23.** Edw. Day, smith, who was bound to appear here for misdemeanour, to stand committed until he pays his fees and is discharged.

**24.** Joan Abell, who appeared after being bound over to this Q.S., discharged on her penitent submission.

**25.** Jn. Longe fined 3s. 4d. after being indicted and found guilty by the jury for an assault and affray on Agnes Clerke.

**26.** Rog. Lane to be whipped next market day after the jury found him guilty of pilfering.

**27.** Thos. Taylor had been bound over at the last Q.S. to be of good behaviour and appear at the Q.S. at the instance of Thos. Simpson for abusing him. He is discharged as Simpson did not prosecute further.  p. 148

**28.** The court debated the controversy between Thos. Penton and Jn. Woodward referred to in their petitions and advised them to avoid further trouble between them.

They agreed to be bound to each other not to start a suit in the king's court at Westminster or elsewhere for any cause arising up to now and to refer all quarrels between them to Dr. Hawley and Ald. Smyth for final determination.

**29.** Hen. Gunn's wife to be put in the ducking stool next market day for beastly and barbarous scolding and this to be repeated every time such misdemeanours are proved against her.

**30.** Edw. Chittell is in prison after being committed by Dr. James and his petition, which was read, was referred to Dr. James.

**31.** Hugh Shawe, Nat. Cooper, Widow Smyth and Ann Hart, widow, licensed to victual.

**32.** Warrants to be made according to the statute against all butchers presented for slaughtering in Lent last, and against all who left the court without paying their fees, and against all gamblers.

**33.** Estreats to be made out for all fines at this and the last Q.S.

**34.** Jn. Harvy, who was indicted and found guilty by the jury of feloniously stealing eight rams, claimed benefit of clergy and was burnt on the hand.

**35.** Jn. Munn(e), barber, who was indicted and found guilty of stealing  p. 149
5s. 6d., a silk and silver lace, a silk girdle and a box from the chest of

Ann Hart, widow, claimed benefit of clergy and was burnt on the hand.

**36.** Hart the beadle to be committed to Bocardo for abusing the court by pretending to burn ('counterfeit burning of') Jn. Munne on the hand.

**37.** Wm. Phillis was indicted, arraigned and found not guilty by the jury of stealing two silver spoons from Wm. Hearne of Abingdon which were sold to Thos. Berry, goldsmith, of Oxf. for 11s. 6d. or 12s. nevertheless the court orders that, if Hearne comes or sends for the spoons, Berry shall give them to him for the same price for which he bought them.

**38.** Wm. Robinson, who is suspected of stealing a riding cloak from Jn. Clarke, is to stay in prison until he returns it or puts in sureties to return or give satisfaction for it.

## [1622c]

Quarter Sessions at the Guildhall Thurs. 20 June 1622. Jn., Bp. of Oxf., Wm. Peirse, Vice-Chancellor, Thos. Harris esq., Mayor, Thos. James D.D., Jn. Rawlinson D.D., Jn. Hawley D.C.L., Thos. Flexney esq., Wm. Wright ald., Oliver Smyth ald., Jn. Bird gent., J.P.s.

**1.** Each absentee from the grand jury to be fined 3s. 4d. and be distrained for this except Thos. Nicholls, tailor, who is discharged. Estreats to be made out quickly.

**2.** Ant. Ives appeared after being bound over on the prosecution of Wm. Hughes and discharged as no further complaint was made.

p. 150 **3.** Francis Whitby had been indicted at the last Q.S. for killing Thos. Barnett. The petty jury found it to be in self-defence and he was bound for his good behaviour and appearance at this Q.S. He appeared but did not bring his pardon so he is to remain bound until the next Q.S. when he is to be discharged if he brings his pardon. Thos. Whitbye and Jas. Fisher gent. bound in the sum of £20 each and Francis bound in the sum of £40.

**4.** Wm. Gough had been bound over for his good behaviour for false, saucy and ill-mannered words about Mr. Davenante, the late Mayor, after his death and against Ald. Harris, now Mayor, in his presence and that of other J.P.s. He humbly acknowledged his offence and promised never to offend in the same way again and is discharged.

**5.** Rob. Jenkenson, tapster, and Wm. Allen, ostler, were bound over to appear at the next Q.S. after complaints in court about their misdemeanours. Ric. Paynter, fellmonger, and Ralph Quinny, victualler, were sureties in the sum of £10 each. Rob. and Wm. were bound in the sum of £20 each.

**6.** Jn. Wells appeared on his recogn. and is discharged by proclamation as no further prosecution was brought.

**7.** Ric. Jackson bound to appear at the next Q.S. on suspicion of killing Jn. Daye. Alex. Hill of the psh. of St. Thos., alebrewer, and Jn. Paynton, embroiderer, were bound in £50 each and Ric. in £100. The coroner's inquest was viewed and gave grounds for suspicion but nobody was bound to prosecute and so it was thought fit that Jackson be bailed. Dr. Hawly is asked to ensure that Daye's wife is bound or brought to prosecute at the next Q.S.

**8.** Jn. Brierwood is strongly suspected of being deceitful and hypocritical and cheating his late mistress, Lady Price, of £20, as appears p. 151 from his own confession but no witness or testimony to the matter is available. The court, 'intending to do justice to all men indifferently', order that he is to be bailed if he can put in good sureties to appear and answer at the next Q.S.

**9.** Ric. Poole, who appeared on his recogn. for allowing unlawful games in his house, is discharged this time because of the court's good opinion of him and is to obey the order of two J.P.s.

**10.** Thos. Garrett of London, goldsmith, is to enter into recogn. in the sum of £20 to prosecute Jn. Smith at the next Q.S. for felony and Thos. Offly as an accessory. Garrett's former recogn. to prosecute Offly was declared void and he was dismissed.

**11.** Wm. Jones, joiner, to be committed to jail and put in irons for saucy and ill-mannered words to some of the Bench and putting his hat on in the presence of the court.

**12.** Mr. Thos. Almond and Mr. Chas. Russaile, late city bailiffs, to pay Mr. Jn. Smyth (Smith) 16s. for the grand jury's dinner at a session during their bailiwick when the fines and forfeitures were very profitable to them. If they refuse to pay their goods are to be distrained and sold and any surplus returned to them. If cunning is used to hinder the constable or other officer or Mr. Smythe or any other person employed to distrain cannot enter their houses

p. 152 they shall be apprehended by warrant made out by the clerk of the court for contempt. They shall be brought before the next J.P. to be committed to prison until they pay.

**13.** Thos. Harwood indicted, arraigned and confessed to stealing various goods from Wm. Manninge's house. He claimed benefit of clergy and was burnt on the hand and sent away with a pass.

**14.** Warrants to be made out against Hen. Pidgley and Jn. Haynes for unlicensed victualling contrary to an order at the Q.S. of 4 Oct. 1621. On their apprehension to be committed and punished according to the statute.

**15.** Nic. Padbury, Rob. Painter and Frances Proffitt *alias* Parfett, widow, allowed to victual for a year.

**16.** Nineteen rings taken from Thos. Offly now in the hands of Mr. Bird, J.P., to be placed in the custody of the present city bailiffs until they are needed by due order of the law.

**17.** Thos. Ofley (Offley) and Jn. Smyth to be bailed with good sureties before any two J.P.s.

**18.** Hen. Gunn, a lewd fellow, to be put in the pillory next market day from 1 p.m. to 3 p.m. and then kept in custody until he enters into recogn. for his future behaviour with good sureties according to a former order.

## [1622D]

p. 153 Gaol Delivery at the Guildhall 27 Sept. 1622. Thos. Harris esq., Mayor, Thos. Wentworth esq., Recorder, Thos. Flexney esq., Wm. Potter ald., Jn. Bird gent., justices for G.D.

**1.** Jn. Chaundler, constable of Holywell, and Thos. Hawkins, tithingman, fined £5 each to be paid on demand for not returning their precept to summon men of Holywell to serve here.

**2.** Phil. Browne had been committed to Bocardo as a wandering rogue but without formal charge ('no just accusation layd to his charge'). Yet because of his rude behaviour and because he is a travelling metalman he is to be well whipped and sent away with a pass to Malmesbury, Wilts., where he says he lives.

**3.** Wm. Allen, indicted and arraigned for killing Jn. Sarney of Oxf. Univ., yeoman, was found guilty of manslaughter by the petty jury and claimed benefit of clergy. As Jn. Vowell affirmed in court that he had been burnt on the hand before, he was sent back to prison pending a certificate from the clerk of the court where he formerly claimed.

**4.** Wm. Gardner is indicted, arraigned and found guilty by the petty jury of the felony of stealing three silver bowls from Thos. Hallam of Oxf., vintner, and condemned to death according to the law.

**5.** Warrants to be made out against all unlicensed victuallers to have their licences renewed.

**6.** Gaol Delivery adjourned to 3 Oct.

# [1622E]

Quarter Sessions at the Guildhall Thurs. 3 Oct. 1622. Wm. Peirse, p. 154 Vice-Chancellor, Wm. Boswell esq., Mayor, Jn. Prideaux D.D., Thos. James D.D., Jn. Hawley D.C.L., Thos. Flexney esq., Thos. Harris ald., Wm. Potter ald., Wm. Wright ald., Jn. Byrd gent., J.P.s.

**1.** Thos. Currall's complaint that Rob. Jenkenson, tapster, and Wm. Allen, ostler, cheated him of a horse is referred to the Vice-Chancellor and they are to be discharged of their recogns.

**2.** Jn. Hill, formerly porter to the Abp. of Canterbury, had wrongfully abused him. The Abp. had been asked to forgive Hill and had written a letter to the Mayor which was read in court. He is to remain bound for his good behaviour until the Abp. asks for his discharge. Any one J.P. of this Bench may take his recogn. with sufficient sureties to appear at the next Q.S.

**3.** Wm., son of Ric. Peirse of Hinksey, is to complete his apprenticeship with Simon Fox of Oxf., baker. Ric. to be bound to Simon in the sum of £5 'for the truth' [? honest behaviour] of Wm. during his service, and Simon to be bound to Ric. in the sum of £5 to treat Wm. well and have him taught to write.

**4.** Jn. Gardner was indicted and found guilty by the grand jury and p. 155 confessed to assaulting Edw. Clifford. He paid his fine of 3s. 4d. and is discharged.

**5.** Edw. Willyams of Oxf., tailor, was bound by recogn. to prosecute Francis Burneham for treasonable words, namely that the king was king of England but not of Wales. He refused to prosecute or offer a bill of indictment after being told by the court to proceed with a legal hearing. On close examination the court found no witness to prove the matter, so each is to be fined 5s. for being drunk at the time of the alleged words, the money to be disposed of according to the statute. As Edw. made a false claim he is to pay Francis's fees and charges.

**6.** As ordered at the last Q.S. Francis Whitby is to remain bound for his good behaviour and appearance at the next Q.S. on the surety of Jas. Fisher gent. and Wm. Carpenter, yeoman, and to bring in and plead his pardon in court.

**7.** Thos. Garrett appeared on his recogn. to prosecute Jn. Smyth as principal and Thos. Offly (Offley) as an accessory but refused to do so, so they are absolutely discharged of their recogns.

p. 156 **8.** Hen. Gunne (Gunn) appeared on his recogn. and admitted and asked to be pardoned for his insufferable abuse of Mr. Bird, J.P. He promised never to offend in this way again and is discharged in hope of his better behaviour in future.

**9.** Mic. Penn discharged after he appeared on his recogn. for the peace at the prosecution of Jn. Peirson and no further prosecution was brought.

**10.** Hen. Cripps of Oxf. Univ., bookbinder, appeared on his recogn. to prosecute Wm. Budg(e) for the felony of stealing some books from his shop. When asked to offer his bill of indictment or to prosecute he refused to do so and was delivered by open proclamation.

**11.** Edw. Willyams committed to Bocardo for three days for giving false information against some of the J.P.s. Before he is released he is to put in sureties to behave well and appear at the next Q.S. and pay the fine of 5s.

**12.** Thos. Bagwell appeared on his recogn. and was charged by some of the Bench with saucy and rash comparisons between his wife and the best wives in the town. He admitted the same penitently, asked the favour of the court and is discharged.

**13.** Francis Comber to be discharged from the service of his master, Thos. Rusly, for misdemeanours against him. The master is to repay the apprentice £4 at or before Christmas and the apprentice is to be whipped. The court ordered this after reference to them by both parties.

p. 157 **14.** Toby Toms, Jn. Brierwood, Geo. Vaughan, Thos. Boughton and Hen. Sherwin discharged by proclamation after they appeared on their recogns. and no further prosecution was brought.

**15.** The charge that Wm. Wirdnam has enticed youth and young scholars to use tobacco and waste time and money is referred to the Vice-Chancellor, and meanwhile he is discharged of his recogn.

**16.** Hen. Gunn's petition against Mr. Ric. Palmer and Hen. Samon, former city bailiffs, is referred to Dr. James to be heard and determined.

**17.** Wm. Egglston (Eggleston) indicted, arraigned and found not guilty by the jury of stealing a goose and discharged.

**18.** A warrant to be made out against Mic. Beesely for trying extort a composition of 20s. from Wm. Eggleston by 'setting a foul face on the matter' of a supposed theft of a goose at Sunningwell. An indictment against Wm. was not found and Mic. is to be bound to answer these charges.

**19.** Jn. Langly and Jn. Nurse, two of the grand jurors, to be fined 10s. each for failing to attend on the last day of the session which had been adjourned until 8 a.m. that day for the giving of the verdict. The whole jury said the two had been the most lax in their attendance throughout.

**20.** Edw. Morris and Wm. Tellen indicted with Wm. Smyth and Edw. Hutchins and found guilty by the grand jury of enticing Mic. Knowles and Geo. Lilegrove, Rob. Budd's apprentices, from his service. Morris and Tellen were fined 3s. 4d. each and Morris is bound for his good behaviour.

**21.** The jury found Ric. Palmer and Hen. Samon (the former bailiffs) p. 158 guilty when their traverse was considered and they are to await their sentence.

**22.** Ant. Slatford, the constable appointed and sworn to look after the jury in the case of Palmer and Samon, to be fined 10s. for allowing Ric. Hemings to go in and talk to the jury.

**23.** Judgement in the case of Ric. Palmer and Hen. Samon to be delayed until the court advises further.

**24.** Joan Plott, Simon Fox and Jn. A'Lee indicted and found guilty of a riot at Jn. Johnson's house and an assault on his wife, Denise. She paid her fine of 5s.

**25.** Ric. Willyams, Julian Willmott and Eliz. Richardson discharged of their recogns. after they appeared and nothing was objected against them.

**26.** Dr. Prideaux and Dr. James to hear and determine the matter concerning Amy, wife of Jas. Booth.

**27.** All those presented here by the grand jury for not selling a full quart of ale or strong beer for a penny according to the statute are to pay 20s. each. Warrants are to be sent to the constables and church-wardens of their pshs. to levy it. If the constables or churchwardens fail to levy the sums or in default of distress do not certify this to the

p. 159 J.P.s within twenty days they shall forfeit 40s. to the poor for each default. These sums shall be levied by distress of goods by warrant to an independent person from a J.P. and if this fails they are to be sent to the common gaol by any J.P. until they pay. This is all provided that the Vice-Chancellor agrees to treat victuallers who are privileged persons in the same way.

**28.** Sim. Fox who was indicted and found guilty of riot fined 5s. and absolutely discharged.

**29.** Warrants to be made out against all unlicensed victuallers and they are to be fined 20s. each and stopped from victualling for three years.

**30.** Agnes Hobbs *alias* Worly to be carted out of town next market day.

**31.** Court of Gaol Delivery adjourned until Tues. 15 Oct.

## [1622F]

p. 160 Adjourned Gaol Delivery at the Guildhall Tues. 15 Oct. 1622. Wm. Peirse, Vice-Chancellor, Wm. Boswell esq., Mayor, Thos. Flexney esq., Thos. Harris ald., Wm. Wright ald.

**1.** A warrant to be made out for Thos. Clarke's wife, a victualler in St. Giles, to be bound over to answer at the next Q.S. for receiving stolen goods.

**2.** A warrant to be made out for Mr. Ric. Cliffe to be bound for his good behaviour, since his failure to prosecute means that Jos. Brad-shawe is kept in prison.

**3.** Mic. Beesely of Sunningwell, Berks., yeoman, bound in the sum of £40 to appear at the next Q.S. and meanwhile behave well. Jn. Slat-tford of Oxf., cutler, and Thos. Poole of Oxf., tailor, sureties in the sum of £20 each.

**4.** Thos. Vaughan appeared on his recogn. and is discharged.

**5.** Jos. Bradshawe discharged by proclamation.

**6.** Wm. Worley to be whipped out of town next market day.

**7.** Thos. Rivans and Jn. Lowe indicted, found guilty by the jury and confessed to using false dice and cards and other cheating. They are to be fined 20s. each, whipped and sent by pass to their last place of residence but this is respited until Thursday week.

**8.** Inito Price found guilty of the same offence of cheating Humph. Jones, servant of Mr. Thos. Flexney, Registrar. He was admitted to his traverse but is to stay in prison until the next Q.S. to await the   p. 161 order of the court unless he puts in good sureties for his appearance at the next Q.S.

## [1623A]

Quarter Sessions at the Guildhall Thurs. 9 Jan. 1623. Wm. Peirse, Vice-Chancellor, Wm. Boswell esq., Mayor, Jn. Prideaux D.D., Jn. Rawlinson D.D., Thos. James D.D., Jn. Hawly D.C.L., Thos. Flexney esq., Thos. Harris ald., Wm. Potter ald., Wm. Wright ald., Oliver Smith ald., Ralph Flexney gent., Jn. Bird gent., J.P.s.

**1.** Jn. Hill, the Abp. of Canterbury's porter, at the request of the Abp. to remain bound for his good behaviour until the Abp. remits his offence. Ald. Harris to take his recogn.

**2.** Mic. Beesly discharged after he appeared as bound at the last G.D. and no prosecution was brought.

**3.** Warrants to be made out against those presented at the last Q.S. for not selling a full quart for a penny and the Vice-Chancellor and the Mayor to sign them. Warrants to be made out for all victuallers to appear on 16 Jan. Those who take in inmates are also to be questioned and the number in each family to be established. The warrants are to say that such orders as the law allows will be made and enforced.

**4.** Francis Whitbee, who appeared on his recogn., is to remain bound   p. 162 until he pleads the King's pardon, on the surety of Jas. Fisher and Nat. Bethwin.

**5.** Hugh Shaw(e) and Leonard Towne discharged after they appeared on their recogns. having been bound by the Vice-Chancellor for assaulting Hen. Pidgly after he arrested Hugh, and no prosecution was brought.

**6.** Jn. Pownall discharged after he appeared on his recogn. and Pidgley's (Pidgly's) complaint that Wm. Robinson and others had been hired to beat him was not proved.

**7.** Hen. Hussy, cook, appeared on his recogn. and Rob. Gardner of Kirtlington accused him of sending away Rob.'s child who had been Hussy's wife's apprentice for three months. She had been sent away for six weeks and had suffered much because of the hardness of the times and the dearth of corn. This was proved and the Hussys are to take the child back and treat her well while she serves out her time. If a complaint is made to any J.P. a special order shall be made. In the meantime Hussy is discharged of his recogn.

**8.** Edw. White of Fyfield appeared on his recogn. for the peace and is discharged as there was no further prosecution, and on a second recogn. for unlicensed victualling is fined 20s. having already been imprisoned for three days according to the statute. He undertook to leave Oxf. when he pays his fine and fees. He is to remain committed until then and then be discharged.

**9.** Wm. Lee was proved to have broken hedges and cut down young trees. He is to be committed to prison and well whipped before the end of the session, this being certified to the court.

**10.** Joan Thacker and Margaret Robinson to be well whipped for breaking and stealing Sir Wm. Ryves's hedges.

**11.** Edw. Tomlins and Jn. Carpenter to be discharged after they appeared on their recogns. and no prosecution was brought.

p. 163 **12.** Jas. Carter to be bound by recogn. to appear at the next Q.S. and answer Maximilian Petty esq.'s complaint of the felony of receiving or stealing sheep.

**13.** Nic. Elliott, who appeared on his recogn. on a complaint of having over beaten his servant, is discharged as the servant was not badly hurt or in in any danger.

**14.** Nic. Woodward, musician, to be fined 10s. and committed until he pays after an indictment was found by the grand jury and he confessed to battery of Wm. White, constable of the psh. of St. Mary Magdalen.

[*Margin*] Discharged.

**15.** The following are discharged by proclamation after the jury did not find the indictments against them: Edith Comber as a common scold; Jas. Lowe for stealing a hat and cloak, value 2s. 8d., from Thos. Vaughan; Edw. Bagwell and Ant. Wells, tailors, for stealing twenty pounds of raisins ('reasons'); Felix Swadlinge for assault and battery of Marian, wife of Wm. Acton, labourer.

**16.** Bart. Day, blacksmith, to be bound for his good behaviour after Wm. Pope, tailor, complained that Day fires guns very dangerously in his rear grounds to the disturbance of his neighbours, especially Pope, whose grounds adjoin his and says he is continually afraid of Day.

**17.** Bart. Day fined 3s. 4d. and discharged after being indicted, found guilty by the jury and confessing to assault and battery of Christian, wife of Rob. Ayres of Cassington, Oxon., yeoman.

**18.** Thos. Leighton of Abingdon, petty chapman, indicted, found guilty by the jury and confessed to making scandalous speeches against the government and chief governors of Oxf. He is to stand on the pillory from 1 p.m. to 3 p.m. with a paper above his head stating his offence and, next Monday, is to be whipped from Northgate to Southgate at a cart's tail.

**19.** A process of outlawry to be made out against Hugh Allen, who p. 164 has escaped after the felony of stealing four bushels of barley, value 12s., from Jn. Browne.

**20.** Thos. Vaughan to be whipped at the post next market day during market time for foul and lewd statements against certain city J.P.s.

**21.** Wm. Tooley (Tooly) to pay the bailiffs 20s. according to the statute for unlicensed victualling. He is to be discharged of his recogn. as he has been imprisoned for three days already.

**22.** Ann, wife of Simon Hasely, entered recogn. on the surety of £20 each from Jn. Stone, tailor, and Jn. Brickland to appear at the next Q.S. as an accessory to Hugh Allen's theft of barley.

**23.** Jn. Newman entered recogn. to appear at the next Q.S. and so was dismissed.

**24.** Lewis Price to be well whipped next market day after confessing in open court to stealing a blanket from Mr. Francis Popman of Balliol Coll., gent.

**25.** Ric. Spurr entered recogn. to appear at the next Q.S. on the surety, acknowledged in court, of Wm. Holbeck and Wm. Carpenter, tailors.

**26.** Rob. Addams and Jn. Comber to be discharged after they appeared on their recogns. and no prosecution was brought.

**27.** Jn. Capell to be well whipped and sent with a pass to Chipping Norton by Dr. James and Dr. Hawley after being indicted and found guilty of petty larceny.

**28.** Thos. Rogers had been found guilty at the Q.S. in Jan. 1622 of the felony of stealing a shirt, value 3s. 4d., from Ant. Ives, and formerly had been indicted for stealing a pair of shoes from Wm. Blackett, for which he had claimed benefit of clergy. Now he admits to being the man formerly tried and arraigned, and is condemned to be hanged.

p. 165 **29.** The following, indicted, arraigned, and found guilty by the petty jury, claimed benefit of clergy and are burnt on the hand: Barnaby Doverson for stealing a box with £30 in gold from his master, Maurice Price; Jos. Cantwell for stealing 5s. 6d. and other money from men sleeping at Mr. Willyams's house, the Star; Thos. Hadly *alias* Kellam for stealing a pair of boots and spurs from Wm. Acton's house; Jn. Weaver and Thos. Hadly again indicted for stealing and selling at Abingdon three store pigs, two from Joan Carpenter, widow, and one from Eliz. Shaw, widow; Thos. Griffin for stealing a black satin suit, a pair of silk stockings, a yellow satin waistcoat, a cloth hood and a cloak bag from unknown persons.

**30.** Jn. Weaver and Thos. Hadly to be imprisoned until they compensate Widow Carpenter and Widow Shaw for their three pigs and put in sureties for their good behaviour.

**31.** The following discharged by proclamation after being indicted, arraigned and found not guilty: Wm. Cule, Wm. Bedford, Wm. Robinson, Christian Ives, Hester Stoppard, Jn. Sunton, and Grace Whitfeild.

**32.** Hen. Pidgly who was imprisoned at the start of this Q.S. to be released, finding sureties for his good behaviour.

## [1623B]

p. 166 Gaol Delivery at the Guildhall Mon. 21 April 1623. Wm. Peirse, Vice-Chancellor, Wm. Boswell esq., Mayor, Thos. Wentworth esq., Recorder, Jn. Hawly D.C.L., Jn. Whistler esq., Thos. Flexney esq., Thos. Harris ald., Wm. Potter ald., Wm. Wright ald., Oliver Smith ald., Jn. Bird gent., justices for G.D.

**1.** Each man summoned to serve on the grand jury who did not appear, thus delaying matters, to be fined 6s. 8d. for contempt.

**2.** Ant. Ives and Wm. Gough, who were bound to appear here, to appear at the next Q.S. and remain bound on their recogns.

**3.** The coroner's inquest jury, who were bound to give their verdict here concerning the death of Thos. Taylor, the proctor's man, cannot agree and they are 'adjourned over' until the next Q.S. on pain of £10 each.

**4.** Jn. Allen and Francis Taylor fined 20s. each for departing without leave after being summoned by the serjeants to serve on the petty jury for life and death.

**5.** Thos. Scudamore, Rob. Gray, Rob. Billingsly and Tim. Gray, who were all found guilty on indictments for felony and burglary, are to be hanged.

**6.** Nat. Jones' indictment for stealing ten cheeses from Jn. Smith and Jn. Bailie's indictment for a sorrel nag supposed to belong to Hen. Edwards were not found by the grand jury and they are discharged by proclamation. Yet Jones is an idle vagrant with no place of abode and is to be whipped at the post and sent away with a pass.

**7.** Rob. Budd, the bellman, who was bound to appear here, discharged p. 167 by proclamation as no prosecution was brought.

**8.** Wm. Adkins, companion and bedfellow of Thos. Scudamore who was condemned for many burglaries, is to be well whipped and discharged as he is strongly suspected of having known of Thos.'s felonies.

**9.** Wm. Ryme to be sent to the House of Correction during the court's pleasure for having a false pass and other misdemeanours.

**10.** Wm., father of Tim. and Rob. Gray, to remain in prison without bail or mainprise until the next Q.S. when he is to be tried as an accessory to some of his sons' burglaries.

**11.** Ric. Goddard had harboured Thos. Skidmore[1] and is suspected, though without 'pregnant proof', of having known something of his burglaries. He was bound by recogn. in the sum of £20 to behave well and appear at the Michaelmas session on the surety of £10 each from Hen. Ingram, carpenter, and Jn. Prickett, slater.

**12.** Wm., son of Toby Toms, surgeon of Oxf. Univ., bound on the surety of his father and Justinian Raye to appear at the next Q.S. to answer for cutting a purse.

**13.** The recogns. of Ric. Francklyn of Horley, Ric. Warner of the psh. of St. Giles and Geo. Stevens (Steevens) of the psh. of St. Peter-le-Bailey to be estreated after they failed to appear.

---

[1] Presumably the Scudamore of 1623B8.

95

**14.** Simon Fox as in 1623B13.

**15.** Ellen Rogers, who was bound to appear, found sureties for her appearance at the next Q.S. and is discharged.

**16.** Phil. Norgrove to remain in prison until further order, although not as a condemned man, having had his pardon, which has never been pleaded, but having since fallen into various capital misdemeanours.

[*Margin*] Norgrove discharged.

p. 168   **17.** Job. Eggleston indicted and found guilty by the petty jury of stealing plate from Mr. Francis Harris, vintner. He claimed benefit of clergy, was burnt on the hand and is to be discharged, paying his fees.

**18.** Wm. Twist(e) indicted and found guilty of stealing a silver bowl from Mr. Dan. Bateman of Brasenose Coll. He claimed benefit of clergy and was burnt on the hand.

**19.** Jn. Studly and Geo. Horne, who were indicted and acquitted by the jury of stealing turkeys and poultry, are to be whipped at the post as idle men who can give no good account of their time.

**20.** Geo. Price, Joan Price and Ursula Peirse to remain in prison until the next Q.S.

**21.** Jn. Hedges to appear at the next Q.S. concerning his words about Budd the Bellman.

## [1623c]

Quarter Sessions at the Guildhall Thurs. 24 April 1623. Wm. Peirse, Vice-Chancellor, Wm. Boswell esq., Mayor, Jn. Prideaux D.D., Thos. James D.D., Jn. Hawly D.C.L., Jn. Whistler esq., Thos. Flexney esq., Thos. Harris ald., Wm. Wright ald., Jn. Bird gent., J.P.s.

**1.** Those who failed to attend the Q.S. and are sworn by the serjeant to have been warned in person or by notice at their houses to be fined 3s. 4d. each for contempt.

p. 169   **2.** Ric. Clacy *alias* Clavelsly to be committed until further order for being present at the killing of Thos. Taylor, the proctor's man, and not helping him ('aidinge for the safety of the King's Subiect').

**3.** Francis Whitbee appeared on his recogn., having been bound from Q.S. to Q.S. for killing Thos. Barnett, Mrs. Iverie's man. He had formerly been indicted and found guilty of manslaughter on the grounds of self-defence and is to remain bound for his good behaviour until he pleads the King's pardon in court. His father, Thos. Whitbee of Buckingham, clerk, and Jas. Fisher, gent., stood surety for him and he is discharged.

**4.** Simon Fox was ordered to be bound for his good behaviour for abusing the Mayor and Art. Stranguidge, the constable, who had young Wm. Mondy in custody on the Mayor's warrant for great misdemeanours. As he asked penitently for forgiveness, and in hope of his future behaviour, the order is to be remitted unless he repeats the offence, in which case further punishment will be considered.

**5.** The Bench was equally divided on binding Jn. Hedges *alias* Leacy for his good behaviour concerning Rob. Budd's case. But for his words and behaviour in court he was bound for his good behaviour on the surety of Rob. Hedges, tanner, and Ric. Hore, cordwainer.

**6.** Wm. Gough to appear at the next Q.S. after the testimony on oath of Wm. Jennings, tailor, concerning his 'intended practise' against Mr. Chas. Russell. He was bound for his appearance and good behaviour on the surety of Hen. Harbert and Edw. Carter, tailor.

**7.** Bart. Day, who appeared on his recogn., indicted and found guilty of battery of Christian wife of Rob. Ayres of Cassington, husbandman. He was fined 2s. 6d. and is discharged.

**8.** Dorothy Dew confessed to assaulting her mistress, Mrs. Joyner, and is discharged with an order to submit to her mistress and bring a certificate of that action to the next Q.S.

**9.** The churchwardens of the psh. of St. Martin petitioned the court that [blank] Denton, widow, a lewd woman, conceived a child at the Crown inn. It is expected to be born there soon and may become a burden to such a small psh. along with her other three children who have lived with her there for a year. Since Mr. Pinck, in whose house the child was conceived, is a privileged person the matter is referred to the Vice-Chancellor.

p. 170

**10.** Wm. Gough, tailor, indicted and found guilty by the grand jury of assault and battery in St. Ebbe's church of Rog. Robinson, who prosecuted him. Wm. was admitted to his traverse and entered recogn. to prosecute it.

**11.** Elias Archer indicted and found guilty by the jury of battery of Ann, wife of Art. Stranguidge. He was fined 3s. 4d. and discharged.

**12.** Thos. Vynton, who had been caught with a mould for counterfeiting coins, discharged paying his fees after testimony in his favour.

**13.** Tim. Gray, condemned to death at the last G.D., is reprieved.

**14.** Ric. Hearne discharged after being indicted and acquitted by the petty jury of the felony of stealing a silver bowl from Mr. Harris, vintner.

**15.** Ric. Clacey (Clacy) *alias* Clavesly is indicted and found guilty by the jury of a barbarous assault and battery on Prudence, wife of Phil. Rixon, barber. He is to remain in prison until he pays his fine of £6 13s. 4d. and his fees.

**16.** Wm. Gray, father of Rob. and Tim. Gray, discharged after being indicted and acquitted by the petty jury of being an accessory to his sons' felony and burglary at the houses of Bridget Keene and Sybil Oram.

p. 171 **17.** Edw. Radclyff of Wigan, Lancs., and Griffin Hughes of Raph [? Roath], Glam., who were indicted and found guilty by the jury of being idle vagrants and having counterfeit passes, are to be whipped and sent by pass to the places where they claim to live.

**18.** Wm. Ryme was indicted for having two wives, Jane Mayor in Banbury and Christian Stanly, a widow, and acquitted by the petty jury and discharged as the evidence was very weak.

**19.** Hugh Allen indicted for stealing four bushels of barley from Jn. Browne, is acquitted by the petty jury and discharged.

**20.** Chas. Griffiths, who was indicted at the coroner's inquest on the death of Thos. Taylor, servant of one of the univ. proctors, was found guilty of manslaughter and is to be proceeded against as an outlaw as he has fled. Ric. Clacy *alias* Clavesly, who was indicted with him, was found *ignoramus*[1] by the jury and discharged.

**21.** Phil. Norgrove to remain in prison without bail or mainprise until further order.

**22.** Ald. Smyth to be treasurer[2] and Ald. Harris and Ald. Wright to take the account of Mr. Jn. Bird, the last treasurer.

**23.** Wm. Hicks and Chas. Pitcher, who was Sir Edw. Fenner's man, are to be allowed to continue victualling.

---

[1] A grand jury endorsement on an indictment when prosecution evidence was insufficient to proceed to the petty jury.
[2] i.e. for maimed soldiers.

**24.** Wm., son of Toby Toms, surgeon, who was bound to answer for cutting a woman's purse, is to be bound to appear at the next Q.S. although the woman did not prosecute, as he is strongly suspected. Toby Toms and Nic. Berry, clothworker, stood surety in the sum of £20 each.

**25.** Wm. White to be committed to prison for three days for ill- p. 172 mannered words to the Mayor and abusing his warrant.

**26.** Ric. Clacy *alias* Claversly, Wm. Gray, Wm. Ryme and Hugh Allen discharged by open proclamation after being indicted and found not guilty by the petty jury.

## [1623D]

Quarter Sessions at the Guildhall Thurs. 12 June 1623. Wm. Peirs, Vice-Chancellor, Wm. Boswell esq., Mayor, Thos. James D.D., Jn. Hawley D.C.L., Thos. Harris ald., Wm. Potter ald., Wm. Wright ald., Oliver Smyth ald., J.P.s.

**1.** Each man, who was sworn here to have been given sufficient warning to serve on the grand jury and did not appear, to be fined 2s. 6d.

**2.** Jn. Hedges released after he appeared on his recogn. and no complaint was made.

**3.** Francis Whitbee (Whitbye) to continue bound from Q.S. to Q.S. according to former orders until he obtains the King's pardon and pleads it here. Jas. Fisher, gent., and Ric. Astell, tailor, stood surety.

**4.** Ric. Momford to be committed to prison until further order after being proved by oath in open court to be a common drunkard, brawler, scolder and breaker of the peace.

**5.** The quarrel between Joan Carpenter and Isabel Harbert, which was heard in open court, seems to have arisen from scolding, quarrelling ('brabling'), evil carriage and misdemeanours on both sides. Mr. Loddington, Principal of New Inn, and Mrs. Steevens, wife of the saltpetre man, are said to know about this because of the disturbance caused to them and other neighbours during the night. The case is to be suspended and Mr. Loddington and Mrs. Steevens are to give p. 173 certificates of their knowledge and opinion of who is at fault to the next J.P., who is to call the parties before him and punish the offender or offenders.

**6.** (Mr.) Wm. Jennings discharged after he appeared on the recogn. obtained by Sam. Vicke and it was certified that they were agreed that there should be no prosecution.

**7.** Wm. Hartly appeared on his recogn. and was prosecuted by Ellen Ranklin for defamation. As this was not clearly proved he is to be discharged paying his fees or be committed until he does so.

**8.** Wm. Gough bound for his good behaviour and appearance at the next Q.S. for various misdemeanours in the sum of £20 himself and on the surety of £10 each from Ric. Whetston, tailor, and Thos. Bolton, tailor.

**9.** Wm. Toms was bound with sureties to appear at the next Q.S. and discharged. A warrant to be sent to Dorothy, wife of Thos. Woodson, to go before the next J.P. to be bound to prosecute Wm. for the felony of taking her purse, as alleged in an information taken in writing before Ald. Harris, J.P.

**10.** The court took Wm. Kensall the elder's own recogn. in the sum of £20 for his good behaviour and appearance at the next Q.S. concerning misdemeanours not fit to be recorded, and meanwhile he is dismissed.

p. 174 **11.** Jn. Castle appeared on his recogn. and was discharged after the court was informed of a final friendly agreement with Ralph Nicholas who had prosecuted him.

**12.** Rob. Baylie and Thos. Yeomans (Yeamans) were indicted and prosecuted by Ric. Carter for assault and battery. The grand jury found them guilty and, although denying the offence, they submitted to the order of the court to avoid further trouble. All parties agreed to obey a final determination to be made by Mr. Steph. Gunne and Mr. Wm. Davies. Ric. Carter and Ric. Yeomans, on behalf of Rob. Baylie and Thos. Yeomans, are to enter bonds in the sum of £10 each to obey the determination by 6 July. If the arbitrators cannot agree Ald. Harris is to act as umpire. In the meantime they are to be fined 2s. 6d. each and discharged.

**13.** Warrants to be made out against those who have not paid their fees to the justices' clerk and the officers of the court at this, and the last, Q.S.

**14.** Jn. Collyns and others complained in open court that Ric. Momford is a drunkard and outrageous fellow, who bites viciously, and this was proved. The court knew his character from a former appearance and considered a shameful punishment suitable for 'so irrefragable a fellow'. He is to sit in the stocks from 2 p.m. to 4 p.m. at Carfax on the next two market days with a muzzle on his mouth and his arms tied to stop him pulling it off. Afterwards he is to be discharged if he has borne his punishment patiently and promises to reform.   p. 175

**15.** Warrants to be made out according to the statute against all those presented by the grand jury.

**16.** Hen. Thrupp to remain in prison until he obtains two adequate sureties to come before Dr. Hawley or Ald. Harris to be bound to appear at the next Q.S. on suspicion of making Joan Edwards pregnant.

## [1623E]

Quarter Sessions Thurs. 2 Oct. 1623. Wm. Peirse, Vice-Chancellor, Wm. Potter esq., Mayor, Jn. Prideaux D.D., Thos. James D.D., Jn. Hawley D.C.L., Jn. Whistler esq., Thos. Flexney esq., Thos. Harris ald., Oliver Smith ald., Ralph Flexney gent., J.P.s.

**1.** Francis Whytbye (Whitbye) to be bound over from Q.S. to Q.S. until he obtains the King's pardon and pleads it in court. Mr. Jas. Fisher and Ric. Astell were bound for him.

**2.** Wm. Gough appeared on the recogn. for his good behaviour which he was ordered to enter into at the last Q.S. on the prosecution of Mr. Chas. Russaile. He is to be discharged as he told the court that the parties were now friends.

**3.** Ric. Wright to be committed to prison until tomorrow when he is   p. 176 to sit in the stocks for two hours for excessive drunkenness and lewd words, then to be discharged paying his fees.

**4.** A process (*pluries capias*)[1] to be made out against Chas. Griffith for the felony of killing Thos. Taylor, late servant to the univ. proctor.

**5.** Jn. Durrant, a former constable, to be committed during the pleasure of the court for neglecting to execute a warrant sent to him by Mr. Thos. Flexney, J.P., and using contemptible words. Wm. Mannings, constable, to be committed to prison until he carries out the warrant to bring in Jn. Westbury.

---

[1] For this writ see B.H. Putnam, *Early Treatises on the Practice of Justices of the Peace* (Oxf. Studies in Social and Legal Hist. vii), 85, n. 19, 94.

**6.** Thos. Alcock put in sureties from Thos. Nobes, cordwainer, and Thos. Norland, tailor, to appear tomorrow morning.

**7.** Hen. Thrupp put in sureties for his good behaviour and appearance at the next Q.S. when it will be known if Joan Edwards has borne his child.

**8.** Warrants to be made out for Wm. Ogle *alias* Osney and Wm. Mumford to be committed to Bocardo and whipped on the next three market days for stealing young springs [coppice shoots]. Mumford to wear the devil's yoke for three hours in the stocks in the market for biting Thos. Medcalfe.

**9.** Thos. Evans indicted and discharged after being found not guilty of stealing a silver bowl from Jesus Coll.

**10.** A certificate to be made out to obtain a pardon for Tim. Gray(e), who was condemned after the indictment confused him with Rob.

**11.** Nic. Mundy and Wm. Mundye, boatmen, indicted for robbing a boat and stealing two planks but acquitted by the jury and discharged by proclamation.

**12.** Hen. Kitlebeater and Thos. Metcalfe discharged after they were bound by recogn. to appear at this Q.S. and no prosecution was brought.

p. 177    **13.** Wm., son of Toby Toms, surgeon, immediately discharged by proclamation after the indictment for cutting Joan Woodson's purse was found not guilty by the grand jury.

**14.** Frideswide Younge and Mary Hopkins swore that Rob. Gunn, tailor, was very sick and could not appear as bound.

**15.** Wm. Rose to stop victualling and to be committed until he pays his fine according to the statute after the jury found an indictment against him for holding unlawful games in his house. Jn. Meredith to be committed to prison and fined 6s. 8d. according to the statute for playing unlawful games in that house.

**16.** Ric. Colton to be committed to prison for 'raising of warrants'[1] until he finds sureties for his good behaviour.

**17.** All unlicensed victuallers presented by the grand jury to be proceeded against by warrants according to the statute.

---

[1] Perhaps meaning that warrants had been made out because of false accusations.

**18.** Wm. Kensall sen. discharged of the recogn. by which he was bound to appear to answer for certain misdemeanours on his solemn promise in court of his future good behaviour.

**19.** (Mr.) Wm. Gough had been indicted for battery of Rog. Robinson in the psh. church of St. Ebbe. His traverse was heard in full here and he is to be discharged as the jury found him not guilty.

**20.** Warrants to be sent by special order to the churchwardens of each psh. forbidding them from ever using trunks[1] or allowing anyone to play at trunks under any pretext. Mrs. Sympson to be fined 6s. 8d. for playing. Wm. Acton to be attached by warrant and committed to prison until he pays 6s. 8d. for playing and finds sureties for his good behaviour.

**21.** Rob. Newman and Jn. Sunton to be whipped and discharged after p. 178 being indicted and found guilty of petty larceny.

**22.** Lewis Willyams and Thos. Hadly *alias* Kellam to be hanged after being found guilty by the petty jury.

**23.** Any boatman who ties a boat to the bridge next to the Castle mills opposite Mr. Paynter's, after being given notice, is to be fined 2s. for each offence. All forfeitures to be taken by distress by warrant made out by the clerk of the court.

## [1623F]

Adjourned Special Sessions of the Peace at the Guildhall Tues. 7 Oct. 1623. Wm. Peirse, Vice-Chancellor, Wm. Potter esq., Mayor, Jn. Prideaux D.D., Jn. Hawley D.C.L., Thos. Flexney esq., Thos. Harris ald., Oliver Smith ald., J.P.s.

**1.** Wm. Ogle *alias* Osney discharged from prison and from his former punishment in hope of his future good behaviour.

**2.** And. Pawlinge has obtained indictments for battery against Thos. Fletcher, Wm. Tonge, Wm. Willmott, Rob. Bryann, Thos. Bland, Wm. Hughes, Geo. Constable, Geo. Thacker and Hen. Sherwyn. At his request the case is wholly referred to the Vice-Chancellor, Mayor and other J.P.s here present.

**3.** A complaint that Thos. Lake, a freeman of this city, had been erecting a tenement on the waste ground in Canditch next to Jesse Wilshire's

---

[1] Game in which players bowl flattened balls through apertures in a long piece of wood.

house by virtue of a lease granted by the city was examined. The Lords
p. 179  of the Council had formerly ordered that permission to build a cottage
or tenement within Oxf. and its suburbs should be given or refused
by the Chancellor of the Univ. and the High Steward of the city as
seemed fit according to the rule of good order and the necessity of the
case. The J.P.s in the presence of both bailiffs order that building should
cease until Christmas to allow the Vice-Chancellor and the Mayor time
to meet and settle the question. If they cannot agree the question shall
be referred in writing to the Chancellor and High Steward. Neither the
city's title to the land nor the validity of any lease granted by the city is
to be questioned.

**4.** As for Thos. Lake's request for damages to be awarded for the
breaking of his timber and frame and the pulling down of what had
been erected, it is to be considered by the Vice-Chancellor and the
Mayor. What they order shall be binding on all parties and all suits in
law to be suspended in the meantime.

**5.** Wm. Tonge, Wm. Willmott, Rob. Bryan, Wm. Hughes, Geo.
Constable and Wm. Sherwyn against whom And. Pawlinge had
obtained indictments agreed to perform the order made by the J.P.s.
Thos. Bland submitted similarly. Thos. Bland, Thos. Fletcher and
Wm. Willmott, the mason, to pay 3s. 4d. each, acknowledge their
offence and ask And. Pawlinge to forgive them. Rob. Bryan, Wm.
Tonge, Geo. Constable, Thos. Roberts, Hen. Hughes, Geo. Thacker
and Hen. Sherwyn to pay Pawlinge 20d. each and those who are
absent 2s. 6d. each. They are to pay this week and acknowledge their
fault or Pawlinge may seek remedy by law.

[*Margin*] 'Divers fined for their abuse'.

p. 180  **6.** Jn. Sunton *alias* Joyner, Mat. Toms, Wm. Stapler, Thos. Willyams
and Wm. Robinson to be taken by warrant and put in the stocks for
pulling down Thos. Lake's house at Canditch.

**7.** Thos. Lake, haberdasher's, claim for damages, referred on 7 Oct.
to the Vice-Chancellor and Mayor, has been fully considered.[1]
It is ordered that those he complained about, Mr. Lawr. Alcock, Ant.
Furnifall, Sam. Simpson and Mat. Toms are to pay Thos. Lake or cause
him to be paid £8 on or before 28 Oct., St. Simon and St. Jude's day. If
any part of this is unpaid Lake may seek remedy by law. When it is paid
Lake shall seal and deliver his deed of release to the other parties.

---

[1] Undated entry, evidently between 7 and 28 Oct.

# [1624A]

Quarter Sessions at the Guildhall Thurs. 15 Jan. 1624. Wm. Peirs, p. 181
Vice-Chancellor, Wm. Potter esq., Mayor, Jn. Bancrofte D.D., Jn.
Rawlinson D.D., Wm. Langton D.D., Jn. Prideaux D.D., Thos.
James D.D., Jn. Hawley D.C.L., Jn. Whistler esq., Thos. Flexney
esq., Thos. Harris ald., Wm. Wright ald., Oliver Smith ald., Ralph
Flexney gent., Jn. Bird gent., Wm. Boswell gent., J.P.s.

1. Francis Whitbee to be bound over from Q.S. to Q.S. until he
obtains the King's pardon and meanwhile be of good behaviour. Ric.
Astell, tailor, and Thos. Hawes, tailor, bound in the sum of £20 each
and Whitbee in the sum of £40.

2. The disputes between Wm. Gough and Rog. Robinson and his
wife, Susan, were referred to the court with the consent of both sides.
Dr. Bancroft and Dr. Hawley are to hear and determine the dispute
and the parties have promised to be bound by their decision.

3. Hen. Thrupp appeared on his recogn. after being bound on
suspicion of getting Joan Edwards of Twyford pregnant. He is
discharged after a certificate from the inhabitants and collectors of
Twyford was read, confirming that the child had been born and
was dead.

4. Hen. Pidgley discharged after he appeared on his recogn. for breach
of the peace against Hen. Gunn's wife and no further prosecution was
brought.

5. Ric. Browne was indicted and prosecuted by Wm. Parsons for
feloniously stealing a grey nag. On evidence given in court he was
acquitted by the jury and discharged. Parsons is to pay his fees.

6. Jn. Coales, Rowland Bedbury, Thos. Walter and Wm. Tilcock, p. 182
who were bound to appear here, discharged as no prosecution was
brought.

7. Edw. Tomlinson appeared on his recogn. and was discharged. The
prosecution by Joan Hutchins, a huckster, of Jn. Cleere for felony for
taking a couple of apples was found to be frivolous, malicious and
envious. She is to 'have her wardens'[1] and pay back the groat she took
and the boy is to be whipped by his master.

[*Margin*] 'A triviall Cause ended'.

---

[1] Wardens were a variety of keeping pear.

**8.** All recusants presented by the grand jury to surrender to the bailiffs before the next Q.S. or be convicted according to the statute.

**9.** Thos. Alcock appeared on his recogn. and was discharged as it was not thought right to question him again.

**10.** It is ordered in respect of Denise Beare's petition that the overseers of the poor and churchwardens of the psh. of St. Mic. shall pay her 5s. towards the rent of her house each quarter while they continue in office. She shall be responsible for keeping her children without further charge on the psh. until the officers or their successors provide a cheaper house.

**11.** Ric. Miles found guilty of the manslaughter of Ric. Reynolds. Mic. Shelton found guilty of the felony of stealing sixteen yards of tawny bays worth 40s. from Mr. Steph. Townsend. Wm. Reade *alias* Ogle and his wife, Magdalen indicted for stealing Alex. Hill's faggots; he was acquitted and she was found guilty to the value of 8d. Miles and Shelton claimed benefit of clergy. Reade and his wife to be banished from the city for ever, leaving within three days with a pass to Chester and so on to Ireland, where they should stay.

**12.** Wm. Huett indicted on suspicion of stealing pewter from Exeter Coll., acquitted by the petty jury and discharged by proclamation.

**13.** Wm. Gough, who was indicted and found guilty by the grand jury of assault and battery on Susan, wife of Rog. Robinson, paid his fine of 2s. 6d. and was discharged.

**14.** Chas. Griffith, who killed the proctor's man, to be proceeded against 'to the Exigent'.[1]

**15.** Thos. Wetherall, Jn. Richardson, Ann Cox and Ann Wright discharged by proclamation, paying their fees.

**16.** Wm. Allen, Thos. Comber, Jn. Wildgoose, Ric. Wyatt, Jn. Dunt, Thos. Price and Widow Tomlins licensed to victual.

p. 183   **17.** The jury found an indictment against Edw. Wigmore (Wiggmore) for irreverent and undutiful words about the noble and illustrious Charles, Prince of Wales. Wiggmore confessed, said the words had been spoken rashly and submitted to the court's judgement. Some of the court thought 'so Capitall an offender' should be punished straightaway but the majority thought punishment should be deferred until serious consideration had been given and the advice of Sir Jn.

---

[1] The writ of *exigent* commanded an arrest on pain of outlawry.

Walter, the Prince's attorney, sought. A copy of the indictment and proceedings is to be sent to Sir Jn. and Mr. Whistler is to explain the matter to him and bring back his advice so further proceedings may be taken. In the meantime Wiggmore to be bound with sureties for his good behaviour and to appear within four days of warning being given to him or left at his house. If no such warning is given he is to appear at the next Q.S. Wm. Brookes, vintner, and Leonard Harrison, mercer, were bound for him in the sum of £100 each and Wiggmore in the sum of £200.

**18.** There are six victuallers in the liberties of Holywell, viz. Wm. Wiblin, Wm. Rancklin, Dorothy Hore, widow, Thos. Holt, Ric. Edins and Thos. Willyams, who asked to be accounted within the liberties of the city and be licensed to victual. They are to find good sureties and be licensed to victual for a year.

**19.** Wm. Reade *alias* Ogle *alias* Osney and his wife, Magdalen, are a lewd and intolerable pair and are to leave the city and univ., their suburbs and liberties and the county of Oxon. and not return. If either is seen more than a day after the end of the Q.S., Wm. Reade is to be imprisoned and wear the devil's yoke on two days and they are to be punished as the court thinks fit. In the meantime each is to have a pass to go to Chester and then Ireland, with three weeks allowed for the journey.

**20.** Ric. Miles was found guilty of the manslaughter of Ric. Reynolds and claimed benefit of clergy. He is not to be burnt on the hand until he has had time to obtain the King's pardon and plead it in court. In the meantime he is to be bound from Q.S. to Q.S. and be of good behaviour. Jn. Brookes, tanner, and Alfred Rance, tailor, stood surety for him.

**21.** Warrants to be made out for all unlicensed victuallers presented p. 184 by the grand jury to be dealt with according to the statute.

**22.** An iron chain and two posts to be set up and maintained at the west end of the City mills so that passage of carts and carriages may be hindered at the charge of Mr. Hen. Bosworth and his successors in the house called Swan's Nest.

## [1624B]

Quarter Sessions and Gaol Delivery at the Guildhall Thurs. 8 April 1624. Wm. Peirs, Vice-Chancellor, Wm. Potter esq., Mayor, Thos.

James D.D., Jn. Hawley D.C.L., Thos. Flexney esq., Thos. Harris ald., Oliver Smyth ald., Jn. Byrd gent., J.P.s.

**1.** As previously ordered, Francis Whitbee to be bound from Q.S. to Q.S. until he obtains the King's pardon and meanwhile to be of good behaviour. Jn. Harwood, tailor, and Ric. Astell, tailor, bound for him in the sum of £20 each and Whitbee in the sum of £40.

**2.** Ric. Myles of Oxf., yeoman, who had been convicted of killing Ric. Reynolds, claimed benefit of clergy and was allowed time to obtain the King's pardon, has now brought it in and is discharged.

**3.** Bridget Shereborne accused Wm. Baker of being the father of her child, supported by the testimony of the midwife and others present at the delivery. He is to be committed to prison until he finds good sureties for performing the order to be made by the two next J.P.s, Dr. Hawley and Ald. Harris.

p. 185 **4.** Mary Parris, the 'distracted' woman from Begbroke, who is in custody in Oxf., is to be sent to Begbroke as her lunacy was not known before her apprehension.

**5.** Thos. Birde the younger and Joan Hatton, widow, for reasons best known to the court, allowed to victual for one year.

**6.** Hen. Clare of Clare in the psh. of Pyrton discharged as the grand jury did not find the indictment against him for stealing half a peck of wheat.

**7.** Ant. Lamborne discharged after certificates from Sir Jas. Woolverige and the town of Odiham [Hants.] that he is innocent of the death of a man in Hants., of which he was suspected because of his own foolish affirmation.

**8.** Warrants to be made out to distrain any churchwardens who have not paid the money they ought to collect to the treasurer or collector.[1]

**9.** Wm. Seller indicted by the grand jury, acquitted and discharged.

**10.** Jn. Wyte, smith, discharged.

**11.** Ald. Smyth elected treasurer for maimed soldiers for the next year and Mr. Wm. Fletcher appointed collector.

**12.** A warrant to be made out for the apprehension of Jn. Hearne for contempt against the J.P.s and a breach of the peace on Wm. Stapler.

---

[1] i.e. for maimed soldiers.

**13.** Wm. Tooly [*Entry not filled in*].

**14.** Recusants, who did not surrender to the bailiffs as proclaimed at the last Q.S., convicted according to the statute.

**15.** An *exigent*[1] to be made out against Chas. Griffith.          p. 186

**16.** Jn. Flexney, manciple, discharged after he appeared on his recogn. and no prosecution was brought.

**17.** Thos. Metcalfe appeared on his recogn. and was discharged having publicly acknowledged his rash and ill-mannered words towards Ald. Harris in particular, and also here in court and against women.

**18.** Alice Foord(e), against whom several indictments were found by the grand jury, escaped from the custody of Mr. Arnold.[2] He is not to be indicted until the next Q.S. to give him the chance to bring Alice Foord to be prosecuted.

**19.** Ric. Lucy, apprentice to Wm. Jones, joiner, complained of and proved in open court his master's ill-treatment of him. He is to be absolutely discharged of his apprenticeship and Jones is to return his indentures and clothes to him. Jones is to be imprisoned for ill-mannered behaviour in court.

**20.** Edw. Wigmore of Oxf., confectioner, bound by recogn. in the sum of £40 to behave well and appear at the next Q.S. Wm. Charles of Oxf., maltster, and Ric. Whetstone of Oxf., tailor, were bound for him in the sum of £20 each.

**21.** The dispute concerning a wether lost by Ric. Honnesty (Honesty) p. 187 and found with Wm. Plott referred to Dr. Hawley and Ald. Harris.

**22.** Edith Collins (Collyns) committed to Bocardo for various misdemeanours until she finds sureties for her good behaviour.

**23.** Jn. Collins (Collyns) elder and younger are discharged after they were bound to appear and nothing was objected against them.

**24.** Edw. Badger find 6s. 8d. for contempt after it was sworn that he had been warned to serve on the petty jury.

**25.** Warrants to be made out for all unlicensed victuallers presented at this Q.S. to appear before two J.P.s, one of whom is of the quorum. Warrants to be made out for all who forfeited their recogns. to be

---

[1] See note to 1624A14.
[2] Keeper of Bocardo: see note to 1621C23.

bound for their good behaviour and appearance at the next Q.S. and to spend three days in prison.

**26.** Thos. Bassett indicted, arraigned and found guilty of the felony of stealing pewter dishes to the value of 6s. 8d. from New Coll. He was granted benefit of clergy and he is to stay in prison until he finds sureties for his good behaviour.

**27.** Thos. Gullett indicted for twelve pieces of plate, part of a silver bowl. Though found not guilty by the petty jury he is to remain in prison until he finds sureties for his good behaviour.

p. 188 **28.** Edw. Meddowes indicted and found guilty of stealing five hens and a cock to the value of 12d. Anne Howell indicted and found guilty of stealing plough irons to the value of 12d. Wal. Pope, indicted under the statute of 39 Eliz. for being an incorrigible rogue, is acquitted by the jury but is strongly suspected of being a rogue. All three are to be whipped at the post next market day above the waist until they are 'all bloody', and then have passes to their birthplaces. Pope's whipping is remitted at the request of some scholars.

**29.** Wm. Brierwood *alias* [*blank*] to remain in prison until further order.

**30.** Wm. Hellines (Hellins) allowed to continue victualling at Binsey for a year if he behaves well.

**31.** Elias Archer maliciously caused Art. Stranguadge to be bound by recogn. to appear at this Q.S. and did not prosecute. Archer is to pay his charges on demand or be arrested by warrant and committed until he pays.

**32.** Nic., son of Hen. Mondy (Mundy), boatman, discharged.

## [1624c]

p. 189 Quarter Sessions Thurs. 27 May 1624. Wm. Potter esq., Mayor, Thos. James D.D., Jn. Rawlinson D.D., Jn. Hawley D.C.L., Thos. Flaxney esq., Wm. Wright ald., Oliver Smyth ald., Ralph Flexney gent., J.P.s.

**1.** Francis Whitbye (Whitby) of Buckingham, gent., bound by recogn. in the sum of £40 to appear at the next Q.S. and be of good behaviour. Ric. Astell of Oxf., tailor, and Edw. Bythell of Oxf., gent., bound for him in the sum of £20 each.

**2.** Bart. Daye found guilty of lewd disposition and behaviour, not fit to be described. He and his wife to find sureties for their good behaviour. Daye's former servant, Jn. Garland, who was found guilty of lewd and lascivious behaviour, to sit in the stocks for one hour and find sureties for his good behaviour.

**3.** Edw. Wigmore appeared and was discharged.

**4.** Hugh Shawe appeared and was discharged.

**5.** Jn. Peade appeared and was discharged.

**6.** Hen. Burgess(e) and Thos. Moore appeared on their recogns. for p. 190 various misdemeanours particularly against Mr. Ric. Paynter of St. Thos. psh. They are discharged paying their fees on condition that within ten days they bring a certificate to Dr. Hawley that they have submitted to Mr. Paynter or he shall bind them over.

**7.** Ralph Loddington, who is accused of making Widow Gibbs pregnant, committed until he finds sureties that the psh. of [*blank*] shall not be charged as a result.

**8.** Martha Byby to be discharged after she appeared on her husband's recogn. on suspicion of taking 7s. from Welhead of Headington.

**9.** Stephen Paradice to be discharged as there was no proof that he had harboured Alice Foord, who escaped from prison.

**10.** Rob. Carpenter, who was apprehended by warrant and confessed to unlicensed victualling, to be committed for three days and find sureties not to victual.

**11.** Chris. Skea indicted for stealing a turkey and four cheeses from Joan Heard *alias* Ostler, widow. Young Sherewood indicted for stealing fifty hop poles from Mr. Jn. Lambach and prosecuted by Ric. Fourd. Jane Crooke indicted for stealing a waistcoat 'at the fire'[1] at Thos. Cave's house at Canditch. They were all found guilty by the grand jury but acquitted by the petty jury and are discharged by proclamation.

**12.** Warrants to be made out for Osney (Oseney), Stapler and p. 191 Robynson to be bound to appear next Thursday.

**13.** Warrants to be made out on the grand jury's presentments.

**14.** [*blank*] Baker[2] was committed at the last Q.S. on suspicion of being the father of Bridget Shereborne's child. She has undertaken to make over her estate to the psh. of [*blank*] to indemnify it in respect of the child. If she brings a certificate that she has done so to the Mayor, Baker is to be discharged.

---

[1] Possibly meaning 'at the fireside'.
[2] Called Wm. in 1623B3 and 1624E7.

111

**15.** Jn. Brent *alias* Brunt, who has been imprisoned for a long time for lewd speeches against Queen Elizabeth and the clergy, to be discharged from Bocardo on bail to appear at the Q.S. after Michaelmas and meanwhile to be of good behaviour.

**16.** Bart. Day of Oxf., gunsmith, bound by recogn. in the sum of £20 and Edw. Day of Oxf., locksmith, and Hen. Gun of Oxf., yeoman, bound as sureties in the sum of £10 each. Bart. is to appear and answer at the next Q.S. and G.D., and in the meantime to be of good behaviour.

## [1624D]

p. 192  Quarter Sessions and Gaol Delivery at the Guildhall Thurs. 3 June 1624. Wm. Peirs, Vice-Chancellor, Wm. Potter esq., Mayor, Jn. Rawlinson D.D., Thos. James D.D., Jn. Hawley D.C.L., Thos. Harris ald., Wm. Wright ald., Oliver Smyth ald., J.P.s and justices for G.D.

**1.** The four aldermen and a J.P. to view their wards and note what poor people and 'squabb' houses[1] there are. The Mayor and some of the Doctors, who are J.P.s, to view the suburbs.

**2.** The Treasurer to examine Chris. Davis's petition that he was pressed as a soldier from Oxf. If he was, he is to have relief according to the statute for maimed soldiers.

**3.** The dispute between Jn. Richardson, boatman, and his servant, Wm. Newell, was examined in open court. Newell is at fault in refusing to serve as agreed until the next All Hallows, and from then to Easter for 5s. a week. Ordered in the presence of both parties that Newell is to continue to serve until All Hallows for 6s. a week and from then to Easter for 5s. a week.

p. 193  **4.** Ferryman Moore indicted for stabbing Jn. Crabtree of Balliol Coll. to death and found guilty of manslaughter. He claimed benefit of clergy and was reprieved by the court's order from being burnt on the hand.

**5.** Eliz. Smyth's (Smith's) petition for a licence to victual allowed.

**6.** Wm. Read (Rede) *alias* Ogle *alias* Osney to wear the devil's yoke on two market days as formerly ordered at the Q.S. after Christmas last. To find sureties for the peace especially towards Nic. Edmonds, who

[1] See note to 1620A13.

asked for this on oath in open court.

**7.** Giles Thorme of the Univ., M.A., and Thos. Twitty of North Leigh, Oxon., clerk, bound in the sum of £40 each on condition that Ferryman Moore appears and answers at the next city Q.S. and is meanwhile of good behaviour.

**8.** Wm. Stapler and Wm. Robinson to find sureties of the peace especially towards Nic. Edmonds.

**9.** Rob. Carpenter to have a licence to victual and pay a fine of 20s. to the bailiff for previous unlicensed victualling.

**10.** Leonard Russell, Thos. Vaughan and Chris. Crutch indicted for stealing six Books of Common Prayer from Magdalen Coll. chapel. Russell, who was found guilty by the petty jury to the value of 10d., p. 194 to be whipped at the post next market day from the shoulders to the waist until he bleeds. Crutch (Croutch), who was found guilty as an accessory, to be whipped but not at the post. Thos. Vaughan acquitted.

**11.** Rob. Carpenter of Oxf., brewer, bound by recogn. in the sum of £20 to victual and keep order in his house according to the statute. Jas. Toldervey of Oxf., glover, and Jn. Anstey of the psh. of St. Peter-le-Bailey, yeoman, bound for him in the sum of £10 each.

## [1624E]

Quarter Sessions and Gaol Delivery at the Guildhall Thurs. 7 Oct. 1624. Jn. Prideaux D.D., Vice-Chancellor, Oliver Smyth esq., Mayor, Thos. James D.D., Jn. Hawley D.C.L., Thos. Flexney esq., Thos. Harris ald., Wm. Wright ald., Jn. Bird gent., Wm. Boswell gent., J.P.s and justices for G.D.

**1.** Francis Whitby, gent., who had formerly been indicted and found guilty of manslaughter, appeared in court on his recogn., claimed the benefit of the King's general and free pardon granted in the last Parliament and is to be absolutely discharged by proclamation.

**2.** Jn. Brent of Evesham (Easam), Worcs., was discharged of his recogn. by proclamation after his certificate was read in open court.

**3.** Jn. Edwards discharged of his recogn. p. 195

**4.** Wm. Gough to be committed during the pleasure of the court for buying seven and a half dozen of lace stolen from Mr. Thos. Nickolls by his [? Thos.'s] journeyman, which is an abuse of justice and an offence to the whole Company of Tailors. Because of his words to Ald. Harris he is not to be released until he finds sureties to appear at the next Q.S. and behave well.

**5.** Gilbert Wort(e) discharged after he appeared on his recogn. and no prosecution was brought.

**6.** Giles Thorne of Oxf. Univ., M.A., and Thos. Twitty of North Leigh, Oxon., clerk, bound in the sum of £20 each on condition that Ferryman Moore appears to answer at the next Q.S. and meanwhile is of good behaviour.

**7.** Wm. Baker jun. has been a prisoner in Bocardo for six months for lack of bail on suspicion of being the father of Bridget Sherborne's child. He is to be released and enter into a bond that the church-wardens of the psh. of St. Peter-le-Bailey will not be charged with the child.

**8.** Thos. Newe, tapster, to be discharged.

**9.** The dispute between Hen. Burgess(e) and his wife, and Jn. Buttres(se) and Kath. Jones, his daughter, is referred to Dr. James and Ald. Harris. It appears to the court that Hen. Burges is a very bad husband and p. 196 unkind son-in-law, and Jn. Buttres a harsh brother-in-law to Kath. Jones and a haunter of alehouses. Buttres is to be bound by recogn. to appear at the next Q.S. and meanwhile keep the peace, but Dr. James and Ald. Harris may cancel this.

**10.** Hen. Seaman and his wife, Eliz., were prosecuted by Everard Abell. Eliz. was indicted and found guilty of assault and battery on Everard. Hen. to pay a fine of 3s. 4d. and be discharged.

**11.** Hen. Burges of Oxf., plasterer, bound in the sum of £20 and Geo. Barton and Steph. Asheley of Oxf., freemasons, bound in the sum of £10 each for Hen. to appear at the next Q.S. and keep the peace.

**12.** Thos. Price indicted and found guilty of playing unlawful games and cheating. He is to be fined 20s. and be committed until he pays and enters into recogn. not to play any more.

**13.** Eliz. Tooley and Eliz. Gamon indicted and found guilty of assault and battery on Anne, wife of Steph. Asheley, and fined 20d. each.

p. 197 **14.** Jn. Elliott indicted for cutting and taking pieces of leather brought to Mr. Lovegrove's house to be curried, and Evan Petty indicted as an accessory for receiving and concealing them. They are to pay 10s. each or be well whipped at the post. They are to remain in prison until this order is performed, which should be before the end of this Q.S.

**15.** Jane Sansam to make a public submission to Dorothy Bache and Brian Dyamond for scandalous words and abuse to them and ask their forgiveness.

**16.** Edw. Warland discharged after appearing on his recogn. and paying his fees and those of three other people, who were bound over because of him.

**17.** Joan Norland, for abusive and scandalous speeches against Kath. Clynche, to find sureties to appear at the next Q.S. and be of good behaviour especially towards Jonas Clynche and his wife. Afterwards Thos. Norland and his wife, Joan, asked forgiveness from Jonas and Kath. Clynch and promised not to offend again. It is mutually undertaken in open court that they shall be good neighbours and live in unity so that their neighbours shall approve of their Christian piety and increase in friendship. All actions at law are now remitted.

**18.** Chas. Griffith, who was indicted and found guilty of the manslaughter of Thos. Taylor before the last general pardon, appeared in court and claimed benefit of the King's pardon, which was allowed by the court and read.

**19.** Wm. Bignell of Oxf., tailor, bound by recogn. in the sum of p. 198 £40 to appear and answer at the Q.S. after Easter, and Fulk and Ric. Bignell, tailors of Oxf., bound for him in the sum of £20 each.

**20.** Fulk Bignell of Oxf., tailor, bound by recogn. in the sum of £40 for his and his wife Avice's, appearance to answer at the next Q.S., and Wm. and Ric. Bignell of Oxf., tailors, bound for him in the sum of £20 each.

**21.** Ethelbert Weller of Wolvercote, yeoman, bound by recogn. in the sum of £40 to appear at the Q.S. after Easter to prosecute Wm. Bignell and his wife, Avice, for taking away Anne Revell, a maid under the age of fourteen, and not to depart without licence of the court.

**22.** Thos. Cantyn, fuller, indicted and found guilty of assault and battery on Ursula, wife of Rob. Moorey, tailor, and fined 3s. 4d. For disorder and swearing at St. Giles's Wake, to the amazement of the hearers, Cantyn is also to pay 6s. according to the statute for 'six insufferable oaths which were especially distinguished', or be punished appropriately.

115

p. 199 **23.** Francis Carpenter and his wife, Joan, complained of 'unchaste' violence against Joan by Jn. Burges, plasterer. They are to be absolutely discharged and Burges is to pay their fees.

**24.** The Vice-Chancellor, the Mayor, Dr. James, Dr. Hawley, Ald. Harris, Ald. Wright and Mr. Boswell are asked by the Bench to consider the general complaint by various women and others who have taken the burden of children left to the pshs. by parents leaving Oxf. They are to choose a time as soon as their weightier business allows to call the interested parties before them and make a final order according to the law.

**25.** Wm. Jackson, a constable, to find sureties for his good behaviour and appearance at the next Q.S., for not executing a warrant from a J.P. to arrest a suspect, which he could easily have done but, either wilfully or negligently, failed or, as the court thinks, refused to do.

**26.** Wm. Jackson of Oxf., tailor, bound by recogn. in the sum of £40 to appear and answer at the next Q.S. and meanwhile be of good behaviour. Steph. Fayerbeard of Oxf., mercer, and Jn. Davies of Oxf. Univ., cook, bound for him in the sum of £20 each.

p. 200 **27.** Jn. Davis of Oxf. Univ., cook, bound by recogn. in the sum of £20 to appear at the next Assizes for the county of Oxon. and prosecute Wm. Stapler for felony.

**28.** Wm. Stapler committed to the Castle until he finds sureties for his appearance.

**29.** Nic. Clyffe appeared on his recogn. and is discharged.

**30.** Margaret, wife of Thos. Cranwell, labourer, indicted for cutting a purse and taking 5s. from Anne, wife of Hugh Dewe, mercer, who prosecuted her. The jury of life and death found her not guilty.

**31.** Alex. Roche, a young man, indicted for cutting a purse and taking 5s. from Chris. Smyth and found not guilty by the jury of life and death.

**32.** Simon Wood(e) indicted for entering Wm. Misson's house and taking two kettles worth 5s. The jury found him guilty to the value of 10d.

**33.** Wm. Pickering(e) committed to prison for three days for great injury to his late master, Mr. Thos. Pen, and lewd behaviour to all men. He is not to be released until he finds good sureties to appear at the next Q.S. and be of good behaviour.

116

**34.** Jn. Plott of Brill, Bucks., yeoman, bound by recogn. in the sum of £20 to appear at the next Q.S. to prosecute Wm. Pickering and not leave without the court's licence.

**35.** Wm. Gough was allowed to submit himself to Ald. Harris and then to enter recogn. for his good behaviour.

**36.** Wm. Gough of Oxf., tailor, bound by recogn. in the sum of £20  p. 201 to appear and answer at the next Q.S. and meanwhile be of good behaviour. Jn. Harwood sen. of Oxf., tailor, and Lewis Jones of Oxf. bound for him in the sum of £10 each.

**37.** A warrant from the court to take Thos. Cantyn and break into his house.

**38.** Rob. Williams, Chris. Palmer, Hen. Seaman and Rob. Presley allowed to continue victualling.

**39.** A warrant to the constable of South-East ward to apprehend Ric. Wardell and recite Eliz. Wildegoose's petition.

**40.** Thos. Holland, Wm. Fletcher and Ric. Norgrove absolutely discharged.

**41.** A warrant to be made out against Hen. Seaman.

**42.** Ric. Ewen pawned a gown and a brass pot to Ric. Crawford who re-pawned them to Jn. Blunt. Ewen shall pay Blunt 18s. by All Hallows and then the pot and gown are to be returned.

**43.** Anne Lea swore in open court that she was in bodily fear of Susan Pryce (Price). A warrant to be made out for Susan to be brought before a J.P. to enter recogn. for the peace with sureties.

**44.** There are a great many poor people wandering the city and suburbs begging and often pilfering, breaking into houses and shops and doing other mischief. They have increased because of the number of cottages and 'squabd' houses[1] built in and around the city, and this breeds 'great dislike' in the univ. and city, endangering the commonwealth if, by God's will, the city is visited with sickness. In order to stop any further  p. 202 increase in the numbers of cottages, 'squabd' houses, poor people and idle beggars, no owner of a tenement or cottage in the city, suburbs or liberties shall let it without securing the churchwardens against any charge that may arise from the tenants or their children. Anyone who fails to comply with this order after it has been publicly read out in

---

[1] See note to 1620A13.

their psh. church is to be put in prison until they enter into a sufficient bond with the churchwardens to perform this order.

**45.** Simon Wood, indicted for stealing two kettles and found guilty of petty larceny only, is to be whipped at the post and discharged.

**46.** Alex. Roche indicted and found not guilty by the jury of cutting a purse but, for reasons best known to the Bench, is to be whipped at the post and have a pass to return to where he came from.

**47.** An enquiry to be made by next Saturday whether any felony has been committed at Bicester recently and what goods have been lost. If no felony is reported, Thos. Cranwell and his wife, Margaret are to be whipped at the post on Saturday and sent away.

**48.** Warrants to be made out against all who have failed to appear on their recogns. and they are to be bound to appear at the next Q.S.

**49.** Jn. Collyns of Oxf., baker, bound by recogn. in the sum of £20 and Thos. Collyns of Oxf., baker, in the sum of £10 for Jn. to appear at the next Q.S. and meanwhile keep the peace, especially towards Edith Collyns.

p. 203 **50.** All the matters in dispute between Thos. Collyns and his wife, Edith, are referred to the Vice-Chancellor and the Mayor to settle, if they can.

**51.** Thos. Price of Oxf., yeoman, bound by recogn. in the sum of £40 and Hen. Sherwyn of Oxf., cordwainer, and Ralph Marshe of Oxf., gunsmith, bound in the sum of £20 each that Price should not play unlawful games without licence.

**52.** Rob. Willyams (Williams, Wylliams) of Oxf., cordwainer, bound in the sum of £20 and Ric. Hore and Nic. Barton of Oxf., cordwainers, in the sum of £10 each for Willyams to be allowed to victual for a year.

**53.** Mon. 18 Oct. 1624. At a meeting of the Vice-Chancellor, the Mayor, Dr. James, Dr. Hawley, Ald. Potter, Ald. Wright and Mr. Boswell, J.P.s, the number of poor people and cottages and 'squabd' houses[1] was discussed so action can be taken speedily to stop any further increase and suppress the disorder which is a source of daily complaint. The state of the city and suburbs is to be viewed by the J.P.s and an exact note taken of all the cottages

[1] Corrected from 'squabbe'. See note to 1620A13.

and 'squabd' houses, the number of inhabitants and the names of the owners or lessors. This is to be done by 16 Nov.

For the suburbs: the Vice-Chancellor, the Mayor, Dr. James, Dr. Hawley.

North-East ward: Ald. Harris, Dr. Langton, Dr. Smithe.

South-East ward: Ald. Potter, Dr. Brancrofte, Dr. Preirs, Mr. Boswell.     p. 204

North-West ward: Ald. Wrighte, Dr. Pincke, Dr. Radcliffe, Mr. Flexney.

South-West ward: Mr. Bird, Dr. Rawlinson, Mr. Whistler.

**54.** A warrant to be made out for the churchwardens and inhabitants of the psh. of St. Mary Magdalen to provide relief for Jn., Susan and Anne Hearne, the children of Jn. Hearne, late of Oxf., tailor.

**55.** A warrant to be made out for Ric. Hutchins, glover, to be brought before the next J.P. to find sureties to keep the peace towards Widow Dudley and secure All Saints' psh. against the cost of his children. He has kept part of the allowance from the psh. for keeping his children and is to account for this. The same J.P. to take order for a tenement or house to be found for Denise Beere, widow, formerly of the psh. of St. Mic., who has lived there for seven years. She undertakes to work for her living and provide for her children and free the Univ. and city from any charge.

**56.** Dr. James, Dr. Hawley, Ald. Potter and Mr. Boswell or any three of them to discuss conditions with Mr. Heathe of Osney for his house to become a House of Correction. If his demands are reasonable they are to view the house and its fixtures and report their opinion.

**57.** Dr. Rawlinson and Mr. Jn. Bird or either of them to call Eliz. Wildgoose and Ric. Wardell before them concerning her relief and lodging and order as is just to the poor woman.

**58.** Edw. Tomlyns (Tomlins) of the psh. of St. Thos. allowed to victual for a year on the surety of Nic. Danyell and Francis Burneham.

## [1625A]

Quarter Sessions and Gaol Delivery at the Guildhall Thurs. 13 Jan.  p. 206
1625. Oliver Smythe esq., Mayor, Jn. Rawlinson D.D., Thos. James D.D., Wm. Langton D.D., Wm. Smythe D.D., Jn. Hawley D.C.L., Jn. Whistler esq., Thos. Harris ald., Wm. Potter ald., Wm. Wright ald., Jn. Bird gent., Wm. Boswell gent., J.P.s.

1. Wm. Goughe, tailor, appeared, having been bound at the last Q.S. to be of good behaviour and appear. He is discharged of his recogn. in hope of his future behaviour after being admonished by the court.

2. A warrant to be sent for Ric. Lovesey, saddler, to be brought before some J.P.s to be bound with good sureties for an assault on young Maris.

3. Thos. Astell committed until he pays his fees for two recogns. and his discharge at this Q.S.

4. Wm. Edwards gent., who had been committed by Ald. Harris for bad behaviour and breach of the peace, discharged after confessing and showing penitence for this and for abusing Ald. Harris, the constable and others.

5. Wm. Jackson discharged after he appeared on his recogn. and no further prosecution was brought. Before he left he used foul language to the court and was committed during the pleasure of the court.

6. Thos. Myles *alias* Astell discharged of his recogn.

p. 207   7. Jn. Weaver of the psh. of St. Ebbe and Hugh Moore of the psh. of St. Clement were apprehended and indicted as notorious wood stealers in Magdalen Coll.'s coppice. As they are unable to give compensation as the statute requires they are to be well whipped at the post during this Q.S.

8. Ferryman Moore had formerly been convicted of manslaughter and claimed benefit of clergy but had been spared from burning. He obtained the King's pardon which was read, allowed and recorded in court.

9. Thos. Fishe and Hugh Ward, members of the grand jury who left in contempt of the court, to be fined 10s. with no abatement to be made by the bailiff.

10. Hen. Sansome to find new sureties and be bound for his good behaviour.

11. Nat. Wymacke to be apprehended by warrant and bound for his good behaviour as a common hedge breaker.

12. Hen. Burges appeared and is discharged.

13. Hen. Sansome of Oxf., cordwainer, is bound by recogn. in the sum of £20 to appear at the next Q.S. and be of good behaviour. Jn. Brooks of Oxf., tanner, and Wm. Day of Oxf., tailor, bound for him in the sum of £10 each.

**14.** Ant. Carter appeared on his recogn. and is discharged as no pros- p. 208
ecution was brought.

**15.** The case of Jn. Vaughan, who was bound to appear on the prosecution of Wm. Lute, to be heard by the Vice-Chancellor.

**16.** A process to be made out against Wm. Bignell who was indicted
and found guilty by the grand jury of assault and battery on the prosecution of Ethelbert Weller.

**17.** Jn. Collyns appeared and is discharged of his recogn. as peace has
been established between his parents and himself.

**18.** Warrants to be made out against recusants and others presented by
the grand jury.

**19.** Mr. Arnold to pay 40s. because of the escape of Jn. Weaver and
Hugh Moore who had been committed to him to be whipped.

**20.** Jn. Jarvis indicted, found guilty by the grand jury and confessed
to resisting, beating and imprisoning Edm. Bolte, constable. He is to
pay a fine of £3 6s. 8d., be imprisoned for a week and find sureties for
his good behaviour.

**21.** Ric. Lovesey indicted for abusing the constables sent by warrant to
apprehend him for great misdemeanours, violently resisting them and
beating and wounding them and those assisting them, especially Jn.
Reymond whose life is in danger. He was found guilty by the grand
jury and confessed to two indictments for misdemeanours and breach
of the peace. For his contempt to the court and to the city's sworn p. 209
officers he is to be imprisoned for three months, and twice a week
during that time is to sit in the stocks in the open market wearing the
devil's yoke for half an hour between 2 p. m. and 3 p.m. Before his
release he is to pay 5 marks for each indictment and find good sureties
for his good behaviour.

**22.** Jn. Pownall and Ric. Clerk who were indicted and found guilty
with Wm. Bignell for assault and battery on Ethelbert Weller to be
fined 2s. 6d.

**23.** Wm. Pyckring(e) is to be hanged, having been found guilty by
the jury of life and death on an indictment for felony and burglary at
night at Thos. Penn, chandler's house.

**24.** 17 Jan. 1625. At a meeting at the office the Mayor, Dr. Rawlinson,
Dr. Bankrofte, Dr. Hawley, Mr. Whistler, Mr. Flexney, Ald. Potter
and Ald. Whighte [*recte* Wrighte], J.P.s, considered Hen. Gun(n)'s

intolerable abuse to the Vice-Chancellor. As he is a notorious person he is to be kept in Bocardo until proceeded against at the next Q.S.

**25.** Wm. Allen has not brought in his licence as ordered at the last Q.S., so is to be apprehended by warrant and bound not to victual.

p. 210 **26.** Wm. Pyckringe by general consent is reprieved from execution until the next Q.S.

**27.** The psh. of St. Peter-in-the-East is burdened with the maintenance of Joan Seaman, dau. of Wm. Foreste, who has three children and is said to be able to work and earn part of her living. Foreste is to allow her 10s. a quarter while she remains in the psh.

**28.** Ant. Ives's two children are to be kept at the charge of the psh. of St. Peter-le-Bailey, where they last lived. The psh. of St. Martin to pay 4d., All Saints' 4d., St. Mary 3d., St. Aldate 4d., St. Ebbe 3d. a week until further order. Of this, 6d. a week is to be paid to Goodwife Page for ten weeks and the 12d. is to remain to the children.

## [1625B]

p. 211 Quarter Sessions at the Guildhall Thurs. 28 April 1625. Oliver Smithe esq., Mayor, Jn. Prudeaux D.D., Vice-Chancellor, Jn. Hawley D.C.L., Jn. Whistler esq., Thos. Flexney esq., Thos. Harris ald., Wm. Potter ald., J.P.s.

**1.** Ric. Lovesey, saddler, having been punished at the last Q.S. for grievous offences, appeared on his recogn. for his good behaviour. He asked the favour of the court, protesting earnestly that he was a reformed man, would never transgress again and would live a civil and quiet life among his neighbours. He is to be discharged in hope of his future behaviour.

**2.** Jn. Jarvis appeared on his recogn. for his good behaviour and is discharged as no further complaint was made against him.

p. 212 **3.** Jn. Benwell and Jn. Anderton appeared on suspicion of hedge ('pale') breaking and stealing piles of faggots at night, especially from behind Ric. Spicer's house. They are to be discharged 'for this once', as no prosecution was brought.

**4.** Hen. Sansome appeared on his recogn. and is discharged as he is reconciled with his prosecutor, Burges the plasterer.

**5.** Ric. Hutchins was examined concerning his daughter, Thomasin, who has been left as a charge on the psh. of All Saints for about three years. He is an able man who could work and maintain his children if he wishes. He agreed to work diligently and pay 4d. a week from his earnings to the churchwardens. His employer, Mr. Jas. Toldervey, glover, has promised to make sure that Hutchins pays as long as he works for him. Once his eldest child is placed he is to pay 12d. a week to support Thomasin.

**6.** Ric. Mumford to be well whipped for hedge breaking and then discharged.

**7.** [*blank*] Osney to be well whipped for not leaving Oxf. as ordered.

**8.** Rob. Stayno of Oxf. Univ. bound in the sum of £10 to prosecute Wm. Harris for the felony of stealing a pewter dish from Magdalen Coll.

**9.** Fulk Bignell appeared and is discharged. p. 213

**10.** Mary, wife of And. Askew, and Eliz., dau. of Jn. Powell, were convicted as scolds and the dispute between them was examined. They are to be put in the cucking stool.

**11.** Nat. Wymack(e), who had formerly been whipped for pilfering and using a ladder to get into the backs of premises, is strongly suspected of other pilfering and misdemeanours. He is to sit at Carfax in the stocks for half an hour next market day, wearing the devil's yoke, and then be discharged.

**12.** Jn. Day and Nic. Maris convicted of a barbarous misdemeanour of setting up a horn at the door of St. Mic.'s church.[1] They are to sit in the stocks at the same church door for half an hour during the service next Sunday morning.

**13.** Hen. Gunn appeared on his recogn. for his good behaviour and is discharged.

**14.** A warrant to be made out for the churchwardens and overseers of p. 214 the poor for the psh. of St. Cross *alias* Holywell to provide a home for Kath. Hunt, widow, or otherwise provide for her four children, as she has lived there a long time and was turned out by a hard landlord. If the wardens and overseers fail to obey the warrant they are to appear before Mr. Whistler and Mr. Flexney or two other J.P.s.

**15.** A process of outlawry to be made out against Ellis Kinge who was indicted for felony and found guilty by the grand jury.

---

[1] A custom of swearing 'on the horns' [*Brewer's Dictionary of Phrase and Fable*] seems to have provided a means of extorting drinks from travellers.

**16.** Martha Italy indicted and found guilty by the grand jury of petty larceny for stealing three yards of lace to the value of 10s. from Thos. Sympson, mercer. She is to be whipped next market day and have a pass to go home.

**17.** Wm. Harris glazier indicted for petty larceny and confessed to stealing a pewter dish from Magdalen Coll. He is to find good sureties to appear at the next Q.S. and be of good behaviour.

**18.** Geo. Harding(e), a prisoner in Bocardo, is to pay his fees before being discharged.

**19.** Old Jn. Smyth, late tapster at the Roebuck, who has long had a victualler's licence under the city seal, which was shown, is to have a new licence for a year. Nic. Munday, Wm. Pemberton, Ric. Sciers of the psh. of St. Martin and Jn. Baldwyn (Baldyn), musician, are similarly to have licences if they find good sureties.

p. 215  **20.** Hugh Wallys, who received £6 for promising to keep Anne Copperthwart for twelve years and bring her up cleanly so she could be educated, has turned her out. He was ordered to find good sureties for his good behaviour and be committed to prison until he will keep her again or return the money. He took the child back.

**21.** Alice Ford to be whipped forthwith after confessing to two indictments for petty larceny found against her by the grand jury at the last Q.S.

## [1625c]

p. 216  Quarter Sessions at the Guildhall Thurs. 16 June 1625. Oliver Smithe esq., Mayor, Jn. Prudeaux D.D., Vice-Chancellor, Jn. Hawley D.C.L., Jn. Whistler esq., Thos. Flexney ald., Thos. Harris ald., Wm. Potter ald., Jn. Bird gent., J.P.s.

**1.** Wm. Harris, glazier, to be brought to court by warrant for contempt in not bringing in his recogn. for his good behaviour as ordered at the last Q.S.

**2.** A warrant to be made out for Thos. Crooke of the psh. of St. Peter-in-the-East, gardener, to appear at this Q.S. and, if he cannot be found, to be brought before the next J.P. to be bound with sureties to appear at the next Q.S. and answer the accusations of Ellen Budworthe and meanwhile be of good behaviour.

**3.** Wm. Pyckring (Pickring), who had been convicted of burgling Mr. Thos. Penn the chandler's house, brought the King's pardon and it was read and allowed. He is to find sureties for his good behaviour, not because of any past act but because his former master, Mr. Penn, fears 'some new attempts and desperate adventures'.

**4.** Edw. Dewberry was accused of assaulting a constable and gave the excuse of being drunk. Unless he pays a fine of 5s. according to the statute for being drunk he is to sit in the stocks for four hours and then obey a further order of the court.

**5.** Geo. Tredwell appeared on his recogn. for striking and laying p. 217 violent hands on Nic. Hicks in the psh. of St. Martin. The statute of 5 Edw. VI cap. 4 was read and under this it appeared that the best course was to refer the case to the ordinary of the diocese, this court certifying the facts as here produced.

**6.** Jn. Smithe's recogn. and his sureties to be estreated for not appearing.

**7.** Wm. Pickering of Oxf., chandler, bound by recogn. in the sum of £40 for his good behaviour and Jas. Pickringe of Wolvercote, yeoman, and Wm. Bignell of Souldern, tailor, bound for him in the sum of £20 each.

**8.** Hen. Harberte made a small complaint that his apprentice, Rog. Carpenter, had wandered for a day or two in Whitsun week. Harberte is to take him back and, if he offends again, the Mayor is to make a suitable order.

**9.** Blisset the shoemaker to bring his apprentice, Thos. Hathorne, when sent for by the Mayor to be well whipped for helping Jn. Pownall to beat Beadle the dyer. A warrant was to be made out for Pownall. Afterwards he came to court, and his differences with Beedle p. 218 were referred to Dr. Hawley for report to the next Q.S.

**10.** The dispute between Thos. Striplinge and his apprentice was ended and he is to treat him well. Any further complaint against the apprentice is to be dealt with appropriately. If the master mistreats the apprentice he is to be bound for his good behaviour and release the *assumpsit* of 20s. made by Thos. Pagett and pay back 20s. of the £3 received with the apprentice and release him.

**11.** Jn. Peade of Oxf., mercer, bound by recogn. in the sum of £20 to appear at the next Q.S. and behave well. Wm. Wirdnam of Oxf., mercer, and Thos. Stryplinge of Oxf. Univ., barber, bound for him in the sum of £10 each.

**12.** A warrant to be made out for Hen. Thorneton of the psh. of St. Thos. to be brought before Dr. Hawley for abusing the constable, Jn. Sherle. If he sees cause to bind him for good behaviour, the court will approve.

**13.** In a matter concerning a sack the indictment was found by the grand jury against Wm. Pemmerton on the oath of And. Stringer. It is to be referred to the next Q.S. as Stringer's evidence in court differed from his previous evidence to the jury.

**14.** And. Stringer of Culham, bargeman, bound in the sum of £20 to appear and give evidence against Wm. Pemmerton concerning a sack found in Pemmerton's house.

p. 219 **15.** Martin Knowles, huckster, indicted, found guilty and confessed to a furious assault on Eliz., wife of Evan Petty. He is to be fined 10s. He is a lewd fellow and would be fined more if he were not so poor. He is to be committed until he pays and finds good sureties for his behaviour because of his ill-mannered behaviour to Ald. Harris.

**16.** Wm. Pemerton of the psh. of St. Thos., boatman, bound in the sum of £20 to appear and answer at the next Q.S. Hen. Sherwyn and Ric. West, cordwainers, bound for him in the sum of £20.

**17.** Thos. Crooke to find sureties for his good behaviour.

**18.** Geo. Tredwell to be apprehended by warrant and bound to appear at the next Q.S. in case he refuses to pay the court's fees.

**19.** Jn. Jarrett, Ric. Godard, Jn. Hurst and Thos. New allowed to victual.

**20.** Thos. Frey paid his fees on threat of being returned to prison and was discharged after the jury returned a verdict of *ignoramus*[1] on his indictment.

**21.** Thos. Feyard and Jane Dickason discharged.

**22.** Widow Hussey to be bailed from Bocardo if she brings sureties before a J.P. for her appearance at the next G.D.

## [1625D]

p. 220 Quarter Sessions at the Guildhall Thurs. 6 Oct. 1625. Jn. Prideaux D.D., Vice-Chancellor, Hen. Bosworth esq., Mayor, Thos. James

[1] See note to 1623C20.

D.D., Jn. Whistler esq., Thos. Flexney esq., Thos. Harris ald., Wm. Potter ald., Wm. Wright ald., Oliver Smyth ald., Jn. Byrd gent., J.P.s.

1. Jn. Carter is to hang his mastiff bitch which bites and runs at people. He is to pay for a cure for the daughter of Anne Poole who was attacked by it.

2. An indictment against Wm. Pemberton for taking a sack was found by the grand jury at the last Q.S.[1] Further proceedings are adjourned to the next Q.S. because of the current sickness and the danger from a gathering of people if the Q.S. continues any longer.

3. And. Stringer of Culham, yeoman, bound by recogn. in the sum of £20 to prosecute Wm. Pemberton at the next Q.S. for the felony of stealing a sack of grain.

4. Wm. Pemberton of the psh. of St. Thos., boatman, bound by recogn. in the sum of £20 to appear and answer at the next Q.S. and not leave without licence. Ric. Hartley of Oxf., cordwainer, bound for him in the sum of £10.

5. The distressed condition of [blank] Stanley, a sawyer, was consid- p. 221 ered. He has lived in the psh. of St. Mary Magdalen for forty years and has been turned out of his home and uncharitably left to live out of doors. The overseers of the psh. are to find a home for him in the psh.

6. Dr. James spoke of the dispute between Mrs. Wallis and her two sons. It is to be heard and determined by the Vice-Chancellor and Ald. Smyth.

7. Ric. Bradshawe to be bound over again for his good behaviour. He is to be attached by warrant and committed until he finds sureties.

8. Jn. Vaughan is to find sureties for his good behaviour or be committed.

9. Jn. Hamlyn and Griffin Joyne are to be committed until they find sureties for their appearance at the next Q.S. and good behaviour in the meantime.

10. The dispute between Mr. Giles Swett and Mr. Jn. Sowe and Ric. Budworth, his tenant, is referred to the Vice-Chancellor and the Mayor by consent of the parties. They are to consider Mr. Swett's

[1] A comment here 'but this Court conceaved that there is muche malice in the pros-ecution' was later struck through.

127

complaint that Budworth, a butcher, keeps hogs and throws their offal into a narrow place adjoining Mr. Swett's garden near his house and chamber windows. If they can, they are to mediate between them and, if not, set down a settlement which all parties have agreed in open court to obey.

p. 222 **11.** Ric. Hearne of Binsey bound by recogn. in the sum of £20 to appear at the next Q.S. and prosecute Thos. Peirs for stealing a grey mare.

**12.** Thos. Peirs of Oxf., baker, bound by recogn. in the sum of £20 to appear and answer at the next Q.S. and not leave without licence.

**13.** Griffin Joyne of Oxf., butcher, bound by recogn. in the sum of £20 to appear and answer at the next Q.S. and not leave without licence. Jn. Ball and Jn. Carter sureties in the sum of £10 each.

**14.** Rob. Ketteridg allowed to victual for a year.

**15.** Jn. Vaughan of Oxf., chamberlain, bound by recogn. in the sum of £20 to appear and answer at the next Q.S., not to leave without licence and to be of good behaviour. Geo. Vaughan, cutler, and Edw. Davies, brewer, bound for him in the sum of £10 each.

**16.** Hen. Harbert of the psh. of St. Giles and Wm. Mundy of Oxf., butcher, bound in the sum of £20 to bring Jn. Hamlyn to appear and answer at the next Q.S.

## [1626A]

p. 223 Quarter Sessions at the Guildhall Thurs. 12 Jan. 1626. Jn. Prudeaux D.D., Vice-Chancellor, Hen. Bosworth esq., Mayor, Wm. Peirs, Dean of Peterborough, Jn. Rawlingson D.D., Wm. Langton D.D., Thos. James D.D., [*blank*] Smyth D.D., Jn. Hawley D.C.L., Thos. Flexney esq., Thos. Harris ald., Wm. Potter ald., Wm. Wright ald., Oliver Smyth ald., J.P.s.

**1.** Ric. Garraway (Garway) appeared on his recogn. taken before Ald. Wright because of suspicions of how he came by five gold rings which he sold. He is to be discharged as he produced testimonials of his honesty from Mr. Peter Hayward, a Westminster J.P., and various other burgesses and inhabitants there.

**2.** Griffin Gyne appeared on his recogn. and is discharged. The court accepted his submission in hope of his future behaviour.

**3.** Edw. Tomlyns (Tomlins), carpenter, appeared on his recogn. for wounding a maid with his axe and cutting her hand. He is discharged as she is reconciled and did not prosecute.

**4.** Margaret Benford's petition concerning her dispute with Ric. Wardell was read in court. Dr. Bancroft and Dr. Rawlingson are to mediate or order a settlement.

**5.** In the matter of a petition from the inhabitants of St. Clements concerning one Hollyman and his sureties, Pownall and Biggnell, the parties did not appear. Their recogns. are to be estreated.

**6.** The case of Joan Hussey and her daughter, who was delivered of    p. 224
a child which was left in a window at Christ Church, was heard. The court cannot proceed as the daughter is deaf and dumb. The advice of the Assize Judges for the county of Oxon. is to be sought, as ordered for cases of difficulty by the King's commission.

**7.** A warrant to be made out for the appearance of Jn. Pownall and Fulk Biggnell.

**8.** Edw. Fincher discharged after he appeared on his recogn. and no prosecution was brought.

**9.** Mrs. Mary Bartholmew appeared on an indictment as a recusant. She asked for a fortnight to take advice and promised to conform to the rule of the Church of England and receive Holy Communion.

**10.** On examination Ric. Garraway was found to be such a lewd fellow that he is to be committed until he finds sureties for his appearance at the next Q.S.

**11.** A warrant to be made out for Agnes Daniell to be bound to appear at the next Q.S.

**12.** An indictment was found against Thos. Peirce for a trespass. It was considered to be only an error and of no consequence, and he is fined 12d.

**13.** One Chapman of Holywell received £8 from the psh. of St. Giles    p. 225
to bring up two children and stop them being a burden on the psh. He is now dead and his wife threatens to return them to the psh. Either she is to keep the children or repay the £8.

**14.** Ric. Lewis of Oxf., tailor, bound in the sum of £20 to bring [*blank*] to appear at the next Q.S. and meanwhile keep the peace especially towards Ann, wife of Edw. Williams.

**15.** Mrs. Frances Potter took the Oath of Allegiance under the statute of 3 Jas. cap. 4 in open court after being accused of recusancy.

**16.** Jn. Hamlyn discharged.

**17.** Beatrice Cox, servant of Mrs. Tilliard, bound by recogn. in the sum of £20 to appear at the next Q.S. and prosecute Wm. Read *alias* Oseney and his wife for felony.

**18.** Fawrd (Ford) committed for saucy and rude speeches and behaviour in court. He is to be whipped and brought back to the court for a further order.

**19.** Ralph Gonsborn allowed to continue victualling.

p. 226 **20.** The recogns. of Wm. Blysset and Jn. Harris forfeit for not bringing in Thos. Hawthorne, Blissett's apprentice.

**21.** A promise to be made out against Hen. Pemerton for not appearing on an indictment for felony.

**22.** Nat. Wymake (Wymack), 'standing mute', is reprieved until the next Q.S.

**23.** Nic. Cope to be whipped next market day in open market time.

**24.** Thos. Elzey and Rob. Wixon allowed to continue victualling.

## [1626B]

p. 227 Quarter Sessions at the Guildhall Thurs. 20 April 1626. Jn. Prideaux D.D., Vice-Chancellor, Hen. Bosworth esq., Mayor, Jn. Bancrofte D.D., Thos. James D.D., Jn. Whistler esq., Thos. Flexney esq., Thos. Harris ald., Wm. Potter ald., Wm. Wright ald., J.P.s.

**1.** A note under the hand of Thos. Clerk of the barbarous and lewd behaviour of Ann, wife of Jn. Daniell (Danyell), towards Dr. Hawley was read in court. The Vice-Chancellor and Mr. Flexney are to call Ann Danyell, Thos. Clarke and Brian Dyamond before them. If Ann Danyell is shown on oath to be guilty or if Diamond is found to have accused her falsely the referees shall order a suitable punishment.

**2.** Edw. Tomlyns, glover, indicted by Jn. Wythers (Withers), is found guilty by the jury of assaulting him and fined 12d.

**3.** Wm. Lovegrove is fined 6d. after being indicted and found guilty of breaking and taking away an iron chain belonging to the city bailiffs near the bridge by Fish Row.

**4.** Ric. Astell was indicted and found guilty by the grand jury of p. 228 assaulting Jn. Hunt, a constable, but did not appear and a process of outlawry is to be made out against him. A warrant to be made out to attach him so he can be bound to appear at the next Q.S. and answer for misbehaviour towards Ald. Harris.

**5.** Jn. Wythers (Withers) to be attached by warrant and bound to appear at the next Q.S. after he appeared on his recogn. and left without licence.

**6.** Wm. Powell indicted and found guilty of assaulting Ric. Heminges, one of the officers and bailiff's serjeants of the city while he was on duty. He is to be fined 20s. and stay in prison until he pays the fine and the court's fees.

**7.** The dispute between Widow Tooley and Mr. Ric. Whetstone (Whetston) was heard, and out of compassion for the poor woman and after being entreated by the court Ric. agreed to pay her 30s. in a year and a half, at a rate of 5s. per quarter from next Midsummer. If she dies before or during that term the payments are to be cancelled. It was also agreed between them that the payments are to cease if it is proved before a J.P. that she has misbehaved towards him, either to his face or behind his back.

**8.** Rob. Williams, who was imprisoned for stealing poles from men's p. 229 coppices, confessed and is to be whipped in the market place during this Q.S.

**9.** All ministers and churchwardens of the city and suburbs to publish a notice in their churches that all sports at Whitsuntide and meetings on such occasions are to be prohibited this year because of the danger of infection. Any offenders to be bound over by the next J.P. to answer at the next Q.S.

**10.** Rob. Humfreis and Phil. Pulcher allowed to victual for a year.

**11.** Last year's collectors and overseers of the poor to bring in their accounts on 16 May.

**12.** Ric. Myles *alias* Astell of Oxf., tailor, bound in the sum of £20 to appear and answer at the next Q.S. and not leave without licence from the court. If he complies this recogn. will be void. If not it is to retain its full force. Thos. Wells of Oxf., saddler, and Ant. Croke of Oxf., cutler, sureties in the sum of £10 each.

# [1626c]

p. 230  Quarter Sessions at the Guildhall Thurs. 8 June 1626. Jn. Prudeaux, Vice-Chancellor, Hen. Bosworth esq., Mayor, Thos. James D.D., Thos. Flexney esq., Wm. Potter ald., Oliver Smyth ald., Jn. Bird gent., J.P.s.

**1.** Each man who was returned as a grand juror and did not appear to be fined 2s. 6d. Mr. Ric. Clyffe of the George to be fined 5s. or saying he would not come, as the constable testified.

**2.** Jn. Blunt fined 3s. for swearing three oaths. For his misbehaviour in court especially towards Dr. James he is to be bound for his good behaviour, be committed in the meantime and spend today in prison.

**3.** The bond to young Hales is committed in trust to Ald. Potter.

**4.** Thos. Wytall (Witall) is indicted and found guilty of battery of Agnes, wife of Wm. Rainsford. He is to be imprisoned until he pays his fine of 2s. 6d. and his fees.

p. 231  **5.** An order to be published in each psh. church for the churchwardens and overseers to be bound on pain of 5s. for each default to give a certificate of each newcomer or inmate in a cottage, house or tenement to the next J.P. or at the latest at the next Q.S. on pain of 10s. Warrants to be made out for collections for the poor.

**6.** Mr. Geo. Chambers refuses to enter bonds with sureties to free the city from any charge from the present and future inhabitants of the cottage he has recently erected, as ordered by the Privy Council. A certificate to be sent to the council, as is required.

**7.** Geo. Chambers of Oxf., bookbinder, bound by recogn. in the sum of £200 on condition that he, his heirs, executors and assignees free the Univ., the City and all its pshs. of any charge from the present and future inhabitants, tenants or inmates of his cottages and tenements or any built in the future. If he does so his recogn. to be void, if not, the sum of £200 to be levied from his lands, tenements, goods and chattels. [*Entry struck through*]

[*Margin*] At a special meeting 24 Feb. 1631 of Thos. Cooper esq., Mayor, Jn. Tolson, Deputy Vice-Chancellor, Jn. Banckroft D.D., Sam. Radcliffe D.D., Wm. Potter ald., Oliver Smyth ald., Hen. Bosworth ald. it was agreed that Mr. Chambers's recogn. shall be void as he has entered a new recogn. of £20 for the same purpose. [*Signed*] Carter.[1]

---

[1] Tim. Carter, town clerk.

**8.** Thos. Wildgoose of Oxf., carpenter, bound by recogn. in the sum of £200 as in 1626C7.

**9.** Jas. Deane of Oxf., gent., bound in the sum of £200 as in 1626C7   p. 232 'during the minority'. [*Entry struck through*]

[*Margin*] At a special meeting 8 March 1631 of Thos. Cooper esq., Mayor, Jn. Bancrofte D.D., Jn. Prideaux D.D., Dr. Pincke D.D., Chas. Halloway esq., Ald. Potter, Ald.Wright, Ald. Smyth, Ald. Boswell, Jas. Chesterman gent., Jn. Willmott gent. it was agreed that Mr. Deane's recogn. shall be void as he has entered a new recogn. of £20 for the same purpose. [*Entry struck through*]

[*Margin*] Thurs. after the feast of Trinity [i.e. 9 June] 1631 the said recogn. of £20 is also made void by consent of Dr. Smyth and Thos. Cooper esq., Mayor. [*Signed*] Tim. Carter, Town Clerk.

**10.** Thos. Norland and his wife, Joan, indicted and found guilty by the grand jury of trespass and taking away the bond of £6 binding Jn. Measey to Chris. Horne. They said they were not guilty but accepted a fine of 6d. each to avoid the cost of a traverse.

**11.** Chris. Cruch (Crouch) indicted for murdering Simon Manthrop, a child of nine, with an iron pin. The jury for life and death found it to be manslaughter on evidence given that he was crazy or distracted.

**12.** Jn. Newman had been bound by Mr. Bird to appear with his wife and answer. He is discharged as no prosecution was brought.

**13.** Ric. Morris to be apprehended by warrant.

**14.** Thos. Simondes indicted for stealing a brass pot, an old brass posnet [cooking pot] and certain pewter dishes from Thos. Keene of Woodstock, and found guilty by the petty jury of petty larceny to the value of 10d. As the court thinks he is a lewd fellow and a thief he is to be whipped at the post next Saturday until he bleeds and to be sent to Woodstock with a copy of this order so the Mayor of Woodstock can have him well whipped again next Tuesday.

**15.** Rob. Rainsford to be bound for his good behaviour and to give   p. 233 Keene of Woodstock his goods back in return for what he paid for them.

**16.** Dr. James and Ald. Smyth are to examine the complaint made by Ald. Harris at the last Q.S. against Ric. Myles *alias* Astell on information from Jn. Hunt, and punish whichever is at fault.

**17.** Hutchins's children to be sent to London. Warrants to be made out for the cost to be collected from the pshs.: St. Ebbe 13s. 4d., St. Martin 6s. 8d., St. Mary Magdalen 6s. 8d., All Saints 3s. 4d., St. Mary 3s. 4d.

**18.** The court considered the complaint about the erection of cottages and receiving and harbouring of inmates, and the order of 4 Jan. 1625 from the Privy Council. Each J.P. is to call the churchwardens and overseers of the poor before him to give an account of the cottages, inmates and newcomers and a note of their landlords' names so they can be removed according to the power given by the Privy Council order.

**19.** Jn. Blunt of Oxf., mercer, bound by recogn. in the sum of £10 to appear at the next Q.S. and meanwhile behave well, especially towards Dr. James. The recogn. taken in the presence of Hen. Bosworth, Mayor, and Oliver Smyth ald.

## [1626D]

p. 234 Quarter Sessions Thurs. 5 Oct. 1626. Wm. Juxon D.D., Vice-Chancellor, Jn. Dewe esq., Mayor, Thos. James D.D., Jn. Whistler esq., Thos. Harris ald., Wm. Potter ald., Wm. Wright ald., Oliver Smyth ald., J.P.s.

**1.** All grand jurors who failed to appear to be fined 3s. 4d.

**2.** Thos. Miller appeared on his recogn. on the prosecution of Thos. Noble and is discharged as no further prosecution was brought.

**3.** Ric. Price, lathrender, to be imprisoned until Saturday as a notorious drunkard and lewd fellow and then whipped.

**4.** Ric. Morris's recogn. to be estreated.

**5.** Ald. Harris and Ald. Wright to consider the petition of Rob. Jenings and his wife and order the churchwardens of the psh. of St. Mic. to provide for them.

**6.** Thos. Profitt, a constable of St. Giles, to be committed during the pleasure of the court for neglecting his office, not obeying a warrant from a J.P., throwing away a pass and allowing a lewd woman sent with her pass to go back to the psh. of St. Mary Magdalen.

**7.** Wm. Arnold, the keeper of Bocardo, fined 10s. for not attending the court when offenders were committed.

p. 235 **8.** Rob. Huett and Ric. Morris discharged.

**9.** A warrant for Vincent Ranckle (Rancklyn) to appear tomorrow to answer for receiving inmates.

**10.** A warrant for old Worley and his son to appear.

**11.** Warrants for Hawley and Old Moore to appear.

**12.** The Vice-Chancellor and the Mayor to consider and determine the petition from Eliz. Shann which was referred to them by Mr. Justice Doddridg and read in court.

**13.** The churchwardens and constables of each psh. are to collect and deliver to the treasurer for maimed soldiers the sums due under the statute by St. Luke's Day without further procrastination.

**14.** Jn. Blunt to be released paying his fees or be apprehended by warrant.

**15.** The churchwardens of Holywell to provide a house for Kath. Hunt, a poor woman who has been turned out of her house there, and collect 40s. in the psh. paying her half on St. Thomas's Day and half on Lady Day towards her arrears.

**16.** A process of outlawry to be made out against Wm. Pemerton for several indictments.

**17.** The grand jury found *ignoramus*[1] on an indictment against Wm. Steevens for stealing six silver plates and six silver spoons. Nevertheless he is to be committed to prison until he finds good sureties for his good behaviour because of his 'lewd course' of life.

**18.** A process of outlawry against Ric. Morris.　　　　　　　p. 236

**19.** Mr. Geo. Chambers undertook that Wm. Page would appear tomorrow morning.

**20.** The churchwardens of the psh. of St. Peter-le-Bailey to make their collection for the poor by All Hallows or be punished according to the statute.

**21.** Chris. Attwood to be whipped next market day after being convicted of breaking windows at Pembroke College.

**22.** Nic. Berry, the constable of South-West ward, to be fined 5s. and imprisoned for twenty-four hours, after being convicted of neglecting his duties and throwing a warrant from a J.P. down in the street with bad language.

---

[1] See note to 1623C20.

**23.** Old. Thos. Worley to send his son, his wife and two children from the psh. of St. Mary Magdalen to the psh. of St. Giles where they lived for the last two years or be committed to prison until the Mayor or another J.P. orders otherwise.

**24.** Ric. Dice to be fined 20s., imprisoned for a day and not released until he pays after the jury found an indictment for disorderly behaviour and breaking glass windows at night. A process to be made out against the other parties cited.

**25.** Wm. Fletcher, gent., to be fined 2s. 6d. and imprisoned during the pleasure of the court after the jury found an indictment for setting up a wall which narrowed Shoe Lane. Processes to be issued against other offenders indicted with him.

p. 237 **26.** Wm. Page of the psh. of St. Thos., boatman, bound in the sum of £40 to appear and answer at the next Q.S. Rog. Blackman of Abingdon, glover, and Hen. Munday of the psh. of St. Thos., boatman, bound for him in the sum of £20 each.

**27.** Rog. Blackman of Abingdon, glover, bound in the sum of £40 to appear and answer at the next Q.S.

**28.** Alex Hill jun. allowed to victual for a year.

## [1627A]

p. 238 Quarter Sessions at the Guildhall Thurs. 11 Jan. 1627. Wm. Juxon, Vice-Chancellor, Jn. Dewe esq., Mayor, Thos. James D.D., Jn. Rawlinson D.D., Wm. Peirs D.D., Thos. Flexney esq., Jn. Whistler esq., Thos. Harris ald., Wm. Potter ald., Wm. Wright ald., J.P.s.

**1.** Dr. Rawlinson and Ald. Potter to settle the dispute between Christian Mumford and Mrs. Peto.

**2.** Cecilia Tomes (Toms) to be provided for according to the statute after her complaint that she had lived in the psh. of St. Mary for three years but now had nowhere to live.

**3.** Bernard Hawe, glover, and Jn. Browne, mercer, churchwardens of the psh. of St. Mary, to be bound for their good behaviour for contempt to the warrant issued by the Mayor and Mr. Whistler telling them to receive Cecilia Toms.

**4.** Mr. Jones the Registrar's complaint about excessive taxes on his part of a tenement in the psh. of St. Mary Magdalen is referred to the decision of the Vice-Chancellor.

136

**5.** Wm. King of Oxf., rider,[1] bound by recogn. in the sum of £20  p. 239
to appear at the next Q.S. and be of good behaviour. Lewis Price,
yeoman, and Jn. West of Oxf. bound for him in the sum of £10
each.

**6.** Jn. Browne, cutter, appeared on his recogn.

**7.** Jn. Allam, bookbinder, appeared on his recogn. on the prosecution
of Mr. Thos. Charles. The grand jury found an indictment for trespass
and entering Charles's house, and Allam submitted and is fined 12d.

**8.** Jn. Allam of Oxf., stationer, bound by recogn. in the sum of £40
to appear at the next Q.S. and keep the peace especially towards Anne
Allam. Thos. Swadlinge of Kidlington, Berks. [*recte* Oxon.] and Jn.
Addams of Oxf., bookbinder, bound for him in the sum of £20
each.

**9.** Wm. Holmes (Holms), who was licensed to victual at Binsey, can
continue to victual in the psh. of St. Peter-le-Bailey where he now
lives. Ralph Hodges (Hodgs) allowed to victual for a year.

**10.** Thos. Cogan of Oxf., gent., is bound by recogn. in the sum of
£20 to prosecute his traverse to the indictment found against him on
the prosecution of Jn. Hunt.

**11.** Jn. Addams, indicted and found guilty by the grand jury, is fined
3s. 4d. for assaulting Ann, wife of Jn. Allam.

**12.** Jn. Marigold, formerly of Lincoln Coll., is found guilty of
murdering Rob. Ewen and a process of outlawry is to be issued. Later
he was removed by *habeas corpus*, tried by the Assize Judges and burnt
on the hand.

**13.** The Aldermen to consider the petition for the relief of the psh. of  p. 240
St. Mary Magdalen.

**14.** Geo. Dwight appeared on his recogn., having been bound to
behave well and answer for his scandalous words and behaviour to
his former mistress, Mrs. Stonehouse of Radley, a gentlewoman of
known integrity who relieved him from misery. His humble and
repentant submission was accepted by her and no offence since
then has been proved so the court admonished him and he is to be
discharged in hope of his future behaviour.

---

[1] A rider may have been (as in the 18th century) a kind of commercial traveller or
bagman, delivering for another merchant.

**15.** Jn. Durant and Thos. Stacy to be bound for their good behaviour and be committed until they find sureties.

**16.** Jn. Browne, cutter, and Vincent Rancklin (Rancklyn) to be bound for their good behaviour.

**17.** Jane Crooke and Vincent Rancklin's daughter to be sent to the House of Correction.

**18.** Chris. Gibbons not to victual for three years and to be apprehended by warrant for unlicensed victualling.

**19.** All recusants presented by the grand jury to be proceeded against according to the statute.

**20.** All unlicensed victuallers to be proceeded against.

**21.** Wm. Lee of the psh. of St. Peter-le-Bailey bound by recogn. in the sum of £20 to give evidence against Ellis Kinge for stealing a bridle from Dr. Peirce, the Dean of Peterborough.

**22.** Edw. Rowse of Oxf., yeoman, bound by recogn. in the sum of £20 to prosecute Ellis Kinge for stealing Dr. Pearce's bridle.

**23.** Jn. Ewen and his wife, Mary, to be sent to the House of Correction.

p. 241 **24.** Francis Browne, indicted and found guilty by the jury of life and death of taking five beasts from Mr. Tim. Gates, is to be reprieved and remain in prison until the next Q.S. so that a record of conviction alleged to exist in Gloucs. can be obtained and he can then be punished correctly.

**25.** Jn. Browne of Oxf., cutter, bound by recogn. in the sum of £40 to appear at the next Q.S. and meanwhile be of good behaviour. Wm. Roberts of Kidlington, gent., and Rog. Brookes of the psh. of All Saints, tailor, bound for him in the sum of £20 each.

**26.** Thos. Charles of Oxf., musician, bound in the sum of £40 to appear at the next Q.S. and meanwhile be of good behaviour. Jn. Baldwyne of Oxf., musician, and Edw. Tomlyns of Oxf., wheelwright, bound for him in the sum of £20 each.

## [1627B]

p. 242 Quarter Sessions at the Guildhall Thurs. 5 April 1627. Wm. Juxon D.D., Vice-Chancellor, Jn. Dew esq., Mayor, Thos. James D.D., Jn. Whistler esq., Thos. Flexney esq., Thos. Harris gent., Wm. Potter ald., Wm. Wright ald., Oliver Smyth ald., J.P.s.

**1.** It was testified on oath that all men returned to serve on the grand jury had been lawfully summoned. Each man who did not appear to be fined 2s. 6d. for contempt.

**2.** Ellis King, against whom Edw. Rowse was bound to prosecute, has been sent to be a soldier at the last press. The prosecution and Rowse's recogn. are therefore dispensed with.

**3.** Warrants to be made out for Ric. Butler of Blue Boar Lane, Rob. Bryan and Wm. Carpenter of the psh. of St. Mary Magdalen to be apprehended for unlicensed victualling.

**4.** Wm. King who appeared on his recogn. discharged as no prosecution was brought.

**5.** Thos. Charles and Jn. Allam discharged of their recogns.                      p. 243

**6.** Eleanor Croft(e) appeared on her recogn. and is discharged.

**7.** Wal. Tanner appeared on his recogn. and is discharged.

**8.** Wm. Kymberley, who was bound by recogn. to appear for unlicensed victualling, confessed and is fined 20s. according to the statute. He is discharged as he entered into a bond not to victual.

**9.** Thos. Fishe (Fyshe) of the psh. of St. Nic. *alias* St. Thos. appeared on his recogn. and was bound in the sum of £20 to appear and answer at the next Q.S. and not leave without licence. Wm. Huett of Oxf., cutler, and Wm. Huntley of Oxf., weelmaker, sureties for £10 each.

**10.** Jn. Browne, cutter, who had been presented at the last Q.S. for keeping a 'house of incontinencie', confessed and was fined £5 and ordered to find sureties for his good behaviour. The fine is reduced to 20s., although he does not deserve this, but he is to pay immediately.

**11.** Phil. Beadow indicted and found guilty of breaking glass windows   p. 244
at Edw. Willyams's house in the psh. of St. Mary Magdalen. He is to be fined 3s. 4d. and bound for his good behaviour.

**12.** Nic. Gardner, joiner, and his servant Rob. Palmer, labourer, discharged after the jury did not find an indictment for assaulting Wm. Mundy.

**13.** The jury found an indictment against Griffin Joyne for rescuing Simon Fox(e) from arrest by two constables, Thos. Steevens and Thos. Mynne, on a warrant from Dr. James J.P. He is fined 2s. 6d.

**14.** Phil. Beadow of Oxf., tailor, bound by recogn. in the sum of £40 to appear and answer at the next Q.S., not to leave without licence and meanwhile be of good behaviour. Ant. Chafforne of Oxf., ostler, and Thos. Nobes of Oxf., shoemaker, sureties for £20 each.

**15.** The following referees are to call last year's overseers of the poor before them so that their accounts can be taken, all arrears collected, and new overseers named:

the Mayor and Dr. James – the pshs. of St. Giles, Holywell and St. Mary Magdalen.

Mr. Harris and Ald. Smyth – St. Mic., St. Martin and St. Aldate.

Dr. Bancrofte and Ald. Potter – St. Mary, St Peter-in-the-East and All Saints.

Ald. Wright and Mr. Boswell – St. Peter-le-Bailey, St. Ebbe, St. Thos. and Binsey.

p. 245 **16.** Francis Browne was indicted and found guilty by the jury of life and death at the last Q.S. of stealing five young heifers from Tim. Gates esq. of Gloucs. but judgement was reserved. No other accusation was made at this Q.S. He claimed benefit of clergy, was burnt on the hand and discharged.

**17.** Jn. Browne of Oxf., cutter, bound by recogn. in the sum of £40 to appear at the next Q.S. and meanwhile be of good behaviour. Ric. Lewys of Oxf., tailor, and Thos. Collyns of Oxf., baker, sureties for £20 each.

## [1627c]

p. 246 Quarter Sessions at the Guildhall Thurs. 24 May 1627. [*Bench not named*]

**1.** The constable of North and South Osney to be fined 5s., which is not to be remitted, for not appearing or returning his precept.

**2.** Jn. Price and Jn. Beate, churchwardens of the psh. of St. Aldate, complained that Jn. Gardner, blacksmith, had taken a stranger with a pregnant wife as an inmate and not given surety to the psh. He is to have them removed within a fortnight on pain of 10s. or be committed to prison until this order is performed. The same order is made for Rob. Wickson who had taken an inmate.

**3.** The court heard Jn. Slatford and Jn. Blunt, examined their witnesses and considered their dispute. Jn. Slatford to be discharged of his recogn. and Jn. Blunt to enter recogn. with sureties to appear at the next Q.S. and meanwhile be of good behaviour.

**4.** Jn. Browne, cutter, to be committed to Bocardo until he enters  p. 247
recogn. with good sureties to appear at the next Q.S. and meanwhile
behave well, after his very bad behaviour to the city bailiffs and their
officer was proved.

**5.** Michael, wife of Jn. Browne, as in 1627C4, for the same offence.

**6.** Jn. Browne to remain in prison for three days and be fined 20s.
for unlicensed victualling. Before release he is to enter recogn. not to
victual without a licence.

**7.** Ric. Goddard, carpenter, appeared on his recogn. and is discharged
as the objections against him were weak.

**8.** Thos. Cox and Dorothy Edwards allowed to victual and Wm.
Tailor to have his licence renewed. Warrants to be made out against
Thos. Edwards and Wm. Blea on bills found against them at the
Michaelmas Q.S. A process of outlawry to be made out against
Crooke.

**9.** Thos. Fish appeared on his recogn. and is discharged. Avis Stockwell to be released from prison.

**10.** Jn. Blunt of Oxf., mercer, bound by recogn. in the sum of £40 to
appear and answer at the next Q.S. and meanwhile be of good behaviour. Jn. Bannister of Oxf., shoemaker, and Ric. West of Oxf., cordwainer, sureties for £20 each.

## [1627D]

Quarter Sessions at the Guildhall Thurs. 4 Oct. 1627. Wm. Juxon,  p. 248
Vice-Chancellor, Jn. Sare esq., Mayor, Jn. Whistler esq., Jn. Prudeaux
D.D., Thos. James D.D., Jn. Bancroft D.D., Wm. Peirs D.D., Thos.
Flexney esq., Thos. Harris esq., Wm. Potter ald., Wm. Wright ald.,
Oliver Smyth ald., J.P.s.

**1.** Hen. Burgis to find sureties on the prosecution of Jn. Crutch.

**2.** Ric. Hearne of Oxf., gunsmith, bound in the sum of £20 to bring
his wife, Anne, to answer at the next Q.S.

**3.** Hen. Burgis of Oxf., plasterer, bound in the sum of £20 to appear
at the next Q.S. and keep the peace especially towards Jn. Cruch.
Wm. Lee, sawyer ('saier'), and Ric. Lee, millwright, are sureties for
£10 each.

**4.** Rob. Johnson discharged from his apprenticeship with Widow
Bland, cooper.

**5.** Thos. and Jn. Arpin to find sureties for the peace.

**6.** Ric. Astell *alias* Miles to pay a fine of 10s. and his fees after being found guilty when his traverse was tried.

**7.** Thos. Arpin of Oxf., tinker, bound in the sum of £20 to appear at the next Q.S. and keep the peace towards Edm. Blythe, Wm. Ewen and Ric. Syks. Jn. Arpin, brazier, and Rob. Ewstace, tailor, are sureties for £10 each.

p. 249   **8.** Jn. Arpin of Oxf., brazier, bound in the sum of £20 to appear at the next Q.S. and keep the peace towards Edw. Blithe, Wm. Ewen and Ric. Syks. Thos. Arpin, tinker, and Thos. Ewstace, tailor, are sureties for £10 each.

**9.** Francis Burnham of Oxf., tailor, bound in the sum of £20 to appear and answer at the next Q.S. and meanwhile obey the orders of the Company of Tailors. Thos. Dodge of Oxf., glover, and Hugh Shawe of Oxf., tailor, are sureties for £10 each.

**10.** Wm. Palmer indicted and found guilty of trespass for stealing a pair of shoes from Mr. Wm. Arnold. He is fined 6d. as he is a very poor boy.

**11.** Peter Tilliard found guilty and fined 3s. 4d. on each of two indictments for battering Jane Ashe several times.

**12.** Kath. Badger found guilty and fined 12d. on each of two indictments for battery. She is to be committed until she pays her fines and fees, then to be whipped and have a pass.

**13.** Chris. Tomlinson, Rob. Chittredge and Wm. Todmorton to have new licences.

**14.** All former orders against Jn. Browne, cutter, and his wife, Michael, to be enforced.

p. 250   **15.** A fine of 20s. to be paid to the old bailiffs[1] for not delivering to them copies of three orders under the hands of two J.P.s against Jn. Browne and Michael, his wife.

**16.** Wm. Hudson and Thos. Deane to have licences to victual.

**17.** The recogns. of Wm. Meeke, Barnaby Scudamore, Patrick Breeze, Jn. Weaver, Thos. Shirle, Rob. Hasleigh, Jn. Allam, Thos. Allam, Jn. Peirs, Rob. Wixon, Rob. Kirtland, Ric. Astell and Nat. Kirtland to be estreated.

---

[1] It is not clear who was fined.

**18.** Avis Stockwell to be discharged paying her fees after the jury found her not guilty of felony.

**19.** Nic. Cruch[1] appeared at the bar, claimed benefit of clergy, was burnt on the hand and discharged.

**20.** Agnes, wife of Wm. Dunslett, Kath. Dunslett, and Mary Dunslett appeared on their recogns., were indicted, found guilty and fined 3s. 4d. each for riot and battery.

**21.** The wife of Thos. Collins (Collyns) discharged and to be released from prison.

**22.** Some of the J.P.s affirmed that the psh. of Holywell was about twenty years behind in its payments for the relief of maimed soldiers. The churchwardens and overseers of the poor of the psh. are to collect the arrears by St. Thos. the Apostle's day.

**23.** Agnes, wife of Jn. Slatford, who was indicted as a scold, asked to p. 251 be admitted to her traverse.

**24.** A process to be made out for Geo. Wilson and his wife to take the Oath of Allegiance at the next Q.S.

**25.** The same process to be made out against all recusants.

## [1628A]

Quarter Sessions at the Guildhall [undated, probably Jan. 1628]. Wm. p. 252 Juxon, Vice-Chancellor, Jn. Sare esq., Mayor, Jn. Rawlingson D.D., Jn. Prideaux D.D., Thos. James D.D., Wm. Peirs D.D., Jn. Whistler esq., Thos. Flexney esq., Chas. Holloway esq., Thos. Harris ald., Wm. Potter ald., Wm. Wright ald., Oliver Smyth ald., J.P.s.

**1.** The parishioners of Holywell are to be discharged from their arrears on payment of 40s. to their churchwardens.

**2.** Jn. Price not to victual and to be committed until he pays 20s. to the bailiffs or makes his peace with them.

**3.** Francis Burnham appeared on his recogn. and was found guilty on an indictment for working as a tailor without serving seven years as an apprentice. He was admitted to his traverse.

**4.** Ric. Astell *alias* Miles refused in open court to retain his appren- p. 253 tice, Wm. Powell, after six years of his apprenticeship, which would

---

[1] Probably a clerical error for Chris. Crutch, convicted in 1626 of manslaughter but not sentenced at that time, presumably because of his insanity: cf. above, 1626c11.

prevent Wm. from getting his freedom.[1] Astell is ordered to take him back for the full term in his indentures.

**5.** Wm. Wright of the psh. of St. Thos. to be licensed to victual for a year.

**6.** Ann, wife of Jn. Slatford, cutler, was found guilty by the grand jury at the last Q.S. on an indictment as a common scold but was admitted to her traverse. She is discharged after the jury found her not guilty on evidence in open court.

**7.** Thos. and Jn. Arpyn discharged after they appeared on their recogns. and no further prosecution was brought.

**8.** An indictment for carnal knowledge of a boy was found against Jn. Peirce by the grand jury. He was found not guilty by the petty jury but is to find good sureties for his good behaviour.

**9.** Indictments against Thos. Preston for stealing a cloak and Jos. Godwyn for stealing several books and a pair of boots were found by the grand jury but they were acquitted by the jury for life and death.

**10.** Warrants to be made out against all unlicensed victuallers presented under the statute and directed to two J.P.s. Also warrants against drunkards, hide gashers and those who did not appear on their recogns.

## [1628B]

p. 254   Quarter Sessions at the Guildhall Thurs. 24 April 1628. Jn. Sare esq., Mayor, Jn. Prideaux D.D., Thos. James D.D., Jn. Whistler esq., Thos. Flexney esq., Chas. Holloway esq., Wm. Potter ald., Oliver Smyth ald., J.P.s.

**1.** Mary, wife of Jn. Ewen, to be sent to the House of Correction until the next Q.S. without bail. Jn. Ewen to be committed to prison for three days without bail for unlicensed victualling and before release to be bound with two sureties not to keep an alehouse.

**2.** Thos. Wirley as for Jn. Ewen in 1628B1.

**3.** Geo. Cowles to be whipped for vagrancy and have a pass.

**4.** Wm. Barton was accused of rape by his daughter, Marie, but the indictment was found *ignoramus*.[2] He is to bring a certificate from the most substantial men of his psh. to the Mayor or be bound to appear at the next Q.S. and meanwhile behave well.

---

[1] A comment, 'which this Court doth take in very ill parte', is struck through.
[2] See note to 1623C20.

[*Margin*] He did not bring the certificate, so is bound.

**5.** Marie Barton 'for the like' is to be committed to prison until she finds sureties for her good behaviour. [*Margin*] Later brought a certificate.

**6.** Geo. Shirt, a maimed soldier pressed from Oxf., to have 40s. a year.

**7.** Thos. Browne to be bound to appear at the next Q.S. for his malicious and causeless prosecution of Rob. Duke, musician, concerning a hatband. Meanwhile to behave well. [*Margin*] Later brought a certificate.

**8.** Thos. Price to be punished as a common drunkard.

**9.** [*blank*] Withers, Thos. Monson [?], Miles Godfrey, Wal. Holbidge, Rog. Stevens the elder, Thos. [*damage*], Thos. Collins, Thos. Fitche, Widow Frenche, Nat. Cooper, Wm. Tommes [?], Widow [*damage*], Thos. Sadler, Ralph Goldesbourne and Edw. Williams presented as unlicensed victuallers and warrants to be made out for them to be bound according to the statute.

**10.** Hen. Southam, gent., to be Treasurer for the year[1] in place of   p. 255
Hen. Bosworth.

# [1628c]

Quarter Sessions at the Guildhall Thurs. after Trinity [12 June 1628]. Wm. Juxon, Vice-Chancellor, Jn. Sare esq., Mayor, Jn. Rawlinson D.D., Jn. Prideaux D.D., Thos. James D.D., Thos. Flexney esq., Wm. Potter ald., Wm. Wright ald., J.P.s.

**1.** Warrants to be made out for Thos. Charles, musician, and his daughter, Anne, wife of Jn. Allam, to be brought before two J.P.s. They are to call Jn. Allam before them and settle the differences between the parties or bind them over for the court to deal with.

**2.** Jn. Ewen committed to prison for three days for unlicensed victualling and before release to put in sureties not to keep an alehouse.

**3.** Jane Wise, Jn. Ewen's sister-in-law, to leave his house within three days and live in her own house or elsewhere or be bound with sureties to appear at the next Q.S. and meanwhile be of good behaviour.

---

[1] i.e. for maimed soldiers.

**4.** Jn. Turner and Wm. Clarke to be whipped as vagrants and have passes.

**5.** Rog. Carpenter discharged with his master's consent from his apprenticeship with Wm. Hobbes, plumber, who is to hand over his indentures. Carpenter is to be whipped.

**6.** Eliz. Holdernes, widow, presented for unlicensed victualling, fined but released from imprisonment.

**7.** All alehouse keepers in Oxf. and its suburbs to appear at the Guildhall next Thursday to renew or be discharged from their licences.

**8.** Geo. Tredwell was indicted for fishing with an unlawful net. His fine is referred to the bailiffs as it is fixed by statute.

## [1628D]

p. 256 Quarter Sessions Thursday after Michaelmas [2 Oct.]. Paul Hood D.D., Deputy Vice-Chancellor, Wm. Goode esq., Mayor, Jn. Whistler, Recorder, Jn, Prideaux D.D., Thos. Flexney esq., Wm. Potter esq., Oliver Smyth esq., Wm. Boswell esq., Jn. Willmott gent., J.P.s.

**1.** Geo. Bishoppe, a prisoner in Bocardo on suspicion of felony, who has not been prosecuted, to be whipped and discharged.

**2.** Margaret Welles, who was indicted for felony is acquitted by the petty jury. Being the servant of the owner of the goods at the time of the supposed felony, she is to be whipped and discharged.

**3.** Eliz. Hutchins, who was indicted for felony and acquitted, is to be whipped and discharged.

**4.** Phil. Rixon licensed to victual.

## [1629A]

p. 257 Quarter Sessions Thurs. 15 Jan. 1629. Wm. Goode esq., Mayor, Accepted Fruen, Vice-Chancellor, Jn. Whistler, Recorder, Wm. Peirce D.D., Jn. Bancrofte D.D., Jn. Rawlinson D.D., Jn. Prideaux D.D., Thos. James D.D., Thos. Flexney esq., Chas. Holloway esq., Wm. Potter esq., Wm. Wright esq., Oliver Smyth esq., Jn. Willmott gent., J.P.s.

**1.** The Mayor and another J.P. to consider whether Ric. Yorke should be licensed to victual or stopped from victualling.

**2.** Peter Price to be committed to Bocardo until he 'shall' his hair [*meaning uncertain or verb missing*] in a decent manner or puts in sureties to appear at the next Q.S., and meanwhile be of good behaviour.

**3.** The Mayor and Ald. Potter are asked to consider Rob. Carter, labourer's, claim for wages and other things from Hen. Samon, his former master. Accordingly on 23 Jan. 1629 they called the parties before them. Hen. Samon agreed that Carter should have 26s. 8d. a year and Carter agreed that all except 5s. 8d. had been paid. Samon said he had withheld that sum because Carter had received as much as that from guests during his service, which should be counted as part of his wages, but the J.P.s told him to pay. Samon refused to pay or enter recogn. to appear and answer at the next Q.S. The J.P.s considered this to be contempt but did not commit him until they had the court's opinion. Samon denied breaking open Carter's box and the J.P.s did not interfere as Carter could not prove it.

**4.** On Eleanor Kirke's petition, the churchwardens and overseers of p. 258 the psh. of St. Mic. are to pay her arrears by Candlemas for keeping Jn. Gosse, who was born in the psh. or warrants are to be made out for them to be brought before some J.P.s to be bound to appear and answer at the next Q.S.

**5.** The officers of St. Giles psh. are ordered as in 1629A4 for keeping Wm. Croton.

# [1629B]

Quarter Sessions Thurs. 16 April 1629. Wm. Goode esq., Mayor, Jn. p. 259 Whistler, Recorder, Thos. James D.D., Wm. Potter esq., Wm. Wright esq., Oliver Smith esq., Wm. Boswell esq., Jn. Willmott gent., J.P.s.

**1.** The churchwardens and overseers of the poor of the psh. of St. Martin are to secure the psh. of St. Aldate against any charge from three children of Jn. Sunton, who were born in the psh. of St. Martin. If notice of their refusal to do so is given to any J.P. he is to make a further order according to the statute.

**2.** Jn. Brookes's complaint that his master, Alex. Hill, cordwainer, did not 'use his trade' was heard and he is discharged from his apprenticeship.

**3.** Geo. Bishoppe to have his hair cut off and to be whipped at the post on two market days.

**4.** Thos. Parsons to be whipped and have a pass.

**5.** A warrant to be made out for Geo. Tredwell to be bound to appear at the next Q.S. and meanwhile be of good behaviour.

**6.** Ric. Hearne, gunsmith, as in 1629B5.

**7.** Jn. Price to be sent for by warrant and committed until he pays his fees.

**8.** Jn. Sare, gent., to be Treasurer for next year.[1]

p. 268 **9.** A meeting of the J.P.s is to be held on 20 May to view all alehouses and licence or suppress them.

## [1629c]

Quarter Sessions Thurs. 4 June 1629. Wm. Goode esq., Mayor, Accepted Frewen, Vice-Chancellor, Jn. Rawlinson D.D., Jn. Bancrofte D.D., Thos. James D.D., Wm. Potter ald., Wm. Wright ald., Oliver Smyth ald., J.P.s.

**1.** By the end of this Q.S. the parishioners of St. Martin are to secure the psh. of St. Aldate against any charge from those of Jn. Sunton *alias* Joyner's children who were born in the psh. of St. Martin. If they do not, a warrant is to be made out for the churchwardens and overseers of the poor to be brought before some J.P.s to be bound to appear and answer at the next Q.S. Afterwards Jn. Ryman and Edw. Daniell, churchwardens of the psh. of St. Martin, came to the office and undertook before the Town Clerk to secure the psh. of St. Aldate during their term and asked that their successors be ordered to do the same.

**2.** Jn. Price, carpenter, told that he was to be stopped from victualling.

**3.** On Mary Fyner's complaint Jn. Banckes, cordwainer, was ordered to repay 50s. of the £4 received when her son became his apprentice, as he has left for an unknown place. He was present in court and paid.

p. 269 **4.** Lee's wife, who had formerly been indicted for being drunk, appeared but had no money for her fine, so was put in the stocks in the hall.

**5.** Wm. Turvey, indicted and convicted of petty larceny, is to be whipped and have a pass allowing him a week to travel to Broughton, Hunts.

[1] i.e. for maimed soldiers.

**6.** Warrants to be sent out under the hands of the Vice-Chancellor and the Mayor for all victuallers in the city and suburbs to appear before them and the other J.P.s on 16 June to be licensed or suppressed.

## [1629D]

Quarter Sessions Thurs. 8 Oct. 1629. Hen. Sowtham esq., Mayor, Accepted Frewen, Vice-Chancellor, Wm. Peirce D.D., Thos. Flexney esq., Wm. Potter esq., Wm. Wright esq., Oliver Smyth esq., Jn. Willmott gent., J.P.s.

**1.** The court considered a petition from Ric. Hartley, cordwainer, that he is too poor because of long sickness to support his children. The psh. of St. Martin is to pay a weekly allowance to support the two children born in that psh. until they can be placed in service or their parents can keep them. If the churchwardens and overseers of the poor refuse to do so, a warrant is to be made out to bind them over to answer at the next Q.S.

**2.** [*blank*] Morris is to be put in the stocks at Carfax for an hour for p. 270 abusing the constable of the psh. of St. Mary Magdalen.

**3.** Widow Hussey, who has been in Bocardo for a long time as an accessory to her daughter's felony, is to be bailed until the next Assizes.

**4.** Thos. Lea's punishment for assaulting and beating a constable remitted as he has submitted. As he left without paying his fees, warrants are to be made out against him and others who left the court or did not appear. When apprehended they are to be bound to appear at the next Q.S.

**5.** On the petition of Mary Harmer, widow, the psh. of St. Ebbe is to pay her 8d. a week to keep her children, who were born there, until they can work for a living.

**6.** Jn. Ritington of Binsey is licensed to continue victualling.

## [1630A]

Quarter Sessions 14 Jan. 1630.[1]

**1.** Jn. Male and Jas. Clarke, who failed to appear as bound, and Rob. Williams, who left without licence, to be sent for by warrant to answer for contempt.

---

[1] This entry follows a heading, later struck through, for Thurs. 15 Oct. 1630 [*recte* 1629]. It appears to be a rough minute rather than a formal record.

## [1630B]

p. 271  Quarter Sessions 7 Oct. 1630. Thos. Cooper esq., Mayor, the Vice-Chancellor [Wm. Smith], Jn. Whistler esq., Recorder, Thos. Flexney esq., Wm. Potter ald., Oliver Smyth ald., Hen. Bosworth ald., J.P.s.

**1.** Ric. Morris committed to prison until he finds good sureties to discharge the psh. of St. Mary Magdalen of any costs from those of his children who were born there. 38s. of his money held by the late bailiffs is to be paid to his mother-in-law to relieve his wife who is in great want and lies in childbed.

**2.** Thos. Crooke, gardener, to be committed until he finds sureties for his appearance at the next Q.S. and good behaviour in the meantime, for taking a stranger as an inmate contrary to the orders of the Privy Council.

**3.** Jn. Mathewes *alias* Waspe as in 1630B2 for irreverent behaviour in court.

**4.** Dorothy Marsh *alias* Thatcher as in 1630B2 and fined 10s. for assault and battery on Jn. Debdale B.A.

## [1631A]

p. 272  Quarter Sessions 13 Jan. 1631. Thos. Cooper esq., Mayor, the Vice-Chancellor [Wm. Smith], Jn. Whistler esq., Recorder, Thos. Flexney esq., Wm. Potter ald., Oliver Smyth ald., Hen. Bosworth ald., J.P.s.

**1.** Thos. Bayley the younger, aged about two, was born when Thos. Baylie the elder, barber, lived in the psh. of St. Mic. His parents then moved to the psh. of St. Mary and left him unprovided for there when they went to an unknown place. The child is too young to be found to be a rogue or sent to his birthplace according to the statute. The churchwardens and overseers of the poor of the psh. of St. Mary are to provide relief for the child. If the churchwardens and overseers of the psh. of St. Mic. complain to a J.P. that they have not done so, the churchwardens and overseers of the psh. of St. Mary are to be bound to answer for their contempt at the next Q.S. As Jn. Hynde of the psh. of St. Mary took Baylie into his house without obtaining security for the psh. according to a former order he is to pay 10s. for the relief of the child. [*Signed*] Carter [town clerk].

2. Agreed that the new building outside and near the Northgate and the adjoining corner house or tower is to be the House of Correction. The Recorder dissented.

## [1631B]

Quarter Sessions Thurs. 6 Oct. 1631. Oliver Smith esq., Mayor, Jn. <sub></sub>p. 273 Whistler esq., Recorder, Thos. Flexney esq., Wm. Boswell ald., Hen. Bosworth ald., Jas. Chesterman gent., J.P.s.

1. Mr. Jn. Bird of the psh. of St. Martin complained about a tax of £3 imposed on him by the churchwardens and overseers of the poor and ratified by the two next J.P.s. The court examined the matter in the presence of Mr. Bird, the churchwardens and the overseers, and found that the tax had been levied for the children of widow Wells, who had been allowed to live in one of Mr. Bird's houses from 6 May 1630 until her death about three weeks ago. The court found that he should suffer an extraordinary tax, partly because, by allowing the tenant to stay there, the children became a burden on the psh., and partly to deter him from doing the same again, as his tenants have previously been a great charge on the psh. In hope of more careful choice of tenants, 20s. of the tax is to be abated and 40s. paid straight-away. Ald. Boswell and Mr. Jas. Chesterman are to examine the rest of the tax and make an order binding on all parties except that Geo. Chambers the younger is not to be taxed, as his father swore that he is just his servant and has no trade or stock of his own. The church-wardens and overseers say Thos. Elzey has refused to pay and used contemptuous language about them and the J.P.s who ratified the tax. Ald. Boswell and Mr. Chesterman are to call Elzey before them and if the complaint is true bind him to answer at the next Q.S., and they are to make out warrants to levy the tax or commit to prison anyone who cannot be distrained for it.

## [1632A]

Quarter Sessions Thurs. 12 Jan. 1632. Oliver Smith esq., Wm. Smith, <sub></sub>p. 274 Vice-Chancellor, Jn. Prideaux D.D., Rob. Pincke D.D., Sam. Radcliffe D.D., Jn. Whistler esq., Recorder, Wm. Boswell ald., Hen. Bosworth ald., Jas. Chesterman gent., J.P.s.

1. At the last Q.S. Mr. Jn. Bird was released from 20s. of a tax from the psh. of St. Martin to relieve orphans who formerly lived in his

house and ordered to pay the remaining 40s. As he has not paid, the court has ratified the full tax of £3. If he does not pay, a warrant is to be issued to distrain him according to the statute.

**2.** Since the erection of the House of Correction at the Northgate there have been fewer rogues, vagabonds and wandering beggars in the city, poor children are put to work there and poor people 'willing to labour' can have spinning work. This already benefits the charitable inhabitants of the city. The benefits will increase if action is taken according to the King's directions, which needs the help of those who can contribute. Therefore in each psh., unless spared by the Mayor, half a tax is to be collected each quarter by the churchwardens and overseers and paid to Jn. Mathew, the Mayor's second serjeant, to be paid out according to the Mayor's instructions to set on work and maintain the poor children and the House of Correction.

**3.** The psh. of All Saints is to provide for the children of widow Hartley (Hartlye), a distracted woman, 50s. having been promised by the churchwardens of the psh. of St. Martin as the children were born there.

## [1632B]

p. 275  Quarter Sessions Thurs. 12 April 1632. Oliver Smith esq., Mayor, Wm. Smith, Vice-Chancellor, Jn. Prideaux D.D., Jn. Whistler esq., Recorder, Thos. Flexney esq., Wm. Potter ald., Wm. Wright ald., Hen. Bosworth ald., Jas. Chesterman gent., J.P.s.

**1.** The dispute between the pshs. of St. Mic. and All Saints over providing for a 'nurse child' of one Templer, a tailor, was heard. Templer and his wife came to live in the psh. of All Saints about two years ago and the child was born there but put to nurse in the psh. of St. Mic. where it has remained ever since. The child's mother is dead and about eight weeks ago Templer ran away, leaving the child, and is thought to be in London. As the question of which psh. should maintain the child is unusual the court will seek further advice before its decision. In the interim both parties should seek the opinion of the Assize Judges. Meanwhile the churchwardens and overseers of the two pshs. are to give 12d. each per week to the nurse. When the dispute is resolved the psh. which is to maintain the child is to repay the other psh. what it has paid in the meantime. Any churchwarden or overseer who disobeys this order is to be bound by recogn. to answer for contempt at the next Q.S.

**2.** The churchwardens and overseers of the poor of the psh. of St. Ebbe are to provide for Ralph Loddington's children according to the law.

**3.** Anne Phenixe is to be committed to and punished in the House of   p. 276 Correction during the pleasure of its overseers for lewd misbehaviour. She is then to be sent to St. Mary Gray [Cray], Kent, where she says she was born, to be set to work according to the law. [*Added later*] She is to be sent today from tithing to tithing by the straightest way to St. Mary Cray and allowed ten days for the journey.

**4.** The half tax for the House of Correction ordered at the last Q.S. is to be enforced. Any churchwardens or overseers who are negligent in performing this order are to be bound over to appear at the next Q.S. and answer for contempt.

## [1632C]

Quarter Sessions Thurs. 31 May 1632. Oliver Smith esq., Mayor, Jn. Prideaux D.D., Wm. Potter ald., Wm. Boswell ald., Hen. Bosworth ald., J.P.s.

**1.** Mr. Ric. Reston proved by the oath of three witnesses that Ralph Pope had threatened to kill him with a sheppeck ('sheppicke') or prong. Pope is committed to prison until he finds sureties to appear at the next Q.S. and keep the peace especially to Mr. Reston.

**2.** Thos. Miller was bound for his good behaviour and appearance at this Q.S. for bad language to Thos. Medcalfe. They both appeared and neither brought any witnesses. Miller is to be discharged without paying any fees as the court did not think he should have been bound as Medcalfe abused him as much or more.

**3.** The half tax for the House of Correction is to be enforced straight-   p. 278 away. Any churchwarden or overseer who is negligent in doing so is to be bound to appear at the next Q.S. to answer for contempt.

## [1632D]

Quarter Sessions Thurs. after Michaelmas [4 Oct.] 1632. Brian Duppa, Vice-Chancellor, Wm. Charles esq., Mayor, Jn. Whistler esq., Recorder, Jn. Prideaux D.D., Wm. Potter ald., Oliver Smith ald., Hen. Bosworth ald., Jas. Chesterman gent., J.P.s.

**1.** The half tax for the House of Correction is to be continued. The Vice-Chancellor and the Mayor are to sign new warrants for it to be levied.

**2.** Warrants to be made out for the apprehension of those who did not appear at this Q.S. as bound or left without licence, or their recogns. to be estreated.

## [1633A]

Quarter Sessions Thurs. after Epiphany [10 Jan.] 1633. Brian Duppa, Vice-Chancellor, Wm. Charles esq., Mayor, Dr. Ratcliffe, Jn. Whistler esq., Recorder, Chas. Halloway esq., Thos. Flexney esq., Wm. Potter ald., Wm. Wright ald., J.P.s.

p. 279 **1.** The parishioners of St. Mic. complained that seventeen families live in a messuage owned by Anne French, widow, which was once (within the past twenty-eight years) occupied by one family. They are mostly so poor that they receive or need relief from the psh. They have so little room that the place is very noisome and likely to be infectious to themselves and their neighbours in the hot part of the year. Several of them make fires in their rooms as they have no chimneys, which is likely to be a danger to the city as the messuage is in the high street.[1] Some of the J.P.s know this to be true and a notice is to be issued to Anne French, giving her two months to remove the families who are inmates and are more than can conveniently live in the messuage. She is also to secure the psh. against any charge from the remaining tenants. If she does not perform this order the constable of her ward is to bring her before a J.P. The J.P. is to bind her by recogn. with sureties to appear and answer at the next Q.S., when the parishioners are to bring in a bill of indictment for causing a nuisance.

## [1633B]

Quarter Sessions Thurs. after Easter [25 April] 1633.[2] Wm. Charles esq., Mayor, Jn. Whistler esq., Recorder, and other J.P.s.

**1.** Warrants to be made out for Jeffrey Browne, Wm. Androes and Bernard Bowles, who left the court without leave or paying their fees, to be apprehended and imprisoned until they pay.

## [1634A]

p. 280  Quarter Sessions Thurs. after Epiphany [9 Jan.] 1634. Brian Duppa D.D., Dean of Christ Church and Vice-Chancellor, Francis Harris esq., Mayor, and other J.P.s.

---

[1] Probably Cornmarket Street.
[2] This entry is a rough minute rather than a formal record.

1. Warrants to be made out for the churchwardens and overseers of the poor of each psh. in the city and suburbs to send the names of all strangers and newcomers in their psh. and their landlords to the Mayor and Aldermen each month, or be bound over to answer if they neglect this duty. The Mayor and Aldermen to bind over the landlords to send the strangers where they should go according to the statute or otherwise order their removal.

## [1634B]

Quarter Sessions Thurs. next after Easter [10 April] 1634. Francis Harris esq., Mayor, Jn. Whistler esq., Recorder, J.P.s.

1. The parishioners of St. Peter-le-Bailey complained about their burden of poor relief. The pshs. of St. Martin, St. Mary, All Saints and St. Aldate are to pay 15s. a year each to assist.

## [1635A]

Quarter Sessions Thurs. after Easter [2 April] 1635. Jn. Sare esq., Mayor, Jn. Whistler esq., Recorder, J.P.s.

1. The minister and better parishioners of St. Peter-le-Bailey told   p. 281
the court that there are many poor people, widows and fatherless children in the psh., who cannot be removed by law, and very few of the inhabitants can contribute to poor relief. At their meeting those few wish to make orders to stop strangers and incapable persons coming to the psh., to tax those who are liable better and more fairly and to settle matters for their common good. They cannot do so as many of the meaner people, who cannot contribute, disrupt the business of the meeting. The court orders that only the better people named below, or any six of them, shall meet to consider the business of the psh. and provision for its poor. Their orders are to be enforced if approved by two J.P.s, who are to bind over or commit to prison anyone who hinders proceedings for the good of the psh. Lastly, the pshs. of St. Martin, All Saints and St. Mary are to pay the yearly sums previously ordered to the churchwardens and overseers of St. Peter-le-Bailey until they show the court reasons not to.

Mr. Chris. Rogers, Principal of New Inn Hall, Wm. Sandbrooke, Rector of St. Peter-le-Bailey, Wm. Levens, Wm. Fletcher, Geo. Boxe, Rob. Bowell, Edm. Worland, Wm. Greene, Edm. Bolt, Thos. Bishopp, Jn. Bolt.

155

## [1636A]

p. 283 Quarter Sessions Thurs. 14 Jan. 1636. Rob. Pincke D.D., Vice-Chancellor, Martin Wright esq., Mayor, Jn. Whistler esq., Recorder, Chas. Holloway esq., Oliver Smith ald., Jn. Sare ald., Jas. Chesterman gent., J.P.s.

1. Ric. Jones, a very poor old man, has lived in the psh. of St. Mary Magdalen almost all his life but is now too destitute to provide himself with food and lodging. The churchwardens and overseers of the poor are to provide relief on pain of the statutory penalty if they are negligent. If they fail to do so a J.P. is to bind them to answer at the next Q.S.

## [1637A]

Quarter Sessions Trinity 1637.¹

1. At Trinity Q.S. 1636 Thos. Simpson (Sympson) was ordered to pay 12d. a week to maintain his daughter, Mary Simpson. He is now discharged from paying as his daughter is fit to work and maintain herself, and lives loosely and is undutiful to her parents.


# APPENDIX

### ADDITIONAL MATERIAL

p. 282 **1.** 13 March 1632

Memo. that Rog. Bird, citizen and tailor of Oxf., paid £10 to the keykeepers of the city, which they are to account for as the city's money at the end of their term of office. In the meantime they are to make what profit they can from it and deliver this to Rog. Bird. Their successors are to do this until Rog.'s son, Thos. is 21 and then give him the £10. If Thos. dies earlier the £10 is to be given to Rog., his executors, administrators or assignees. This was done with the consent of Oliver Smith esq., Mayor, for the better maintenance of Thos. Bird.

[*Signed*] Rog. Bird.

**2.** 20 Aug. 1633

Memo. that Rog. Bird, having been paid £6 10s. by Jn. Bartholmewe, mercer, agreed that until Thos. Bird is 21 the keykeepers shall pay

---

¹ A rough note with no precise date.

Bartholmewe, his executors or assignees, 16s. a year in respect of the
£10, and that if Thos. Bird dies before he is 21 the city shall keep the
£10 until he would have been 21 and continue to pay 16s. a year to
Bartholmewe. This agreement was made with the consent of Wm.
Charles esq., Mayor.

[*Signed*] Rog. Bird.

[*Margin*] Witnesses: Tim. Carter and Bernard Lyford [*signatures*],
Alice Bird [*her mark*].

**3.** 'AB having found sureties by Recognizance against the useinge of Title page
unlawfull Games and for useinge and mainteyninge good order & rule
in his house accordinge to the statute in that behalfe is admitted and
allowed by AB & CD Justices of the Peace of the said Citty to kepe an
Alehouse for one whole yeare next [*page torn*] date &c'.

**4.** 'A.B., C.D. come and yeald your bodies to the Bailiffs of the Cittie Endpapers
of Oxon. before the next Quarter Sessions to be holden for the said
Cittie. Or else you and every of you willbe then convicted of Recu-
sancie'.

# INDEX OF NAMES AND PLACES

NOTE. Places are assigned to counties as defined before 1974. Abbreviations include abp., Archbishop; ald., alderman; Alex., Alexander; And., Andrew; Ant., Anthony; app., apprentice; Art., Arthur; Bart., Bartholomew; bp., Bishop; bro., brother; Chas., Charles; Chris., Christopher; Coll., College; Dan., Daniel; dau., daughter; Edm., Edmund; Edw., Edward; Eliz., Elizabeth; fam., family; Geo., George; Gilb., Gilbert; Hen., Henry; Humph., Humphrey; husb., husband; Jas., James; Jn., John; Jos., Joseph; Kath., Katherine; Lawr., Lawrence; Ld., Lord; Marg., Margaret; Mat., Matthew; Mic., Michael; Nat., Nathaniel; Nic., Nicholas; Oxf., Oxford; Phil., Philip; psh., parish; Ric., Richard; Rob., Robert; Rog., Roger; s., son; Sam., Samuel; Sim., Simon; Steph., Stephen; Thos., Thomas; Tim., Timothy; Vct., Viscount; w., wife; Wal., Walter; wid., widow; Wm., William.

A'Lee, *see* Lee
Abbott(e):
  Geo., abp. of Canterbury, 1622E2, 1623A1
  Rob., pro-vice-chancellor, J.P., 1614B, 1615A, 1615B
Abell:
  Everard, 1624E10
  Joan, 1622B24
Abingdon (Berks.), xxi, 1621E16, 1622B37, 1623A18, 29, 1626D26, 27
Acton:
  Marian, 1623A15
  Wm., 1623A15, 29, 1623E20
  —, wid., 1618A24
Adams (Addams):
  Jn., 1620B1, 1620C11, 1620D16, 1621B20, 25, 1627A8, 11
  Rob., 1623A26
Adkins, Wm., 1623B8
Airey (Airay, Ayeray), Hen., pro-vice-chancellor, J.P., 1616E, 1616G
Alcock:
  Frances, 1618E21
  Lawr., 1623F7

Thos., 1617B8, 1618E21, 1623E6, 1624A9
  —, 1618E24
Aldam, Ric., 1621B32
Alder, Bart., 1615A1
All Saints psh., 1616H29, 1617A22, 1618A25, 1619C11, 20, 1620B43, 1624E55, 1625A28, 1625B5, 1626C17, 1627A25, 1627B15, 1632A3, 1632B1, 1634B1, 1635A1
All Souls College, 1617A4
Allam:
  Anne, 1627A8, 11, 1628C1
  Jn., 1621B20, 1627A7, 8, 11, 1627B5, 1627D17, 1628C1
  Thos., 1627D17
Allen:
  Francis, 1617A21
  Hugh, 1623A19, 22, 1623C19, 26
  Jn., 1623B4
  Nic., 1614A6
  Wm., 1622C5, 1622D3, 1622E1, 1624A16, 1625A25
Alley:
  Jn., 1619D6
  (*alias* Leveret) Wm., 1619H14

Alligant, Ric., 1616A20
Allnutt, *see* Alnutt
Almond, Thos., 1620B20, 21, 1620C6, 7,
     1622C12
Alnutt (Allnutt), Mary, *see* Tucky
Alverd, Wm., 1616C21, 1616H15, 29
Ampney, Down (Gloucs.), 1619C2
Anderton, Jn., 1625B3
Andrews (Andrewes, Androes,
     Androwes):
  Kath., 1620B24, 29
  Thos., 1619B3, 1619D9, 10, 1619F10
  Wm., 1633B1
Anstey, Jn., 1624D11
Applebye, Wm., 1620D38
Archer, Elias, 1615A3, 1617B11, 1623C11,
     1624B31
Argo(e), Jn., 1616A16
Argoll, Hen., 1620C8
Arncott (Oxon.), 1619D6
Arnold, Wm., 1618E17, 1620C17, 1621C23
     and n., 1624B18, 1625A19, 1626D7,
     1627D10
Arpin:
  Jn., 1627D5, 7, 8, 1628A7
  Thos., 1627D5, 7, 8, 1628A7
Ashe, Jane, 1627D11
Ashley (Ashly):
  Anne, 1624E13
  Steph., 1621C9, 1624E11, 13
Ashton, Jn., 1622A23
Askew:
  And., 1625B10
  Mary, 1625B10
Astle (Astell):
  Jn., 1621E24
  (*alias* Miles) Ric., 1617C15, 1623D3, 1623E1,
     1624A1, 1624B1, 1624Cl, 1626B4, 12,
     1626C16, 1627D6, 17, 1628A4
  (*alias* Miles) Thos., 1625A3, 6
Attwood:
  Chris., 1626D21
  Marg., Margery, 1616A19, 1621C19, 21

Ayeray, *see* Airey
Aykers, Hen., 1616H6
Ayres:
  Christian, 1623A17, 1623C7
  Rob., 1623A17, 1623C7

Bache, Dorothy, 1624E15
Badger:
  Edw., 1621B9, 1624B24
  Eliz., 1618A25
  Kath., 1627D12
  Wm., 1614A5, 1614B13, 1615D8, 1616B1,
     3, 1617A13, 1617B22, 1618A4, 5,
     12, 25
Bagnoll, Sam., 1618D1, 1619B2
Bagwell:
  Edw., 1623A15
  Thos. and w., 1622E12
Bailey (Bailie, Baylie, Bayly, Baylye):
  Edw., 1621B18
  Jn., 1623B6
  Rob., 1623D12
  Sibyl, 1616D7
  Thos., sen. and jun., 1631A1
  Wm., 1616D5, 7
  Mr., 1616C11
Baker:
  Chris., 1619B5
  Wm., 1624B3, 1624C14 and n., 1624E7
Baldwin (Baldwyn, Baldwyne,
     Baldyn), Jn., 1615A18, 1619A28,
     1622A13, 1622B1, 1625B19,
     1627A26
Ball, Jn., 1625D13
Balliol College, 1623A24, 1624D4
Banbury (Oxon.), 1623C18
Banckes (Bancks), *see* Banks
Bancroft (Banckroft, Bancrofte,
     Bankrofte, Brancrofte), Jn., bp.
     of Oxf., J.P., xiii, 1624A, 1624A2,
     1624E53, 1625A24, 1626A4, 1626B,
     1626C7, 9, 1627B15, 1627D, 1629A,
     1629C

Mr., principal of New Inn Hall, 1623D5

London, 1616H2, 1622C10, 1632B1; *and see* Drury Lane; Inner Temple; Westminster

London, Wm., 1620B18, 1620C15

Longe, Jn., 1619C19, 1622B25

Lovegrove:
Wm., 1626B3
Mr., 1624E14

Lovelace *alias* Oates, Rob., 1615B8

Lovesay (Lovesaye, Lovesey):
Ric., 1620D28, 1621A16, 1625A2, 21, 1625B1
Rob., 1621E14
Thos., 1621E14

Lowe:
Jas., 1623A15
Jn., 1622F7

Lucas, Jn., 1618A2, 1618B20

Lucy, Ric., 1624B19

Lugg, Toby and w., 1621E6

Lute, Wm., 1625A15

Lyford, Bernard, Appendix, 2

Mabbs, Wm., 1617B3, 1617C1

Maddox:
Laur., 1616A10
Wm., 1616A10

Magdalen College, 1624D10, 1625A7, 1625B8, 17; *and see* Langton

Magdalen Hall, 1621B17

Maisters, Thos., 1622B3

Male, Jn., 1630A1

Mallat, Mrs., 1615C2

Malmesbury (Wilts.), 1622D2

Manford (Manthorpe, Manthrop):
Sim., 1626C11
Thos., 1618E25

Manninge (Mannings), Wm., 1622C13, 1623E5

Manthorpe (Manthrop), *see* Manford

March, *see* Marsh

Marigold, Jn., 1627A12

Maris:
Jn., 1621E4
Nic., 1620B16, 1620C14, 1625B12
—, 'Young', 1625A2

Marsh (March, Marshe):
(*alias* Thatcher) Dorothy, 1630B4
Ralph, 1624E51
(*alias* Thatcher) Rob., 1621D9

Marton, And. and w., 1622B3

Mason, Rob., 1622A18

Matthew (Mathew, Mathewe, Mathewes):
Jn., 1632A2
Jn. jun., 1617B4, 13, 18, 1618A23, 1618B18
Jn. sen., 1618A23, 1618B18, 1618E11
(*alias* Waspe) Jn., 1630B3
Goodwife, 1617A26

Mawditt (Mawdytt):
Moses, 1620A8
Goodwife, w. of Moses, 1620A8

Mayler, Edw., 1618A7

Mayor, Jane, 1623C18

Meares, Wal., 1616H2

Measey, Jn., 1626C10

Medcalfe, *see* Metcalfe

Meddowes, Edw., 1624B28

Meeke, Wm., 1627D17

Meredith, Jn., 1623E15

Merton College, 1615C3, *and see* Savile; Symondson

Metcalfe (Medcalfe, Metcalf), Thos., 1618E12, 1623E8, 12, 1624B17, 1632C2

Middleton, Thos., 1616C8

Miles (Myles):
Martha, 1620B40
Ric., 1624A11, 20, 1624B2; *and see* Astell
Thos., *see* Astell

Miller:
Nat., 1622A12
Thos., 1626D2, 1632C2

Milton, Great (Oxon.), 1616H5

Missenden, Little (Bucks.), 1619D7

(*alias* Ogle or Osney) Magdalen, 1624A11,
19, 1626A17
(*alias* Ogle or Osney) Wm., 1623E8,
1623F1, 1624A11, 19, 1624C12,
1624D6, 1625B7, 1626A17
Readinge (Redding, Reddinge):
Alice, 1618C3
Jn., 1619D7
Reason *alias* Hucks, Wm., 1618A3
Redding(e), *see* Readinge
Rede, *see* Read
Reston, Ric., 1632C1
Revell, Anne, 1624E21
Rewley, 1619F5
Reymond, Jn., 1625A21
Reynolds, Ric., 1624A11, 20, 1624B2
Rice (Ryce):
Eliz., 1621A17
Wm., 1621A17
Richardson:
Eliz., 1622E25
Jn., 1614A6, 1619A15, 1624A15,
1624D3
Thos., 1618A24, 1621C5, 15, 1621D7
Richmont, Jn., 1618A24
Ritington, Jn., 1629D6
Rivans, Thos., 1622F7
Rives, *see* Ryves
Rixon:
Phil., 1623C15, 1628D4
Prudence, 1623C15
Wm., 1616G7, 1616I5
Roath, *see* Raph
Roberts:
Thos., 1616C16, 1622A12, 1623F5
Wm., 1627A25
Robins:
Eliz., 1618B14
Isobel, 1618B4
Robinson (Robynson):
Jas., 1621B17
Marg., 1623A10
Ric., 1616A23

Rob., 1616D4
Rog., 1623C10, 1623E19, 1624A2, 13
Susan, 1624A2, 13
Thos., 1620D5
Wm., 1616D3, 1622B38, 1623A6, 31, 1623F6,
1624C12, 1624D8; *and see* Sutton
Roche, Alex., 1624E31, 46
Roebuck inn, 1625B19
Rogers:
Chris., principal of New Inn Hall,
1635A1
Dorothy, 1620C18, 1620D41 and n.
Ellen, 1623B15
Thos., 1620A9, 1620B37, 1621B13,
1622A20, 1623A28
Romane, Peter (*alias* Earlsman, Thos.),
1619D17
Rose, Wm., 1616I9, 1623E15
Rosterne, Jn., 1618B15
Rounsevale (Rounsevall), *see* Rownsefall
Rowland, Jn., 1616A8
Rownsefall (Rounsevale, Rounsevall),
Hen., 1617B16, 1618E15, 1621A29,
1622B6
Rowse, Edw., 1627A22, 1627B2
Rudland, Rob., 1622A9
Rusly, Thos., 1622E13
Russell (Russaile):
Chas., 1621E1, 35, 1622C12, 1623C6,
1623E2
Leonard, 1624D10
Mr., 1615D2, 1621B4
Ryce, *see* Rice
Rycote (Oxon.), 1620A12
Ryman, Jn., 1629C1
Ryme:
Geo., 1614B1
Jn., 1617C14
Wm., 1623B9, 1623C18, 26
Ryves (Rives), Wm. (later Sir Wm.), J.P.,
xiv, xvi, 1614B, 1614B1, 1615A, D,
1616A, E, F, 1617A, B, 1618A, 1618D1,
1619A, B, 1623A10

Scott:
  Geo., 1621E29, 1622A14
  Joan, 1615F8
Scudamore (Skidmore):
  Barnaby, 1627D17
  Thos., 1623B5, 8, 11 and n.
Seaman (Seamon):
  Eliz., 1624E10
  Hen., 1624E10, 38, 41; *and see* Symon
  Joan and children, 1625A27
  Jn., 1618E1
Searle, Sam., 1615C2, 1615F3
Seller, Wm., 1624B9
Selwood (Sellwood):
  Eliz., 1618E24
  Eliz., w. of Sheene, 1618B7, 1619A17
  Sheene, 1618B7, 1619A17
Shann, Eliz., 1626D12
Shaw(e):
  Abraham, 1616H7
  Edw., 1620D10
  Eliz., 1623A29, 30
  Frances, 1620D10
  Francis, 1621A30, 1621B37
  Hugh, 1621C20, 1622B31, 1623A5, 1624C4, 1627D9
Sheene, Eliz., 1615B7
Shelton, Mic., 1624A11
Shepherd (Sheppard, Shepparde):
  (*alias* Hore) Frances, 1618A15, 1619C16
  —, 1618A15
Shepreve, Mrs., 1618A25
Sherborne (Shereborne), Bridget and child, 1624B3, 1624C14, 1624E7
Sherewood, —, 'Young', 1624C11
Sherle (Shirle):
  Jn., 1625C12
  Thos., 1627D17
Sherwin (Sherwyn):
  Hen., 1622E14, 1623F2, 5, 1624E51, 1625C16
  Wm., 1623F5
Shirle, *see* Sherle

Shirt, Geo., 1628B6
Shoe Lane, 1626D25
Short(e):
  Alice, 1621E8
  Peter, 1617B9
Shury, Kath., 1617D3
Simondes, *see* Symonds
Simpson (Sympson):
  Joan, 1621E10, 21, 27, 1622A3
  Mary, 1637A1
  Sam., 1623F7
  Thos., 1621E10, 21, 27, 1622A3, 1622B27, 1625B16, 1637A1
  Mrs., 1623E20
Singleton:
  Thos., vice-chancellor, J.P., 1614A
  Wm., 1620A4
Skea, Chris., 1624C11
Skevington, Steph., 1620B6
Skidmore, *see* Scudamore
Slatford:
  Agnes (Ann), 1627D23, 1628A6
  Ant., 1622E22
  Jn., 1621D5, 1622F3, 1627C3, 1627D23, 1628A6
Slayman:
  Edm., 1619D14, 1619E5, 1620C21
  Marg. (Mary), 1619D14, 1619H6, 1620C21, 1621B22, 1621C3, 8; *and see* Stokes
Sly(e):
  Edw., 1620A7, 1620C4
  Eliz., 1615A5, 10
Smale, Lawr., 1618A5
Smith (Smithe, Smyth, Smythe):
  Ann, 1621E23
  Chris., 1624E31
  Eliz., 1624D5
  Geo., 1616A9, 20
  Joan, 1619A3
  Jn., 1616A9, 1616H5, 1622B3, 11, 1622C10, 12, 17, 1622E7, 1623B6, 1625B19, 1625C6

Striblehill *alias* Striplinge, Jn., 1620B32, 33
Stringer, And., 1625C13, 14, 1625D3
Striplinge (Stryplinge):
  Jn., *see* Striblehill
  Thos., 1625C10, 11
Stronge, Sampson, 1622A13
Stryplinge, *see* Striplinge
Stubbs (Stubbes):
  Edw., 1617B18, 1617C2, 15, 1617D2,
    1618A23, 1618B17, 1618E13
  Wm., 1618B9, 1618E13
Studley (Studly):
  Dorothy, 1618B13
  Jn., 1616H19, 1623B19
Stukeley, —, 1622B14
Styles, Alice, 1618D4
Sumpton, *see* Sunton
Sunningwell (Berks.), 1622E18, 1622F3
Sunton (Sumpton):
  Ellis, 1620D39
  Jn., 1618C12, 1620D39, 1623A31,
    1623E21, 1629B1; *and see* Joyner
  Thos., 1616B5; *and see* Joyner
Sutton *alias* Robinson, Wm., 1616C1
Swadling(e):
  Felix, 1621E31, 1623A15
  Thos., 1627A8
Swan inn, 1616A9, 1616H5
Swan's Nest, 1624A22
Swayne, Thos., 1618A16
Swett, Giles, 1625D10
Swifte (Swyfte):
  Eliz., 1618A13
  Ric., 1619E7
Syks, Ric., 1627D7, 8
Sylly, Thos., 1618A24
Symes:
  And., 1617A24
  Ric., 1615A15; *and see* Williams, Ric.
Symon *alias* Seaman, Hen., 1620D8
Symonds (Simondes):
  Eliz., 1618E8
  Hen., 1618E8

Joan, 1620A19, 1621B34
  Thos., 1626C14
Symondson, Mr., sub-warden of
  Merton Coll., 1619F3
Sympson, *see* Simpson

Tailor, *see* Taylor
Tanner, Wal., 1627B7
Tavy, Wm., 1616A23
Tawney, Wm., 1621E18
Taylor (Tailor, Tayler):
  Francis, 1623B4
  Susan and child, 1614B14, 1615A6,
    1615B1
  Thos., 1616H18, 1621A13, 1622A3,
    1622B27, 1623B3, 1623C2, 20,
    1623E4, 1624A14, 1624E18
  Wm., 1627C8
Teasler:
  Amy, 1616C11
  Thos., 1622B13
Tellen, Wm., 1622E20
Templer, — and fam., 1632B1
Tew, Jn., 1620D40, 1621A14
Thacker:
  Geo., 1623F2, 5
  Joan, 1623A10
Thackham, Goodwife, 1621A21
Thatcher, *see* Marsh, Dorothy and Rob.
Thomas, Jn. (Jn. ap), 1620B31, 42
Thomlyns, *see* Tomlins
Thompson, Wm., 1619H5
Thorne (Thorme), Giles, 1624D7,
  1624E6
Thorneton:
  Edw., 1621B1
  Hen., 1625C12
Thrupp, Hen., 1623D16, 1623E7,
  1624A3
Tilcock (Tylcock):
  Mary, 1619A24
  Wm., 1619A24, 1621B19, 1624A6
  —, 1617B9

# INDEX OF SUBJECTS

*and see* maimed soldiers
squab houses, *see* cottages
State, officers of, xii
stationer, 1627A8
stocks, xx–xxi, 1616H18, 1617B2, 10,
  20, 23, 26, 1618E20, 1619A2, 15,
  1619E8, 1619G2, 1619H12, 1620B17,
  1620C4, 1620D29, 1623D14, 1623E3,
  8, 1623F6, 1624C2, 1625A21,
  1625B11, 12, 1625C4, 1629C4,
  1629D2
stolen goods:
  receiving, 1615A12, 14, 1616H8, 1617D2,
    1618D3, 1619A27, 1622F1, 1623A12,
    1624E4, 14
  recovery of, 1619E4
strangers, 1630B2, 1634A1, 1635A1
Sunday observance, xxvi, 1615F8,
  1616A24, 1616D13
*supersedeas* [writ], 1614B1, 1615F3
Supremacy, Oath of, 1614B4
surgeons, 1616H26, 1617B25, 1618A3,
  1618B13, 1623B12, 1623C24, 1623E13
Suspect, Oath of a, 1615D4, 1616B5
swearing, 1624E22, 1626C2, 1632C2; *and
  see* lewd words

tailors, 1615B4, 1615C5, 1616H1, 1617C15,
  1618B17, 1621A4, 18, 24, 1621B4,
  1621E1, 1622B3, 1622C1, 1622E5,
  1622F3, 1623A15, 16, 22, 25, 1623C6,
  10, 1623D3, 8, 1623E6, 14, 1624A1,
  20, 1624B1, 20, 1624C1, 1624E19,
  20, 22, 26, 36, 54, 1625A1, 13,
  1625C7, 1626A14, 1626B12, 1627A25,
  1627B14, 17, 1627D7, 8, 9, 1628A3,
  1632B1, Appendix, 1
  Company of, 1624E4, 1627D9
tanners, 1623C5, 1624A20, 1625A13
tapsters, 1622C5, 1622E1, 1624E8, 1625B19
taxation, 1616H29, 1627A4, 1631B1,
  1632A1, 2, 1632B4, 1632C3, 1632D1,
  1635A1

theft, petty larceny, pilfering, xviii–xxi,
  1615A15, 16, 1616A15, 1616C17,
  1616D9, 1616H20, 1617B20, 1617C11,
  1618A17, 1618A23, 1619C4, 1620C16,
  1620D32, 1621B13, 19, 1622A13, 20,
  21, 1622B26, 1622C13, 1623A27,
  1623E21, 1624E44, 1625B11, 21,
  1629C5
of bedding, 1621B18, 1622A16, 23,
  1623A24
of books, 1621B17, 20, 1622E10,
  1624D10, 1628A9
of cattle, sheep, pigs, xix, 1619C9,
  1619F6, 1621A24, 1622B34,
  1623A12, 29, 30, 1624B21,
  1627A24, 1627B16
of cloth, textiles, etc., 1614B2, 1616A11,
  1616C14, 1617C9, 1618A16, 1621C18,
  1624A11, 1624E4, 1625B16
of clothing, footwear etc., xx,
  1616A12, 1618C10, 1618D2, 3, 1619C5,
  1619F10, 1619H14, 1619I1, 2, 1620B37,
  1621C17, 1622A16, 1622B35, 38,
  1623A15, 28, 29, 1624C11, 1627D10,
  1628A9
of food (cheese, fruit, etc.), 1623B6,
  1624A7, 1624C11
of grain, 1619G3, 1623A19, 22,
  1623C19, 1624B6, 1625C13, 14,
  1625D2, 3, 4
of horses, 1617A4, 1617C9, 1619C2,
  1619D12, 1621E2, 1623B6, 1624A5,
  1625D11
of miscellaneous, unusual items,
  1620C14 (building materials),
  1621A15 (tools), 1621E33 (swans),
  1623E11 (boat planks), 1624B28
  (plough irons), 1624C11 (hop poles),
  1624E14, 32, 45 (leather, kettles),
  1626B3 (iron chain), 1627A21, 22
  (bridle)
of poultry, 1616A10, 13, 14, , 1622E17,
  18, 1623B19, 1624B28, 1624C11